Forging the

American Character

Forging the American Character

Readings in United States History To 1877

Volume I

John R. M. Wilson, Editor
Southern California College

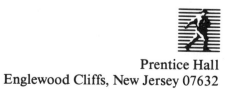

Prentice Hall
Englewood Cliffs, New Jersey 07632

Library of Congress Cataloging-in-Publication Data

Forging the American character : readings in United States history /
edited by John R.M. Wilson.

    p. cm.
   ISBN 0-13-326703-2 (v. 1). — ISBN 0-13-326711-3 (v. 2)
   1. United States—Civilization. I. Wilson, John R. M.
 E169.1.F745 1991   90-7131
 973—dc20   CIP

Editorial/production supervision and interior design: JENNIFER WENZEL
Cover design: BEN SANTORA
Manufacturing buyer: ED O'DOUGHERTY

© 1991 by Prentice Hall, Inc.
A Division of Simon & Schuster
Englewood Cliffs, New Jersey 07632

Printed in the United States of America

10 9 8 7 6 5 4 3 2 1

ISBN   0-13-326703-2 2361- 3978 9/00

Prentice-Hall International (UK) Limited, *London*
Prentice-Hall of Australia Pty. Limited, *Sydney*
Prentice-Hall Canada Inc., *Toronto*
Prentice-Hall Hispanoamericana, S.A., *Mexico*
Prentice-Hall of India Private Limited, *New Delhi*
Prentice-Hall of Japan, Inc., *Tokyo*
Simon & Schuster Asia Pte. Ltd., *Singapore*
Editora Prentice-Hall do Brasil, Ltda., *Rio de Janeiro*

Contents

Preface

A long United States history textbook may run to 1,000 pages. Although that length may seem intimidating to students, it does not allow extended treatment of a wide variety of fascinating topics. A book of readings does. The theme of this reader is the American character. I trust that the concept will illuminate American history without being overly restrictive.

A reader like this enables students to explore subjects ranging from the exploits of Tecumseh to the morality of American foreign policy, from the idealized "cult of true womanhood" in the 1840s to the significance of Watergate, in readable, thoughtful excerpts by outstanding specialists. The nature of the selections varies. Some offer new interpretations of the past; others introduce readers to new findings; while still others synthesize the writings in a historical subfield. The readings do not pretend to cover every possible topic; rather, they explore various areas that shed light on the American character yet suffer comparative neglect in many textbooks.

Trying to define the American character can be very frustrating. No one has been able to develop a widely accepted definition of the concept. Authors often use different meanings in the same piece of writing—for instance, referring interchangeably to the character of the individual

American and to the character of the mass of Americans. National character, especially in a country as big and heterogeneous as the United States, can be useful only as a large-scale generalization to cover the most prominent characteristics of the national culture. Some scholars have criticized efforts to capture the national character, suggesting that in many cases they may be merely intellectually sophisticated forms of racial stereotyping. Yet the practice persists, perhaps because it is so convenient to group people and thus make them more manageable. Perhaps the most useful definition would be that national character means generalizations about a nation or nationality developed to elucidate the ways in which it is distinctive.

A national character suggests tendencies on the part of a people, not fixed positions held by everyone. It means that, all things being equal, the people of a given nation are more likely to believe or behave a certain way than those of another nation. There is an inherent comparison implied in suggesting a national character, although studies of the American character generally tend not to explicitly explore other nationalities.

The genre began very early in the history of the United States with the publication in 1782 of J. Hector St. John de Crévecoeur's *Letters from an American Farmer;* the immigrant asked the famous question, "What then is this American, this new man?" Crévecoeur's pioneering inquiry into the American character ran up against geographical and cultural heterogeneity, which has become a vastly greater obstacle in the succeeding two centuries. The most famous inquiry came in the 1830s when Alexis de Tocqueville wrote *Democracy in America* and provided penetrating French insight into the nature of the conforming, religious, liberty-loving joiners he observed. Over the years, historians and other social observers have sought to explain American distinctiveness through such characteristics as abundance, exposure to the frontier, pragmatism, belief in progress, and mobility. They have debated the relative influence of mother England and the wilderness, and in so doing have illuminated American self-understanding—without providing any final answers. The quest continues, as the popularity of *Habits of the Heart* (1985) attests.

This collection suggests that Americans have defined themselves not only by what they are, but by what they are not, and the latter negative definition is an important component of Americanism. By and large, native Americans have not been allowed to share their heritage with Europeans. For other nationalities, conformity to the English cultural model was long required for acceptance in the United States, although a more pluralistic, open society seems to be emerging in the late twentieth century. Yet over the past half century, the increasingly diverse American population has frequently defined itself less by what it is than by what it is not—as antifascist and, especially, anticommunist.

This book should help to clarify some of the various forces, ideologies, people, and experiences that have helped forge today's distinctive American character. If, as Socrates said, the unexamined life is not worth living, then this excursion into the life of a people should help make it more worth living.

In closing, I'd like to thank the reviewers of my book, Anthony N. Stranges, Texas A&M University; William Woodward, Seattle Pacific University; Harry Stegmaier, Jr., Frostburg State University; and Ralph Beebe, George Fox College, for their helpful suggestions.

John R. M. Wilson
Costa Mesa, California

Forging the
American Character

1

Myths That Hide the American Indian

Oliver La Farge

Too many historical accounts have begun American history with the arrival of English settlers at Jamestown, Plymouth, and Massachusetts Bay. This Anglo-centrism conveniently overlooks earlier Spanish settlements in the Southwest and Florida. Even more disturbing, Americans speak of Columbus (or Leif Ericson) "discovering" America, though to claim discovery of a continent with a million people already living there is a trifle presumptuous. (In fact, some recent scholars calculate the population at ten, or even a hundred, million.)

In this article, Oliver La Farge tries to penetrate beneath three often contradictory myths of the American Indian—Noble Red Man, Bloodthirsty Savage, and Indolent Drunk—to reveal the intricate and divergent types of civilization that the first Americans created. He deals with the three centers of high Indian culture at the time the whites first arrived—Southeast-Mississippi Valley, Southwest, and Northwest Coast—and demonstrates the chasm between the popular image of the Indian and the reality.

A native of New York City, La Farge (1901–1963) lived much of his life in New Mexico, where the Indians were his special interest as an anthropologist, ethnologist, and novelist. He wrote numerous books about them, including The Changing Indian *(1942) and* A Pictorial History of the American Indian *(1956). He also served as president of the Association on American Indian Affairs (except during World War II military duty) from 1937 until his death and was official advisor to the Hopi Indians. As a youth, La Farge nicknamed himself "Indian Man"; as an adult, according to former Secretary of the Interior Stewart Udall, he knew "more about the American Indian than any non-Indian." In this article, written in 1956, he shares some of that knowledge.*

The role of the Native Americans, as the American Indians now prefer to be known, in forging the American character has been more significant than one might guess. As La Farge makes clear, diversity distinguished both their various civilizations and their responses to the European incursion—and diversity would become a critical component of the American character. In different ways, the Cherokee's ill-fated adoption of the white's ways and the Plains Indian's more successful adaptation to the horse reflected the need to adjust to the dominant culture. One final thought: as La Farge notes, French philosophers were so taken with the equalitarian ideal of the noble savage that their writings influenced both American and French revolutionaries to seek some measure of equality in their political upheavals. Ironically, native Americans received very little equal treatment from the political system they helped inspire.

Ever since the white men first fell upon them, the Indians of what is now the United States have been hidden from white men's view by a number of conflicting myths. The oldest of these is the myth of the Noble Red Man or the Child of Nature, who is credited either with a habit of flowery oratory of implacable dullness or else with an imbecilic inability to converse in anything more than grunts and monosyllables.

That first myth was inconvenient. White men soon found their purposes better served by the myth of ruthless, faithless savages, and later, when the "savages" had been broken, of drunken, lazy good-for-nothings. All three myths coexist today, sometimes curiously blended in a schizophrenic confusion such as one often sees in the moving pictures. Through the centuries the mythical figure has been variously equipped; today he wears a feather headdress, is clothed in beaded buckskin, dwells in a tepee, and all but lives on horseback.

It was in the earliest period of the Noble Red Man concept that the Indians probably exerted their most important influence upon Western civilization. The theory has been best formulated by the late Felix S. Cohen, who, as a profound student of law concerning Indians, delved into early white–Indian relations, Indian political economy, and the white men's view of it. According to this theory, with which the present writer agrees, the French and English of the early seventeenth century encountered, along the East Coast of North America from Virginia southward, fairly advanced tribes whose semihereditary rulers depended upon the acquiescence of their people for the continuance of their rule. The explorers and first settlers interpreted these rulers as kings, their people as subjects. They found that even the commonest subjects were endowed with many rights and freedoms, that the nobility was fluid, and that commoners existed in a state of remarkable equality.

Constitutional monarchy was coming into being in England, but the divine right of kings remained firm doctrine. All European society was stratified in many classes. A somewhat romanticized observation of Indian society and government, coupled with the idea of the Child of Nature, led to the formulation, especially by French philosophers, of the theories of inherent rights in all men, and of the people as the source of the sovereign's authority. The latter was stated in the phrase "consent of the governed." Both were carried over by Jefferson into our Declaration of Independence in the statement that "all men are created equal, that they are endowed by their Creator with certain unalienable Rights" and the governments derive "their just powers from the consent of the governed. . . . "

Thus, early observations of the rather simple, democratic organization of the more advanced coastal tribes, filtered through and enlarged by the minds of European philosophers whose thinking was ripe for just such material, at least influenced the formulation of a doctrine, or pair of doctrines, that furnished the intellectual base for two great revolutions and profoundly affected the history of mankind.

In the last paragraph I speak of "the more advanced" tribes. Part of the myth about the first Americans is that all of them, or most of them, had one culture and were at the same stage of advancement. The tribes and nations that occupied North America varied enormously, and their condition was anything but static. The advent of the white men put a sudden end to a phase of increasingly rapid cultural evolution, much as if a race of people, vastly superior in numbers, in civilization, and above all in weapons, had overrun and conquered all of Europe in Minoan times. Had that happened, also, the conquerors would undoubtedly have concluded, as so many white men like to conclude about Indians, that that peculiar race of light-skinned people was obviously inferior to their own.

Human beings had been in the New World for at least 15,000 years. During much of that time, as was the case in the beginning everywhere, they advanced but little from a Paleolithic hunting culture. Somewhere around 2500 B.C. farming began with the domestication of corn either in Peru or in Meso-America in the vicinity of western Guatemala. Farming brought about the sedentary life and the increased food supply necessary for cultural progress. By the time of the birth of Christ, the influence of the high cultures, soon to become true civilizations, in Meso-America was beginning to reach into the present United States. Within the next 1,500 years the Indians of parts of North America progressed dramatically. When the white men first landed, there were three major centers of high culture: the Southeast-Mississippi Valley, the Southwest, and the Northwest Coast. None of the peoples of these regions, incidentally, knew about war bonnets or lived in tepees.

The Southeast-Mississippi Valley peoples (for brevity, I shall refer to the area hereafter simply as "Southeast") seem to have had the strongest influences from Meso-America, probably in part by land along the coast of Texas, in part by sea across the Gulf of Mexico, whether direct from Mexico or secondhand through the peoples of the West Indies. There is a striking resemblance between some of their great earthen mounds, shaped like flat-topped pyramids, with their wood-and-thatch temples on top, and the stone-and-mortar, temple-topped pyramids of Meso-America. Some of their carvings and engravings strongly suggest that the artists had actually seen Meso-American sculptures. The list of similarities is convincingly long.

There grew up along the Mississippi Valley, reaching far to the north, and reaching also eastwards in the far south, the high culture generally called "Mound Builder." It produced a really impressive art, especially in carving and modeling, by far the finest that ever existed in North America. The history of advancing civilization in the New World is like that of the Old—a people develops a high culture, then barbarians come smashing in, set the clock part way back, absorb much of the older culture, and carry it on to new heights. A series of invasions of this sort seems to have struck the Mound Builders in late prehistoric times, when they were overrun by tribes mainly of Muskhogean and Iroquoian linguistic stock. Chief among these were the ancestors of the well-known Five Civilized Tribes—the Seminoles, Creeks, Choctaws, Chickasaws, and Cherokees. When white men first met them, their culture was somewhat lower than that of the earlier period in the land they occupied. Nonetheless, they maintained, in Florida, Alabama, Mississippi, Louisiana, and Georgia, the highest level east of the Rockies. A late movement of Iroquoian tribes, close relatives of the Cherokees, among them the Iroquois themselves, carried a simpler form of the same culture into Pennsylvania, New York, Ohio, and into the edge of Canada.

All of these people farmed heavily, their fields stretching for miles. They were few in a vast land—the whole population of the present United States was probably not over a million. Hunting and fishing, therefore, were excellent, and no reasonable people would drop an easy source of abundant meat. The development of their farming was held in check quantitatively by the supply of fish and game. They farmed the choice land, and if the fields began to be exhausted, they could move. They moved their habitations somewhat more freely than do we, but they were anything but nomadic. The southern tribesmen lived neither in wigwams nor tepees, but in houses with thatched roofs, which in the extreme south often had no walls. They had an elaborate social structure with class distinctions. Because of their size, the white men called their settlements "towns." The state of their high chiefs was kingly. They were a people well on the road toward civilization.

The Natchez of Mississippi had a true king, and a curious, elaborate social system. The king had absolute power and was known as the Sun. No ordinary man could speak to him except from a distance, shouting and making obeisances. When he went out, he was carried on a litter, as the royal and sacred foot could not be allowed to touch the ground. The Natchez nation was divided into two groups, or moieties: the aristocracy and the common people. The higher group was subdivided into Suns (the royal family), Nobles, and Honored Ones. The common people were known simply as Stinkers. A Stinker could marry anyone he pleased, but all the aristocrats had to marry out of their moiety, that is, marry Stinkers. When a female aristocrat married a Stinker man, her children belonged to her class; thus, when a Sun woman married a Stinker, her children were Suns. The children of the men, however, were lowered one class, so that the children of a Sun man, even of the Sun himself, became Nobles, while the children of an Honored One became lowly Stinkers.

This system in time, if nothing intervened, would lead to an overwhelming preponderance of aristocrats. The Natchez, however, for all their near-civilization, their temples, their fine crafts and arts, were chronically warlike. Those captives they did not torture to death they adopted, thus constantly replenishing the supply of Stinkers (a foreigner could become nothing else, but his grandchildren, if his son struck a royal fancy, might be Suns).

The Indians of the Southeast knew the Mexican-West Indian art of feather weaving, by means of which they made brilliant, soft cloaks. The Sun also wore a crown of an elaborate arrangement of feathers, quite unlike a war bonnet. In cloak and crown, carried shoulder-high on a litter, surrounded by his retainers, his majesty looked far more like something out of the Orient than anything we think of ordinarily when we hear the word "Indian."

The Natchez were warlike. All of the southeasterners were warlike. War was a man's proper occupation. Their fighting was deadly, ferocious, stealthy if possible, for the purpose of killing—men, women, or children, so long as one killed—and taking captives, especially strong males whom one could enjoy torturing to death. It is among these tribes and their simpler relatives, the Iroquois, that we find the bloodthirsty savage of fiction, but the trouble is that he is not a savage. He is a man well on the road toward civilization.

With the Iroquois, they shared a curious pattern of cruelty. A warrior expected to be tortured if captured, although he could, instead, be adopted, before torture or at any time before he had been crippled. He entered into it as if it were a contest, which he would win if his captors failed to wring a sign of pain from him and if he kept taunting them so long as he was conscious. Some of the accounts of such torture among the Iroquois, when the victim was a member of a tribe speaking the same language and holding to the same customs, are filled with a quality of mutual affection. In at least one case, when a noted enemy proved to have been too badly wounded before his capture to be eligible for adoption, the chief, who had hoped that the man would replace his own son, killed in battle, wept as he assigned him to his fate. At intervals between torments so sickening that one can hardly make one's self read through the tale of them, prisoner and captors exchanged news of friends and expressions of mutual esteem. Naturally, when tribes who did not hold to these customs, including white men, were subjected to this treatment it was not well received.

This pattern may have come into North America from a yet more advanced, truly civilized source. The Mexicans—the Aztecs and their neighbors—expected to be sacrificed if they were captured, and on occasion might insist upon it if their captors were inclined to spare them. They were not tortured, properly speaking, as a general rule, but some of the methods of putting them to death were not quick. What we find in North America may have been a debasement of the Mexican practices developed into an almost psychopathic pleasure among people otherwise just as capable of love, of kindness, of nobility, and of lofty thought as anywhere—or what the conquistadores found in Mexico may have been a civilized softening of earlier, yet more fearful ways. The Aztecs tore fantastic numbers of hearts from living victims, and like the people of the Southeast, when not at war said "We are idle." They were artists, singers, dancers, poets, and great lovers of flowers and birds.

The Iroquois and Muskhogeans had a real mental sophistication. We observe it chiefly in their social order and what we know of their religions. The Iroquois did not have the royalty and marked divisions of classes that we find farther south, but their well-organized, firmly knit tribes were what enabled them, although few in numbers, to dominate the Algonkians who surrounded them. The Iroquois came nearer to having the matriarchy that popular fable looks for among primitive people than any other American tribe. Actual office was held by the men, but the women's power was great, and strongly influenced the selection of the officers.

Five of the Iroquois tribes achieved something unique in North America, rare anywhere, when in the sixteenth century they formed the

League of the Five Nations—Senecas, Onondagas, Mohawks, Cayugas, and Oneidas—to which, later, the Tuscaroras were added. The League remained united and powerful until after the American Revolution, and exists in shadowy form to this day. It struck a neat balance between sovereignty retained by each tribe and sovereignty sacrificed to the league, and as so durable and effective a union was studied by the authors of our Constitution.

The league was founded by the great leader Hiawatha. Any resemblance between the fictional hero of Longfellow's poem and this real, dead person is purely coincidental. Longfellow got hold of the name and applied it to some Chippewa legends, which he rewrote thoroughly to produce some of the purest rot and the most heavy-footed verse ever to be inflicted upon a school child.

The Iroquois lived in "long houses," which looked like extended Quonset huts sheathed in bark. Smaller versions of these, and similarly covered, domed or conical structures, are "wigwams," the typical housing of the Northeast. Many people use the word "wigwam" as synonymous with "tepee," which is incorrect. A tepee, the typical dwelling of the Plains Indians of a later period, is a functional tent, usually covered with hides or, in recent years, canvas, and one of its essential features is that it is the shelter of constantly mobile people. A tepee, incidentally, is about the most comfortable tent ever invented, winter or summer—provided you have two or three strong, competent women to attend to setting it up and striking it.

The great tribes we have been discussing showed their sophistication in a new way in their response to contact with Europeans. Their tribal organizations became tighter and firmer. From south to north they held the balance of power. The British success in establishing good relations with many of them was the key to driving the French out of the Mississippi area; to win the Revolution, the Americans had to defeat the Iroquois, whose favor up to then had determined who should dominate the Northeast. The southern tribes radically changed their costume, and quickly took over cattle, slaves, and many arts. By the time Andrew Jackson was ready to force their removal, the Cherokees had a stable government under a written constitution, with a bicameral parliament, an alphabet for writing their language, printing presses, a newspaper, schools, and churches.

Had it not been for the white men's insatiable greed and utter lawlessness, this remarkable nation would have ended with a unique demonstration of how, without being conquered, a "primitive" people could adapt itself to a new civilization on its own initiative. They would have become a very rare example of how aborigines could receive solid profit from the coming of the white men.

After the five Civilized Tribes were driven to Oklahoma, they formed a union and once again set up their governments and their public schools. Of course we could not let them have what we had promised them; it turned out that we ourselves wanted that part of Oklahoma after all, so once again we tore up the treaties and destroyed their system. Nonetheless, to this day they are a political power in the state, and when one of their principal chiefs speaks up, the congressmen do well to listen.

The tribes discussed until now and their predecessors in the same general area formed a means of transmission of higher culture to others, east and west. Their influence reached hardly at all to the northwards, as north of the Iroquois farming with native plants was difficult or impossible. On the Atlantic Coast of the United States the tribes were all more or less affected. Farming was of great importance. Even in New England, the status of chiefs was definite and fairly high. Confederacies and hegemonies, such as that of the Narragansetts over many of the Massachusetts tribes, occurred, of which more primitive people are incapable. Farther south, the state of such a chief as Powhatan was royal enough for Europeans to regard him as a king and his daughter as a true princess.

To the westward, the pattern of farming and sedentary villages extended roughly to the line that runs irregularly through Nebraska and Kansas, west of which the mean annual rainfall is below twenty inches. In wet cycles, there were prehistoric attempts to farm farther west, and in historic times the Apaches raised fair crops in the eastern foothills of the southern tip of the Rockies, but only the white men combined the mechanical equipment and the stupidity to break the turf and exhaust the soil of the dry, high plains.

An essay as short as this on so large a subject is inevitably filled with almost indefensible generalizations. I am stressing similarities, as in the case of the Iroquois-Southeast tribes, ignoring great unlikenesses. Generalizing again, we may say that the western farmers, whose cultures in fact differed enormously, also lived in fairly fixed villages. In the southern part, they built large houses covered with grass thatch. At the northwestern tip of the farming zone we find the Mandans, Hidatsa, and Crows, who lived in semi-subterranean lodges of heavy poles covered with earth, so big that later, when horses came to them, they kept their choice mounts inside. These three related, Siouan-speaking tribes living on the edge of the Plains are the first we have come to whose native costume, when white men first observed them, included the war bonnet. That was in the early nineteenth century; what they wore in 1600, no one knows.

The western farmers had their permanent lodges; they also had tepees. Immediately at hand was the country of the bison, awkward game for men on foot to hunt with lance and bow, but too fine a source of meat to ignore. On their hunting expeditions they took the conical tents. The size of the tepees was limited, for the heavy covers and the long poles had to be dragged either by the women or by dogs. Tepee life at the time was desirable only for a short time, when one roughed it.

The second area of Meso-American influence was the Southwest, as anthropologists define it—the present states of New Mexico and Arizona, a little of the adjacent part of Mexico, and various extensions at different times to the north, west, and east. We do not find here the striking resemblances to Meso-America in numbers of culture traits we find in the Southeast; the influence must have been much more indirect, ideas and objects passing in the course of trade from tribe to tribe over the thousand miles or so of desert northern Mexico.

In the last few thousand years the Southwest has been pretty dry, although not as dry as it is today. A dry climate and a sandy soil make an archaeologist's paradise. We can trace to some extent the actual transition from hunting and gathering to hunting plus farming, the appearance of the first permanent dwellings, the beginning of pottery-making, at least the latter part of the transition from twining and basketry to true weaving. Anthropologists argue over the very use of the term "Southwest" to denote a single area, because of the enormous variety of the cultures found within it. There is a certain unity, nonetheless, centering around beans, corn, squashes, tobacco, cotton, democracy, and a preference for peace. Admitting the diversity, the vast differences between, say, the Hopi and Pima farmers, we can still think of it as a single area, and for purposes of this essay concentrate on the best-studied of its cultures, the Pueblos.

The name "Pueblo" is the Spanish for "village," and was given to that people because they lived—and live—in compact, defensible settlements of houses with walls of stone laid up with adobe mortar or entirely of adobe. Since the Spanish taught them how to make rectangular bricks, pure adobe construction has become the commoner type. They already had worked out the same roofing as was usual in Asia Minor and around the Mediterranean in ancient times. A modern Pueblo house corresponds almost exactly to the construction of buildings dating back at least as far as 600 B.C. in Asia Minor.

The Pueblos, and their neighbors, the Navahos, have become well enough known in recent years to create some exception to the popular stereotype of Indians. It is generally recognized that they do not wear feathers and that they possess many arts, and that the Pueblos are sedentary farmers.

Farming has long been large in their pattern of living, and hunting perhaps less important than with any people outside the Southwest. Their society is genuinely classless, in contrast to that of the Southeast. Before the Spanish conquest, they were governed by a theocracy. Each tribe was tightly organized, every individual placed in his niche. The power of the theocracy was, and in some Pueblos still is, tyrannical in appearance.

Physical punishment was used to suppress the rebellious; now more often a dissident member is subjected to a form of being sent to Coventry. If he be a member of the tribal council, anything he says at meetings is pointedly ignored. If he has some ceremonial function, he performs it, but otherwise he is left in isolation. I have seen a once self-assertive man, who for a time had been a strong leader in his tribe, subjected to this treatment for several years. By my estimation, he lost some thirty pounds, and he became a quiet conformist.

The power of the theocracy was great, but it rested on the consent of the government. No man could overstep his authority, no one man had final authority. It went hard with the individual dissident, but the will of the people controlled all.

The Pueblos had many arts, most of which still continue. They wove cotton, made handsome pottery, did fine work in shell. Their ceremonies were spectacular and beautiful. They had no system of torture and no cult of warfare. A good warrior was respected, but what they wanted was peace.

The tight organization of the Pueblo tribes and the absolute authority over individuals continues now among only a few of them. The loosening is in part the result of contact with whites, in part for the reason that more and more they are building their houses outside of the old, solid blocks of the villages, simply because they are no longer under constant, urgent need for defense.

It is irony that the peace-loving southwestern farmers were surrounded by the worst raiders of all the wild tribes of North America. Around A.D. 1100 or 1200 there began filtering in among them bands of primitives, possessors of a very simple culture, who spoke languages of the Athabascan stock. These people had drifted down from western Canada. In the course of time they became the Navahos and the Apaches. For all their poverty, they possessed a sinew-backed bow of Asiatic type that was superior to any missile weapon known to the Southwest. They traded with the Pueblos, learned from them, stole from them, raided them. As they grew stronger, they became pests. The Navahos and the northeastern branch of the Apaches, called Jicarilla Apaches, learned farming. The Navahos in time became artists, above all the finest of weavers, but they did not give up their raiding habits.

These Athabascans did not glorify war. They made a business of it. Killing enemies was incidental; in fact, a man who killed an enemy had to be purified afterwards. They fought for profit, and they were about the only North Americans whose attitude toward war resembled professional soldiers'. This did not make them any less troublesome.

The last high culture area occupied a narrow strip along the Pacific Coast, from northern California across British Columbia to southern Alaska, the Northwest Coast culture. There was no Meso-American influence here, nor was there any farming. The hunting and fishing were so rich, the supply of edible wild plants so adequate, that there was no need for farming—for which in any case the climate was unfavorable. The prerequisite for cultural progress is a food supply so lavish that either all men have spare time, or some men can specialize in non-food-producing activities while others feed them. This condition obtained on the Northwest Coast, where men caught the water creatures from whales to salmon, and hunted deer, mountain sheep, and other game animals.

The area was heavily forested with the most desirable kinds of lumber. Hence wood and bark entered largely into the culture. Bark was shredded and woven into clothing, twined into nets, used for padding. Houses, chests, dishes, spoons, canoes, and boats were made of wood. The people became carvers and woodworkers, then carried their carving over onto bone and horn. They painted their houses, boats, chests, and their elaborate wooden masks. They made wooden armor, including visored helmets, and deadly wooden clubs. In a wet climate, they made raincloaks of bark and wore basketry hats, on the top of which could be placed one or more cylinders, according to the wearer's rank. The chiefs placed carvings in front of their houses that related their lineage, tracing back ultimately to some sacred being such as Raven or Bear—the famous, so-called totem poles.

I have said that the finest prehistoric art of North America was that of the Mound Builders; in fact, no Indian work since has quite equaled it—but that is, of course, a matter of taste. The greatest historic Indian art was that of the Northwest Coast. Their carvings, like the Mound Builder sculptures, demand comparison with our own work. Their art was highly stylized, but vigorous and fresh. As for all Indians, the coming of the white men meant ruin in the end, but at first it meant metal tools, the possession of which resulted in a great artistic outburst.

Socially they were divided into chiefs, commoners, and slaves. Slaves were obtained by capture, and slave-raiding was one of the principal causes of war. Generosity was the pattern with most Indians, although in the dry Southwest we find some who made a virtue of thrift. In the main, a man was respected because he gave, not because he possessed. The Northwest Coast chiefs patterned generosity into an ugliness. A chief would invite a rival to a great feast, the famous potlatch. At the feast he would shower his rival and other guests with gifts, especially copper disks and blankets woven of mountain sheep wool, which were the highest units of value. He might further show his lavishness by burning some possessions, even partially destroy a copper disk, and, as like as not, kill a few slaves.

If within a reasonable time the other chief did not reply with an even larger feast, at which he gave away or destroyed double what his rival had got rid of, he was finished as a chief—but if he did respond in proper form, he might be beggared, and also finished. That was the purpose of the show. Potlatches were given for other purposes, such as to authenticate the accession of the heir to a former chief, or to buy a higher status, but ruinous rivalry was constant. They seem to have been a rather disagreeable, invidious, touchy people. The cruelty of the southeasterners is revolting, but there is something especially unpleasant about proving one's generosity and carelessness of possessions by killing a slave—with a club made for that special purpose and known as a "slave-killer."

The Meso-American culture could spread, changing beyond recognition as it did so, because it carried its food supply with it. The Northwest Coast culture could not, because its food supply was restricted to its place of origin.

North and east of the Northwest Coast area stretched the sub-Arctic and the plains of Canada, areas incapable of primitive farming. To the south and east were mountains and the region between the Rockies and the Coastal ranges called the Great Basin. Within it are large stretches of true desert; most of it is arid. Early on, Pueblo influences reached into the southern part, in Utah and Nevada, but as the climate grew drier, they died away. It was a land to be occupied by little bands of simple hunters and gatherers of seeds and roots, not strong enough to force their way into anywhere richer.

In only one other area was there a natural food supply to compare with the Northwest Coast's, and that was in the bison range of the Great Plains. But, as already noted, for men without horses or rifles, hunting bison was a tricky and hazardous business. Take the year 1600, when the Spanish were already established in New Mexico and the English and French almost ready to make settlements on the East Coast, and look for the famous Plains tribes. They are not there. Some are in the mountains, some in the woodlands to the northeast, some farming to the eastward, within the zone of ample rainfall. Instead we find scattered bands of Athabascans occupying an area no one else wanted.

Then the white men turned everything upside down. Three elements were most important in the early influence: the dislodgment of eastern tribes, the introduction of the horse, and metal tools and firearms. Let us look first at the impact on the centers of high culture.

White men came late to the Northwest Coast, and at first only as traders. As already noted, early contact with them enriched the life of the Indians and brought about a cultural spurt. Then came settlers. The most advanced, best organized tribes stood up fairly well against them for a time, and they are by no means extinct, but of their old culture there are now only remnants, with the strongest survivals being in the arts. Today, those Indians who are in the "Indian business," making money from tourists, dress in fringed buckskin and war bonnets, because otherwise the tourists will not accept them as genuine.

The tribes of the Atlantic Coast were quickly dislodged or wiped out. The more advanced groups farther inland held out all through colonial times and on into the 1830s, making fairly successful adjustments to the changed situation, retaining their sovereignty, and enriching their culture with wholesale taking over of European elements, including, in the South, the ownership of Negro slaves. Finally, as already noted, they were forcibly removed to Oklahoma, and in the end their sovereignty was destroyed. They remain numerous, and although some are extremely poor and backward, others, still holding to their tribal affiliations, have merged successfully into the general life of the state, holding positions as high as chief justice of the state supreme court. The Iroquois still hold out in New York and in Canada on remnants of their original reservations. Many of them have had remarkable success in adapting themselves to white American life while retaining considerable elements of their old culture. Adherents to the old religion are many, and the rituals continue vigorously.

The British invaders of the New World, and to a lesser degree the French, came to colonize. They came in thousands, to occupy the land. They were, therefore, in direct competition with the Indians and acted accordingly, despite their verbal adherence to fine principles of justice and fair dealing. The Spanish came quite frankly to conquer, to Christianize, and to exploit, all by force of arms. They did not shilly-shally about Indian title to the land or Indian sovereignty; they simply took over, then granted the Indians titles deriving from the Spanish crown. They came in small numbers—only around 3,000 settled in the Southwest—and the Indian labor force was essential to their aims. Therefore they did not dislodge or exterminate the Indians, and they had notable success in modifying Indian culture for survival within their regime and contribution to it.

In the Southwest the few Spaniards, cut off from the main body in Mexico by many miles of difficult, wild country, could not have survived alone against the wild tribes that shortly began to harry them. They needed the Pueblo Indians and the Pueblos needed them. The Christian Pueblos were made secure in their lands and in their local self-government. They approached social and political equality. During the period when New Mexico was under the Mexican Republic, for two years a Taos Indian, braids, blanket, and all, was governor of the territory. Eighteen pueblos survive to this day, with a population now approaching 19,000, in addition to nearly 4,000 Hopis, whose culture is Pueblo, in Arizona. They are conservative progressives, prosperous on the whole, with an excellent chance of surviving as a distinctive group for many generations to come. It was in the house of a Pueblo priest, a man deeply versed in the old religion as well as a devout Catholic, that I first saw color television.

The Spanish, then, did not set populations in motion. That was done chiefly from the east. The great Spanish contribution was loosing the horses. They did not intend to; in fact, they made every possible effort to prevent Indians from acquiring horses or learning to ride. But the animals multiplied and ran wild; they spread north from California into Oregon; they spread into the wonderful grazing land of the high Plains, a country beautifully suited to horses.

From the east, the tribes were pressing against the tribes farther west. Everything was in unhappy motion, and the tribes nearest to the white men had firearms. So the Chippewas, carrying muskets, pushed westward into Minnesota, driving the reluctant Dakotas, the Sioux tribes, out of the wooded country into the Plains as the horses spread north. At first the Dakotas hunted and ate the strange animals, then they learned to ride them, and they were off.

The Sioux were mounted. So were the Blackfeet. The semi-civilized Cheyennes swung into the saddle and moved out of the farming country into the bison range. The Kiowas moved from near the Yellowstone to the Panhandle; the Comanches came down out of the Rocky Mountains; the Arapahos, the Crows, abandoning their cornfields, and the Piegans, the great fighting names, all followed the bison. They built their life around the great animals. They ate meat lavishly all year round; their tepees, carried or dragged now by horses, became commodious. A new culture, a horse-and-bison culture, sprang up overnight. The participants in it had a wonderful time. They feasted, they roved, they hunted, they played. Over a serious issue, such as the invasion of one tribe's territory by another, they could fight deadly battles, but otherwise even war was a game in which shooting an enemy was an act earning but little esteem, but touching one with one's bare hand or with a stick was the height of military achievement.

This influx of powerful tribes drove the last of the Athabascans into the Southwest. There the Apaches and the Navahos were also mounted and on the go, developing their special, deadly pattern of war as a business. In the Panhandle country, the Kiowas and Comanches looked westward to the Spanish and Pueblo settlements, where totally alien peoples offered rich plunder. The Pueblos, as we have seen, desired to live at peace. The original Spanish came to conquer; their descendants, becoming Spanish-Americans, were content to hold what they had, farm their fields, and graze their flocks. To the north of the two groups were Apaches and Utes; to the east, Kiowas and Comanches; to the south, what seemed like unlimited Apaches; and to the west the Navahos, of whom there were several thousands by the middle of the seventeenth century.

The tribes named above, other than the Kiowas and Comanches, did not share in the Plains efflorescence. The Navahos staged a different cultural spurt of their own, combining extensive farming with constant horseback plundering, which in turn enabled them to become herdsmen, and from the captured wool develop their remarkable weaving industry. The sheep, of course, which became important in their economy, also derived from the white men. Their prosperity and their arts were superimposed on a simple camp life. With this prosperity, they also developed elaborate rituals and an astoundingly rich, poetic mythology.

The Dakotas first saw horses in 1722, which makes a convenient peg date for the beginning of the great Plains culture. A little over a hundred years later, when Catlin visited the Mandans, it was going full blast. The memory of a time before horses had grown dim. By 1860 the Plains tribes were hardpressed to stand the white men off; by 1880 the whole pattern was broken and the bison were gone. At its height, Plains Indian culture was brittle. Materially, it depended absolutely on a single source of food and skins; in other aspects, it required the absolute independence of the various tribes. When these two factors were eliminated, the content was destroyed. Some Indians may still live in tepees, wear at times their traditional clothing, maintain here and there their arts and some of their rituals, but these are little more than fringe survivals.

While the Plains culture died, the myth of it spread and grew to become embedded in our folklore. Not only the Northwest Coast Indians but many others as unlikely wear imitations of Plains Indian costume and put on "war dances," to satisfy the believers in the myth. As it exists today in the public mind, it still contains the mutually incongruous elements of the Noble Red Man and the Bloodthirsty Savage that first came into being three centuries and a half ago, before any white man had ever seen a war bonnet or a tepee, or any Indian had ridden a horse.

2

Were the Puritans "Puritanical?"

Carl N. Degler

Carl N. Degler (1921–   ), president of the Organization of American Historians from 1979–80, has enjoyed a long and fruitful academic career. Since earning his Ph.D. at Columbia University in 1952, he has spent most of his career teaching at Vassar (1954–1968) and Stanford (since 1968). His primary research interests have been the history of the American South and American social history, particularly women and the family, as exemplified by his outstanding book At Odds: Women and the Family in America from the Revolution to the Present *(1980). He won several awards for his penetrating comparative study* Neither Black Nor White: Slavery and Race Relations in Brazil and the United States *(1971). The article that follows is taken from* Out of Our Past *(1959), a stimulating social and intellectual history of the United States.*

In the pleasure-oriented 1920s, satirist H. L. Mencken defined a Puritan as a person who was desperately afraid "that someone, some-where, may be happy," a theme used as a counterpoint for Hugh Hefner's "playboy philosophy" in the 1960s and 1970s. In this article, Degler takes issue with the Mencken image and sets the record straight in a responsible historical reevaluation. He refutes the "puritanical" nature of the Puritans in the areas of drinking, dress, music, art, and sex. Tempered by such twentieth-century horrors as two world wars, Stalin, Hitler, and a nuclear arms race, Degler finds the negative Puritan view of human nature more realistic than did earlier, more optimistic historians.

The Puritans played a disproportionately large part in forging the American character. Their Calvinistic view of humans as inherently sinful has been a powerful force in the nation's history and has contributed to Americans' being among the most morality-conscious people in the world. Their emphasis on the importance of education, given secular support by Thomas Jefferson, reflects a continuing fundamental American attitude. All in all, Degler demonstrates that the American character has not changed as much over the centuries as many people believe.

To most Americans—and to most Europeans, for that matter the core of the Puritan social heritage has been summed up in Macaulay's well-known witticism that the Puritans prohibited bearbaiting not because of torture to the bear, but because of the pleasure it afforded the spectators. And as late as 1925, H. L. Mencken defined Puritanism as "the haunting fear that someone, somewhere, may be happy." Before this chapter is out, much will be said about the somber and even grim nature of the Puritan view of life, but quips like those of Macaulay and Mencken distort rather than illumine the essential character of the Puritans. Simply because the word "Puritan" has become encrusted with a good many barnacles, it is worth while to try to scrape them off if we wish to gain an understanding of the Puritan heritage. Though this process is essentially a negative one, sometimes it is clarifying to set forth what an influence is *not* as well as what it is.

Fundamental to any appreciation of the Puritan mind on matters of pleasure must be the recognition that the typical, godly Puritan was a worker in the world. Puritanism, like Protestantism in general, resolutely and definitely rejected the ascetic and monastic ideals of medieval Catholicism. Pleasures of the body were not to be eschewed by the Puritan, for, as Calvin reasoned, God "intended to provide not only for our necessity, but likewise for our pleasure and delight." It is obvious, he wrote in his famous *Institutes,* that "the Lord have endowed flowers with such beauty . . . with such sweetness of smell" in order to impress our senses; therefore, to enjoy them is not contrary to God's intentions. "In a word," he concluded, "hath He not made many things worthy of our estimation independent of any necessary use?"

It was against excess of enjoyment that the Puritans cautioned and legislated. "The wine is from God," Increase Mather warned, "but the

Drunkard is from the Devil." The Cambridge Platform of the Church of 1680 prohibited games of cards or dice because of the amount of time they consumed and the encouragement they offered to idleness, but the ministers of Boston in 1699 found no difficulty in condoning public lotteries. They were like a public tax, the ministers said, since they took only what the "government might have demanded, with a more *general imposition* . . . and it employes for the welfare of the public, all that is raised by the *lottery*." Though Cotton Mather at the end of the century condemned mixed dancing, he did not object to dancing as such; and his grandfather, John Cotton, at the beginning saw little to object to in dancing between the sexes so long as it did not become lascivious. It was this same John Cotton, incidentally, who successfully contended against Roger Williams' argument that women should wear veils in church.

In matters of dress, it is true that the Massachusetts colony endeavored to restrict the wearing of "some new and immodest fashions" that were coming in from England, but often these efforts were frustrated by the pillars of the church themselves. Winthrop reported in his *History*, for example, that though the General Court instructed the elders of the various churches to reduce the ostentation in dress by "urging it upon the consciences of their people," little change was effected, "for divers of the elders' wives, etc., were in some measure partners in this general disorder."

We also know now that Puritan dress—not that made "historical" by Saint-Gaudens' celebrated statue—was the opposite of severe, being rather in the English Renaissance style. Most restrictions on dress which were imposed were for purposes of class differentiation rather than for ascetic reasons. Thus long hair was acceptable on an upper-class Puritan like Cromwell or Winthrop, but it was a sign of vanity on the head of a person of lower social status. In 1651 the legislature of Massachusetts called attention to that "excess in Apparell" which has "crept in upon us, and especially amongst people of mean condition, to the dishonor of God, the scandall of our profession, the consumption of Estates, and altogether unsuitable to our poverty." The law declared "our utter detestation and dislike, that men or women of mean condition, should take upon them the garb of Gentlemen, by wearing Gold or Silver Lace, or Buttons, or Points at their knees, or to walk in great Boots; or Women of the same rank to wear Silk or Tiffany hoods, or Scarfes, which tho allowable to persons of greater Estates, or more liberal education, is intolerable in people of low condition." By implication, this law affords a clear description of what the well-dressed Puritan of good estate would wear.

If the Puritans are to be saved from the canard of severity of dress, it is also worth while to soften the charge that they were opposed to music and art. It is perfectly true that the Puritans insisted that organs be removed from the churches and that in England some church organs were smashed by zealots. But it was not music organs as such which they opposed, only music in the meetinghouse. Well-known American and English Puritans, like Samuel Sewell, John Milton, and Cromwell, were sincere lovers of music. Moreover, it should be remembered that it was under Puritan rule that opera was introduced into England—and without protest, either. The first English dramatic production entirely in music—*The Siege of Rhodes*—was presented in 1656, four years before the Restoration. Just before the end of Puritan rule, John Evelyn noted in his diary that he went "to see a new opera, after the Italian way, in recitative music and scenes. . . . " Furthermore, as Percy Scholes points out, in all the voluminous contemporary literature attacking the Puritans for every conceivable narrow-mindedness, none asserts that they opposed music, so long as it was performed outside the church.

The weight of the evidence is much the same in the realm of art. Though King Charles' art collection was dispersed by the incoming Commonwealth, it is significant that Cromwell and other Puritans bought several of the items. We also know that the Protector's garden at Hampton Court was beautified by nude statues. Furthermore, it is now possible to say that the Puritan closing of the theaters was as much a matter of objection to their degenerate lewdness by the 1640s as an objection to the drama as such. As far as American Puritans are concerned, it is not possible to say very much about their interest in art since there was so little in the seventeenth century. At least it can be said that the Puritans, unlike the Quakers, had no objection to portrait painting.

Some modern writers have professed to find in Puritanism, particularly the New England brand, evidence of sexual repression and inhibition. Though it would certainly be false to suggest that the Puritans did not subscribe to the canon of simple chastity, it is equally erroneous to think that their sexual lives were crabbed or that sex was abhorrent to them. Marriage to the Puritan was something more than alternative to "burning," as the Pauline doctrine of the Catholic Church would have it. Marriage was enjoined upon the righteous Christian; celibacy was not a sign of merit. With unconcealed disapprobation, John Cotton told a recently married couple the story of a pair "who immediately upon marriage, without ever approaching the *Nuptial Bed*," agreed to live apart from the rest of the world, "afterwards from one another, too. . . . " But, Cotton advised, such behavior was "no other than an effort of blind zeal, for they are the dictates of a blind mind they follow therein and not of the Holy Spirit which saith, *It is not good that man should be alone*." Cotton set himself against not only Catholic asceticism but also the view that women were the "unclean vessel," the tempters of men. Women, rather than being "a necessary Evil are a necessary Good," he wrote. "Without them there is no comfortable Living for Man. . . . "

Because, as another divine said, "the Use of the Marriage Bed" is "founded in man's Nature" the realistic Puritans required that married men unaccompanied by wives should leave the colony or bring their wives over forthwith. The Puritan settlements encouraged marriages satisfactory to the participants by permitting divorces for those whose spouses were impotent, too long absent, or cruel. Indeed, the divorce laws of New England were the easiest in Christendom at a time when the eloquence of a Milton was unable to loosen the bonds of matrimony in England.

Samuel Eliot Morison in his history of Harvard has collected a number of examples of the healthy interest of Puritan boys in the opposite sex. Commonplace books, for example, indicate that Herrick's poem beginning "Gather ye rosebuds while ye may" and amorous lines from Shakespeare, as well as more erotic and even scatological verse, were esteemed by young Puritan men. For a gentleman to present his affiance with a pair of garters, one letter of a Harvard graduate tells us, was considered neither immoral nor improper.

It is also difficult to reconcile the usual view of the stuffiness of Puritans with literally hundreds of confessions to premarital sexual relations in the extant church records. It should be understood, moreover, that these confessions were made by the saints or saints-to-be, not by the unregenerate. That the common practice of the congregation was to accept such sinners into church membership without further punishment is in itself revealing. The civil law, it is true, punished such transgressions when detected among the regenerate or among the nonchurch members, but this was also true of contemporary non-Puritan Virginia. "It will be seen," writes historian Philip A. Bruce regarding Virginia, "from the various instances given relating to the profanation of Sunday, drunkenness, swearing, defamation, and sexual immorality, that, not only were the grand juries and vestries extremely vigilant in reporting these offenses, but the courts were equally prompt in inflicting punishment; and that the penalty ranged from a heavy fine to a shameful exposure in the stocks . . . and from such an exposure to a very severe flogging at the county whipping post." In short, strict moral surveillance by the public authorities was a seventeenth-century rather than a Puritan attitude.

Relations between the sexes in Puritan society were often much more loving and tender than the mythmakers would have us believe. Since it was the Puritan view that marriage was eminently desirable in the sight of God and man, it is not difficult to find evidence of deep and abiding love between a husband and wife. John Cotton, it is true, sometimes used the Biblical phrase "comfortable yoke mate" in addressing his wife, but other Puritan husbands come closer to our romantic conventions. Certainly John Winthrop's letters to his beloved Margaret indicate the depth of attachment of which the good Puritan was capable. "My good wife . . . My sweet wife," he called her. Anticipating his return home, he writes,

"So . . . we shall now enjoy each other again, as we desire. . . . It is now
bed time; but I must lie alone; therefore I make less haste. Yet I must kiss
my sweet wife; and so, with my blessing to our children . . . I commend
thee to the grace and blessing of the lord, and rest. . . . "

Anne Bradstreet wrote a number of poems devoted to her love for
her husband in which the sentiments and figures are distinctly romantic.

> To my Dear and loving Husband
> I prize thy love more than whole Mines of gold
> Or all the riches that the East doth hold.
> My love is such that Rivers cannot quench,
> Nor aught but love from thee give recompense.

In another poem her spouse is apostrophized as

> My head, my heart, mine Eyes, my life, nay more
> My joy, my Magazine of earthly store

and she asks:

> If two be one, as surely thou and I,
> How stayest thou there, whilst I at Ipswich lye?

Addressing John as "my most sweet Husband," Margaret Winthrop
perhaps epitomized the Puritan marital ideal when she wrote, "I have
many reasons to make me love thee, whereof I will name two: First,
because thou lovest God and, secondly, because thou lovest me. If these
two were wanting," she added, "all the rest would be eclipsed."

It would be a mistake, however, to try to make these serious, dedicated men and women into rakes of the Renaissance. They were sober if
human folk, deeply concerned about their ultimate salvation and intent
upon living up to God's commands as they understood them, despite
their acknowledgement of complete depravity and unworthiness. "God
sent you not into this world as Play-House, but a Work-House," one
minister told his congregation To the Puritan this was a world drenched
in evil, and, because it truly is, they were essentially realistic in their
judgments. Because the Puritan expected nothing, Perry Miller has
remarked, a disillusioned one was almost impossible to find. This is
probably an exaggeration, for they were also human beings; when the
Commonwealth fell, it was a Puritan, after all, who said, "God has spit in
our faces." But Professor Miller's generalization has much truth in it.
Only a man convinced of the inevitable and eternal character of evil
could fight it so hard and so unceasingly.

The Puritan at his best, Ralph Barton Perry has said, was a "moral
athlete." More than most men, the Puritan strove with himself and with

his fellow man to attain a moral standard higher than was rightfully to be expected of so depraved a creature. Hence the diaries and autobiographies of Puritans are filled with the most torturous probing of the soul and inward seeking. Convinced of the utter desirability of salvation on the one hand, and equally cognizant of the total depravity of man's nature on the other, the Puritan was caught in an impossible dilemma which permitted him no rest short of the grave. Yet with such a spring coiled within him, the Puritan drove himself and his society to tremendous heights of achievement both material and spiritual.

Such intense concern for the actualization of the will of God had a less pleasant side to it, also. If the belief that "I am my brother's keeper" is the breeding ground of heightened social conscience and expresses itself in the reform movements so indigenous to Boston and its environs, it also could and did lead to self-righteousness, intolerance and narrow-mindedness, as exemplified in another product of Boston: Anthony Comstock. But this fruit of the loins of Puritanism is less typical of the earthy seventeenth-century New Englander than H. L. Mencken would have us think. The Sabbatarian, antiliquor, and antisex attitudes usually attributed to the Puritans are a nineteenth-century addition to the much more moderate and essentially wholesome view of life's evils held by the early settlers of New England.

To realize how different Puritans could be, one needs only to contrast Roger Williams and his unwearying opponent John Cotton. But despite the range of differences among Puritans, they all were linked by at least one characteristic. That was their belief in themselves, in their morality and in their mission to the world. For this reason, Puritanism was intellectual and social dynamite in the seventeenth century; its power could behead kings, overthrow governments, defy tyrants, and disrupt churches.

The Reformation laid an awesome burden on the souls of those who broke with the Roman Church. Proclaiming the priesthood of all believers, Protestantism made each man's relationship to God his own terrifying responsibility. No one else could save him; therefore no one must presume to try. More concerned about his salvation than about any mundane matter, the Puritan was compelled, for the sake of his immortal soul, to be a fearless individualist.

It was the force of this conviction which produced the Great Migration of 1630–40 and made Massachusetts a flourishing colony in the span of a decade. It was also, ironically, the force which impelled Roger Williams to threaten the very legal and social foundations of the Puritan Commonwealth in Massachusetts because he thought the oligarchy wrong and himself right. And so it would always be. For try as the rulers of Massachusetts might to make men conform to their dogma, their own rebellious example always stood as a guide to those who felt the truth was being denied. Such individualism, we would call it today, was flesh and bone of the religion which the Puritans passed on. Though the theocracy soon withered and died, its harsh voice softened down to the balmy breath of Unitarianism, the belief in self and the dogged resistance to suppression or untruth which Puritanism taught never died. Insofar as Americans today can be said to be individualistic, it is to the Puritan heritage that we must look for one of the principal sources.

In his ceaseless striving for signs of salvation and knowledge of God's intentions for man, the Puritan placed great reliance upon the human intellect, even though for him, as for all Christians, faith was the bedrock of his belief. "Faith doth not relinquish or cast out reason," wrote the American Puritan Samuel Willard, "for there is nothing in Religion contrary to it, tho' there are many things that do transcend and must captivate it." Richard Baxter, the English Puritan, insisted that "the *most Religious,* are the *most* truly, and *nobly rational*." Religion and reason were complementary to the Puritan, not antithetical as they were to many evangelical sects of the time.

Always the mere emotion of religion was to be controlled by reason. Because of this, the university-trained Puritan clergy prided themselves on the lucidity and rationality of their sermons. Almost rigorously their sermons followed the logical sequence of "doctrine," "reasons," and "uses." Conscientiously they shunned the meandering and rhetorical flourishes so beloved by Laudian preachers like John Donne, and in the process facilitated the taking of notes by their eager listeners. One of the unforgivable crimes of Mistress Anne Hutchinson was her assertion that one could "feel" one's salvation, that one was "filled with God" after conversion, that it was unnecessary, in order to be saved, to be learned in the Bible or in the Puritan writers. It was not that the Puritans were cold to the Word—far from it. A saint was required to testify to an intense religious experience—almost by definition emotional in character—before he could attain full membership in the Church. But it was always important to the Puritans that mere emotion—whether it be the anarchistic activities of the Anabaptists or the quaking of the Friends—should not be mistaken for righteousness or proper religious conduct. Here, as in so many things, the Puritans attempted to walk the middle path—in this instance, between the excessive legalism and formalism of the Catholics and Episcopalians and the flaming, intuitive evangelism of the Baptists and Quakers.

Convinced of reason's great worth, it was natural that the Puritans should also value education. "Ignorance is the mother (not of Devotion but) of Heresy," one Puritan divine declared. And a remarkably well-educated ministry testified to the Puritan belief that learning and scholarship were necessary for a proper understanding of the Word of God. More than a hundred graduates of Cambridge and Oxford Universities settled in New England before 1640, most of them ministers. At the same date not five men in all of Virginia could lay claim to such an educational background. Since Cambridge University, situated on the edge of Puritan East Anglia, supplied most of the graduates in America, it was natural that Newtown, the site of New England's own college, would soon be renamed in honor of the Alma Mater. "After God had carried us safe to New-England," said a well-known tract, some of its words now immortalized in metal in Harvard Yard, "one of the next things we longed and looked after, was to advance learning, and perpetuate it to posterity; dreading to leave an illiterate ministry to the churches, when the present ministers shall lie in the dust." "The College," founded in 1636, soon to be named Harvard, was destined to remain the only institution of higher learning in America during almost all the years of the seventeenth century. Though it attracted students from as far away as Virginia, it remained, as it began, the fountainhead of Puritan learning in the New World.

Doubt as one may Samuel Eliot Morison's claims for the secular origins of Harvard, his evidence of the typically Renaissance secular education which was available at the Puritan college in New England is both impressive and convincing. The Latin and Greek secular writers of antiquity dominated the curriculum, for this was a liberal arts training such as the leaders had received at Cambridge in England. To the Puritans the education of ministers could be nothing less than the best learning of the day. So important did education at Harvard seem to the New Haven colony in 1644 that the legislature ordered each town to appoint two men to be responsible for the collection of contributions from each family for "the mayntenaunce of scolars at Cambridge. . . . "

If there was to be a college, preparatory schools had to be provided for the training of those who were expected to enter the university. Furthermore, in a society dedicated to the reading of the Bible, elementary education was indispensable. "It being one chief project of that old deluder Satan to keep men from the knowledge of the Scriptures" began the first school laws of Massachusetts (1647) and Connecticut (1650). But the Puritans supported education for secular as well as religious reasons. The Massachusetts Code of 1648, for instance, required children to be taught to read inasmuch "as the good education of children is of singular behoof and benefit to any Commonwealth."

The early New England school laws provided that each town of fifty families or more was to hire a teacher for the instruction of its young; towns of one hundred families or more were also directed to provide grammar schools, "the master thereof being able to instruct youths so far as they may be fitted for the University." Though parents were not obliged to send their children to these schools, if they did not they were required to teach their children to read. From the evidence of court cases and the high level of literacy in seventeenth-century New England, it would appear that these first attempts at public-supported and public-controlled education were both enforced and fruitful.

No other colony in the seventeenth century imposed such a high educational standard upon its simple farming people as the Puritans did. It is true, of course, that Old England in this period could boast of grammar schools, some of which were free. But primary schools were almost nonexistent there, and toward the end of the seventeenth century the free schools in England became increasingly tuition schools. Moreover, it was not until well into the nineteenth century that the English government did anything to support schools. Primary and secondary education in England, in contrast with the New England example, was a private or church affair.

Unlike the Puritans, the Quakers exhibited little impulse toward popular education in the seventeenth and early eighteenth centuries. Because of their accent on the Inner Light and the doctrine of universal salvation, the religious motivation of the Puritans for learning was wanting. Furthermore, the Quakers did not look to education, as such, with the same reverence as the Puritans. William Penn, for example, advised his children that "reading many books is but a taking off the mind too much from meditation." No Puritan would have said that.

Virginia in the seventeenth century, it should be said, was also interested in education. Several times in the course of the century, plans were well advanced for establishing a university in the colony. Free schools also existed in Virginia during the seventeenth century, though the lack of village communities made them inaccessible for any great numbers of children. But, in contrast with New England, there were no publicly supported schools in Virginia; the funds for the field schools of Virginia, like those for free schools in contemporary England, came from private or ecclesiastical endowment. Nor was Virginia able to bring its several plans for a college into reality until William and Mary was founded at the very end of the century.

Though the line which runs from the early New England schools to the distinctly American system of free public schools today is not always progressively upward or uniformly clear, the connection is undeniable. The Puritan innovation of public support and control on a local level was the American prototype of a proper system of popular education.

American higher education in particular owes much to religion, for out of the various churches' concern for their faiths sprang a number of colleges, after the example of the Puritans' founding of Harvard. At the time of the Revolution, there were eight colleges besides Harvard in the English colonies, of which all but one were founded under the auspices of a church. William and Mary (1693) and King's College, later Columbia (1754), were the work of the Episcopalians; Yale (1701) and

Dartmouth (1769) were set up by Congregationalists not comforted by Harvard; the College of New Jersey, later Princeton (1747), was founded by the Presbyterians; Queens College, later Rutgers (1766), by the Dutch Reformed Church; the College of Rhode Island, later Brown (1764), by the Baptists. Only the Academy of Philadelphia, later the University of Pennsylvania (1749), was secular in origin.

The overwhelming importance of the churches in the expansion of American higher education during the colonial period set a pattern which continued well into the nineteenth century and to a limited extent is still followed. Well-known colleges like Oberlin, Wesleyan, Haverford, Wittenberg, Moravian, Muhlenberg, and Notre Dame were all founded by churches in the years before the Civil War. By providing a large number of colleges (recall that England did not enjoy a third university until the nineteenth century), the religious impulses and diversity of the American people very early encouraged that peculiarly American faith in the efficacy and desirability of education for all.

When dwelling on the seminal qualities of the seventeenth century, it is tempting to locate the source of the later American doctrine of the separation of Church and State and religious freedom in the writings of Roger Williams and in the practices of provinces like New York, Maryland, and Pennsylvania. Actually, however, such a line of development is illusory. At the time of the Revolution all the colonies, including Rhode Island, imposed restrictions and disabilities upon some sects, thus practicing at best only a limited form of toleration, not freedom of religion—much less separation of Church and State. Moreover, Roger Williams' cogent and prophetic arguments in behalf of religious freedom were forgotten in the eighteenth century; they could not exert any influence on those who finally worked out the doctrine of religious freedom enshrined in the national Constitution. In any case, it would have been exceedingly difficult for Williams to have spoken to Jefferson and the other Virginians who fought for religious freedom. To Williams the Puritan, the great justification for freedom of religion was the preservation of the purity of the Church; to the deistic Virginians, the important goal was the removal of a religious threat to the purity and freedom of the State.

3

The Quest
for the National
Character

David M. Potter

*After earning his Ph.D. in history at Yale in 1940, David Potter (1910–
1971) spent his career teaching at Yale and Stanford. His major interests were his native South, particularly the Civil War period (see his*
Lincoln and His Party in the Secession Crisis *and* The South and
the Secession Crisis*), and, later in his career, social history. His People of Plenty (1954), a landmark in the analysis of American society,
suggested that abundance, rather than democracy, was the determining
factor in forming the American character. The implications of his thesis
are profound, for American efforts to remake the world in the image of
the United States have reflected a far greater ability and willingness to
export democracy than to export the abundance that Potter feels is
necessary to make it work.*

*This 1962 essay goes right to the heart of the forging of the Ameri-
can character. Potter holds that almost all theories of the American character fit into one of two molds. The first, initially proclaimed by Thomas
Jefferson, describes the American as an idealistic individualist. The*

This reading, "The Quest for the National Character," by David M. Potter, is
reprinted from *The Reconstruction of American History*, John Higham, ed., by permission of
Unwin Hyman, Ltd.

second, articulated by France's Alexis de Tocqueville, calls the Ameri-can a materialistic conformist. Potter seeks to reconcile the contradic-tions between these two theories by focusing on their common commitment to equality. This resolution may not answer all questions raised by the conflict, but it does afford a means of harmonizing two dissonant views of the American character.

Potter, clearly intrigued by the concept of the American character, also wrote an article found in the second volume of this collection. In "American Women and the American Character," he raises some serious questions about the inclusiveness of any theories of national character, since they omit the female half of the population. Keep that reservation in mind as you read this essay.

Unlike most nationality groups in the world today, the people of the United States are not ethnically rooted in the land where they live. The French have remote Gallic antecedents; the Germans, Teutonic; the English, Anglo-Saxon; the Italians, Roman; the Irish, Celtic; but the only people in America who can claim ancient American origins are a rem-nant of Red Indians. In any deep dimension of time, all other Americans are immigrants. They began as Europeans (or in the case of 10 percent of the population, as Africans), and if they became Americans it was only, somehow, after a relatively recent passage westbound across the Atlantic.

It is, perhaps, this recency of arrival which has given to Americans a somewhat compulsive preoccupation with the question of their Ameri-canism. No people can really qualify as a nation in the true sense unless they are united by important qualities or values in common. If they share the same ethnic, or linguistic, or religious, or political heritage, the foun-dations of nationality can hardly be questioned. But when their ethnic, religious, linguistic, and political heritage is mixed, as in the case of the American people, nationality can hardly exist at all unless it takes the form of a common adjustment to conditions of a new land, a common commitment to shared values, a common esteem for certain qualities of character, or a common set of adaptive traits and attitudes. It is partly for this reason that Americans, although committed to the principle of free-dom of thought, have nevertheless placed such emphasis upon the obli-gation to accept certain undefined tenets of "Americanism." It is for this same reason, also, that Americans have insisted upon their distinctive-ness from the Old World from which they are derived. More than two centuries ago Hector St. John de Crevecoeur asked a famous question, "What then is the American, this new man?" He simply assumed, without arguing the point, that the American is a new man, and he only inquired wherein the American is different. A countless array of writers, includ-ing not only careful historians and social scientists but also professional

patriots, hit-and-run travelers, itinerant lecturers, intuitive-minded am-
ateurs of all sorts, have been repeating Crevecoeur's question and seeking to answer it ever since.

A thick volume would hardly suffice even to summarize the diverse
interpretations which these various writers have advanced in describing
or explaining the American character. Almost every trait, good or bad,
has been attributed to the American people by someone, and almost
every explanation, from Darwinian selection to toilet-training, has been
advanced to account for the attributed qualities. But it is probably safe to
say that at bottom there have been only two primary ways of explaining
the American, and that almost all of the innumerable interpretations
which have been formulated can be grouped around or at least oriented
to these two basic explanations, which serve as polar points for all the
literature.

The most disconcerting fact about these two composite images of
the American is that they are strikingly dissimilar and seemingly about
as inconsistent with one another as two interpretations of the same phe-
nomenon could possibly be. One depicts the American primarily as an
individualist and an idealist, while the other makes him out as a conformist and a materialist. Both images have been developed with great
detail and elaborate explanation in extensive bodies of literature, and
both are worth a close scrutiny.

For those who have seen the American primarily as an individualist, the story of his evolution as a distinctive type dates back possibly to
the actual moment of his decision to migrate from Europe to the New
World, for this was a process in which the daring and venturesome were
more prone to risk life in a new country while the timid and the conventional were more disposed to remain at home. If the selective factors in
the migration had the effect of screening out men of low initiative, the
conditions of life in the North American wilderness, it is argued, must
have further heightened the exercise of individual resourcefulness, for
they constantly confronted the settler with circumstances in which he
could rely upon no one but himself, and where the capacity to improvise
a solution for a problem was not infrequently necessary to survival.

In many ways the colonial American exemplified attitudes that
were individualistic. Although he made his first settlements by the removal of whole communities which were transplanted bodily—
complete with all their ecclesiastical and legal institutions—he turned
increasingly, in the later process of settlement, to a more and more
individualistic mode of pioneering, in which one separate family would
take up title to a separate, perhaps an isolated, tract of land, and would
move to this land long in advance of any general settlement, leaving
churches and courts and schools far behind. His religion, whether
Calvinistic Puritanism or emotional revivalism, made him individually

responsible for his own salvation, without the intervention of ecclesiastical intermediaries between himself and his God. His economy, which was based very heavily upon subsistence farming, with very little division of labor, also impelled him to cope with a diversity of problems and to depend upon no one but himself.

With all of these conditions at work, the tendency to place a premium upon individual self-reliance was no doubt well developed long before the cult of the American as an individualist crystallized in a conceptual form. But it did crystallize, and it took on almost its classic formulation in the thought of Thomas Jefferson.

It may seem paradoxical to regard Jefferson as a delineator of American national character, for in direct terms he did not attempt to describe the American character at all. But he did conceive that one particular kind of society was necessary to the fulfillment of American ideals, and further that one particular kind of person, namely the independent farmer, was a necessary component in the optimum society. He believed that the principles of liberty and equality, which he cherished so deeply, could not exist in a hierarchical society, such as that of Europe, nor, indeed, in any society where economic and social circumstances enabled one set of men to dominate and exploit the rest. An urban society or a commercial society, with its concentration of financial power into a few hands and its imposition of dependence through a wage system, scarcely lent itself better than an aristocracy to his basic values. In fact, only a society of small husbandmen who tilled their own soil and found sustenance in their own produce could achieve the combination of independence and equalitarianism which he envisioned for the ideal society. Thus, although Jefferson did not write a description of the national character, he erected a model for it, and the model ultimately had more influence than a description could ever have exercised. The model American was a plain, straightforward agrarian democrat, an individualist in his desire for freedom for himself, and an idealist in his desire for equality for all men.

Jefferson's image of the American as a man of independence, both in his values and in his mode of life, has had immense appeal to Americans ever since. They found this image best exemplified in the man of the frontier, for he, as a pioneer, seemed to illustrate the qualities of independence and self-reliance in their most pronounced and most dramatic form. Thus, in a tradition of something like folklore, half-legendary figures like Davy Crockett have symbolized America as well as symbolizing the frontier. In literature, ever since J. Fenimore Cooper's Leatherstocking tales, the frontier scout, at home under the open sky, free from the trammels of an organized and stratified society, has been cherished as an incarnation of American qualities. In American politics the voters showed such a marked preference for men who had been born in log cabins that many an ambitious candidate pretended to pioneer origins which were in fact fictitious.

The pioneer is, of course, not necessarily an agrarian (he may be a hunter, a trapper, a cowboy, a prospector for gold), and the agrarian is not necessarily a pioneer (he may be a European peasant tilling his ancestral acres), but the American frontier was basically an agricultural frontier, and the pioneer was usually a farmer. Thus it was possible to make an equation between the pioneer and the agrarian, and since the pioneer evinced the agrarian traits in their most picturesque and most appealing form there was a strong psychological impulse to concentrate the diffused agrarian ideal into a sharp frontier focus. This is, in part, what Frederick Jackson Turner did in 1893 when he wrote *The Significance of the Frontier in American History.* In this famous essay Turner offered an explanation of what has been distinctive in American history, but it is not as widely realized as it might be that he also penned a major contribution to the literature of national character. Thus Turner affirmed categorically that:

> The American intellect owes its striking characteristics to the frontier. That coarseness and strength, combined with acuteness and acquisitiveness; that practical inventive turn of mind, quick to find expedients; that masterful grasp of material things, lacking in the artistic but powerful to effect great ends; that restless, nervous energy; that dominant individualism, working for good and for evil; and withal, that buoyancy and exuberance which comes with freedom—these are traits of the frontier, or traits called out elsewhere because of the existence of the frontier.

A significant but somewhat unnoticed aspect of Turner's treatment is the fact that, in his quest to discover the traits of the American character, he relied for proof not upon descriptive evidence that given traits actually prevailed, but upon the argument that given conditions in the environment would necessarily cause the development of certain traits. Thus the cheapness of land on the frontier would make for universal land-holding which in turn would make for equalitarianism in the society. The absence of division of labor on the frontier would force each man to do most things for himself, and this would breed self-reliance. The pitting of the individual man against the elemental forces of the wilderness and of nature would further reinforce this self-reliance. Similarly, the fact that a man had moved out in advance of society's institutions and its stratified structure would mean that he could find independence, without being overshadowed by the institutions, and could enjoy an equality unknown to stratified society. All of this argument was made without any sustained effort to measure exactly how much recognizable equalitarianism and individualism and self-reliance actually were in evidence either on the American frontier or in American society. There is little reason to doubt that most of his arguments were valid or that most of the traits which he emphasized did actually prevail, but it is nevertheless ironical that Turner's interpretation, which exercised such vast influence upon historians, was not based upon the historian's kind of proof, which is from evidence, but upon an argument from logic which so often fails to work out in historical experience.

But no matter how he arrived at it, Turner's picture reaffirmed some by-now-familiar beliefs about the American character. The American was equalitarian, stoutly maintaining the practices of both social and political democracy; he had a spirit of freedom reflected in his buoyance and exuberance; he was individualistic—hence "practical and inventive," "quick to find expedients," "restless, nervous, acquisitive." Turner was too much a scholar to let his evident fondness for the frontiersman run away with him entirely, and he took pains to point out that this development was not without its sordid aspects. There was a marked primitivism about the frontier, and with it, to some extent, a regression from civilized standards. The buoyant and exuberant frontiersman sometimes emulated his Indian neighbors in taking the scalps of his adversaries. Coarse qualities sometimes proved to have more survival value than gentle ones. But on the whole this regression was brief, and certainly a rough-and-ready society had its compensating advantages. Turner admired his frontiersman, and thus Turner's American, like Jefferson's American, was partly a realistic portrait from life and partly an idealized model from social philosophy. Also, though one of these figures was an agrarian and the other was a frontiersman, both were very much the same man—democratic, freedom-loving, self-reliant, and individualistic.

An essay like this is hardly the place to prove either the validity or the invalidity of the Jeffersonian and Turnerian conception of the American character. The attempt to do so would involve a review of the entire range of American historical experience, and in the course of such a review the proponents of this conception could point to a vast body of evidence in support of their interpretation. They could argue, with much force, that Americans have consistently been zealous to defend individualism by defending the rights and the welfare of the individual, and that our whole history is a protracted record of our government's recognizing its responsibility to an ever broader range of people—to men without property, to men held in slavery, to women, to small enterprises threatened by monopoly, to children laboring in factories, to industrial workers, to the ill, to the elderly, and to the unemployed. This record, it can further be argued, is also a record of the practical idealism of the American people, unceasingly at work.

But without attempting a verdict on the historical validity of this image of the American as individualist and idealist, it is important to bear in mind that this image has been partly a portrait, but also partly a model.

In so far as it is a portrait—a likeness by an observer reporting on Americans whom he knew—it can be regarded as authentic testimony on the American character. But in so far as it is a model—an idealization of what is best in Americanism, and of what Americans should strive to be, it will only be misleading if used as evidence of what ordinary Americans are like in their everyday lives. It is also important to recognize that the Jefferson–Turner image posited several traits as distinctively American, and that they are not all necessarily of equal validity. Particularly, Jefferson and Turner both believed that love of equality and love of liberty go together. For Jefferson the very fact, stated in the Declaration of Independence, that "all men are created equal," carried with it the corollary that they are all therefore "entitled to (and would be eager for) life, liberty, and the pursuit of happiness." From this premise it is easy to slide imperceptibly into the position of holding that equalitarianism and individualism are inseparably linked, or even that they are somehow the same thing. This is, indeed, almost an officially sanctioned ambiguity in the American creed. But it requires only a little thoughtful reflection to recognize that equalitarianism and individualism do not necessarily go together. Alexis de Tocqueville understood this fact more than a century ago, and out of his recognition he framed an analysis which is not only the most brilliant single account of the American character, but is also the only major alternative to the Jefferson–Turner image.

After traveling the length and breadth of the United States for ten months at the height of Andrew Jackson's ascendancy, Tocqueville felt no doubt of the depth of the commitment of Americans to democracy. Throughout two volumes which ranged over every aspect of American life, he consistently emphasized democracy as a pervasive factor. But the democracy which he wrote about was far removed from Thomas Jefferson's dream.

"Liberty," he observed of the Americans, "is not the chief object of their desires; equality is their idol. They make rapid and sudden efforts to obtain liberty, and if they miss their aim resign themselves to their disappointment; but nothing can satisfy them without equality, and they would rather perish than lose it."

This emphasis upon equality was not, in itself, inconsistent with the most orthodox Jeffersonian ideas, and indeed Tocqueville took care to recognize that under certain circumstances equality and freedom might "meet and blend." But such circumstances would be rare, and the usual effects of equality would be to encourage conformity and discourage individualism, to regiment opinion and to inhibit dissent. Tocqueville justified this seemingly paradoxical conclusion by arguing that:

> When the inhabitant of a democratic country compares himself individually with all those about him, he feels with pride that he is the equal of any

one of them; but when he comes to survey the totality of his fellows, and to place himself in contrast with so huge a body, he is instantly overwhelmed by the sense of his own insignificance and weakness. The same equality that renders him independent of each of his fellow citizens, taken severally, exposes him alone and unprotected to the influence of the greater number. The public, therefore, among a democratic people, has a singular power, which aristocratic nations cannot conceive; for it does not persuade others to its beliefs, but it imposes them and makes them permeate the thinking of everyone by a sort of enormous pressure of the mind of all upon the individual intelligence.

At the time when Tocqueville wrote, he expressed admiration for the American people in many ways, and when he criticized adversely his tone was abstract, bland, and free of the petulance and the personalities that characterized some critics, like Mrs. Trollope and Charles Dickens. Consequently, Tocqueville was relatively well received in the United States, and we have largely forgotten what a severe verdict his observations implied. But, in fact, he pictured the American character as the very embodiment of conformity, of conformity so extreme that not only individualism but even freedom was endangered. Because of the enormous weight with which the opinion of the majority pressed upon the individual, Tocqueville said, the person in the minority "not only mistrusts his strength, but even doubts of his right; and he is very near acknowledging that he is in the wrong when the greater number of his countrymen assert that he is so. The majority do not need to force him; they convince him." "The principle of equality," as a consequence, had the effect of "prohibiting him from thinking at all," and "freedom of opinion does not exist in America." Instead of reinforcing liberty, therefore, equality constituted a danger to liberty. It caused the majority "to despise and undervalue the rights of private persons," and led on to the pessimistic conclusion that "Despotism appears . . . peculiarly to be dreaded in democratic times."

Tocqueville was perhaps the originator of the criticism of the American as conformist, but he also voiced another criticism which has had many echoes, but which did not originate with him. This was the condemnation of the American as a materialist. As early as 1805 Richard Parkinson had observed that "all men there (in America) make it (money) their pursuit," and in 1823 William Faux had asserted that "two selfish gods, pleasure and gain, enslave the Americans." In the interval between the publication of the first and second parts of Tocqueville's study, Washington Irving coined his classic phrase concerning "the almighty dollar, that great object of universal devotion throughout the land." But it remained for Tocqueville, himself, to link materialism with equality, as he had already linked conformity.

"Of all passions," he said, "which originate in or are fostered by equality, there is one which it renders peculiarly intense, and which it also infuses into the heart of every man: I mean the love of well-being. The taste for well-being is the prominent and indelible feature of democratic times. . . . The effort to satisfy even the least wants of the body and to provide the little conveniences of life is uppermost in every mind."

He described this craving for physical comforts as a "passion," and affirmed that "I know of no country, indeed, where the love of money has taken stronger hold on the affections of men."

For more than a century we have lived with the contrasting images of the American character which Thomas Jefferson and Alexis de Tocqueville visualized. Both of these images presented the American as an equalitarian and therefore as a democrat, but one was an agrarian democrat while the other was a majoritarian democrat; one an independent individualist, the other a mass-dominated conformist; one an idealist, the other a materialist. Through many decades of self-scrutiny Americans have been seeing one or the other of these images whenever they looked into the mirror of self-analysis.

The discrepancy between the two images is so great that it must bring the searcher for the American character up with a jerk, and must force him to grapple with the question whether these seemingly antithetical versions of the American can be reconciled in any way. Can the old familiar formula for embracing opposite reports—that the situation presents a paradox—be stretched to encompass both Tocqueville and Jefferson? Or is there so grave a flaw somewhere that one must question the whole idea of national character and call to mind all the warnings that thoughtful men have uttered against the very concept that national groups can be distinguished from one another in terms of collective group traits.

Certainly there is a sound enough basis for doubting the validity of generalizations about national character. To begin with, many of these generalizations have been derived not from any dispassionate observation or any quest for truth, but from superheated patriotism which sought only to glorify one national group by invidious comparison with other national groups, or from a pseudo-scientific racism which claimed innately superior qualities for favored ethnic groups. Further, the explanations which were offered to account for the ascribed traits were as suspect as the ascriptions themselves. No one today will accept the notions which once prevailed that such qualities as the capacity for self-government are inherited in the genes, nor will anyone credit the notion that national character is a unique quality which manifests itself mystically in all the inhabitants of a given country. Between the chauvinistic purposes for which the concept of national character was used, and the irrationality with which it was supported, it fell during the 1930s into a disrepute from which it has by no means fully recovered.

Some thinkers of a skeptical turn of mind had rejected the idea of national character even at a time when most historians accepted it without question. Thus, for instance, John Stuart Mill as early as 1849 observed that "of all vulgar modes of escaping from the consideration of the effect of social and moral influences on the human mind, the most vulgar is that of attributing diversities of character to inherent natural differences." Sir John Seely said, "no explanation is so vague, so cheap, and so difficult to verify."

But it was particularly at the time of the rise of Fascism and Naziism, when the vicious aspects of extreme nationalism and of racism became glaringly conspicuous, that historians in general began to repudiate the idea of national character and to disavow it as an intellectual concept, even though they sometimes continued to employ it as a working device in their treatment of the peoples with whose history they were concerned. To historians whose skepticism had been aroused, the conflicting nature of the images of the American as an individualistic democrat or as a conformist democrat would have seemed simply to illustrate further the already demonstrated flimsiness and fallacious quality of all generalizations about national character.

But to deny that the inhabitants of one country may, as a group, evince a given trait in higher degree than the inhabitants of some other country amounts almost to a denial that the culture of one people can be different from the culture of another people. To escape the pitfalls of racism in this way is to fly from one error into the embrace of another, and students of culture—primarily anthropologists, rather than historians—perceived that rejection of the idea that a group could be distinctive, along with the idea that the distinction was eternal and immutable in the genes, involved the ancient logical fallacy of throwing out the baby along with the bath. Accordingly, the study of national character came under the special sponsorship of cultural anthropology, and in the forties a number of outstanding workers in this field tackled the problem of national character, including the American character, with a methodological precision and objectivity that had never been applied to the subject before. After their investigations, they felt no doubt that national character was a reality—an observable and demonstrable reality. One of them, Margaret Mead, declared that "In every culture, in Samoa, in Germany, in Iceland, in Bali, and in the United States of America, we will find consistencies and regularities in the way in which newborn babies grow up and assume the attitudes and behavior patterns of their elders—and this we may call 'character formation.' We will find that Samoans may be said to have a Samoan character structure and Americans an American character structure." Another, the late Clyde Kluckhohn, wrote: "The statistical prediction can safely be made that a hundred Americans, for example, will display certain defined characteristics more frequently than will a hundred Englishmen comparably distributed as to age, sex, social class, and vocation."

If these new students were correct, it meant that there was some kind of identifiable American character. It might conform to the Jeffersonian image; it might conform to the Tocqueville image; it might conform in part to both; or it might conform to neither. But in any event discouraged investigators were enjoined against giving up the quest with the conclusion that there is no American character. It has been said that a philosopher is a blind man in a dark room looking for a black cat that isn't there; the student of national character might also, at times, resemble a blind man in a dark room, looking for a black cat, but the cultural anthropologists exhorted him to persevere in spite of the problems of visibility, for the cat was indubitably there.

Still confronted with the conflicting images of the agrarian democrat and the majoritarian democrat, the investigator might avoid an outright rejection of either by taking the position that the American character has changed, and that each of these images was at one time valid and realistic, but that in the twentieth century the qualities of conformity and materialism have grown increasingly prominent, while the qualities of individualism and idealism have diminished. This interpretation of a changing American character has had a number of adherents in the last two decades, for it accords well with the observation that the conditions of the American culture have changed. As they do so, of course the qualities of a character that is derived from the culture might be expected to change correspondingly. Thus, Henry S. Commager, in his *The American Mind* (1950), portrayed in two contrasting chapters "the nineteenth-century American" and "the twentieth-century American." Similarly, David Riesman, in *The Lonely Crowd* (1950), significantly sub-titled *A Study of the Changing American Character*, pictured two types of Americans, first an "inner-directed man," whose values were deeply internalized and who adhered to these values tenaciously, regardless of the opinions of his peers (clearly an individualist), and second an "other-directed man," who subordinated his own internal values to the changing expectations directed toward him by changing peer groups (in short, a conformist).

Although he viewed his inner-directed man as having been superseded historically by his other-directed man, Riesman did not attempt to explain in historical terms the reason for the change. He made a rather limited effort to relate his stages of character formation to stages of population growth, but he has since then not used population phase as a key. Meanwhile, it is fairly clear, from Riesman's own context, as well as from history in general, that there were changes in the culture which would have accounted for the transition in character. Most nineteenth-century Americans were self-employed; most were engaged in agriculture; most produced a part of their own food and clothing. These facts meant that their well-being did not depend on the goodwill or the services of their associates, but upon their resourcefulness in wrestling with the elemental forces of Nature. Even their physical isolation from their fellows added something to the independence of their natures. But most twentieth-century Americans work for wages or salaries, many of them in very large employee groups; most are engaged in office or factory work; most are highly specialized; and are reliant upon many others to supply their needs in an economy with an advanced division of labor. Men now do depend upon the goodwill and the services of their fellows. This means that what they achieve depends less upon stamina and hardihood than upon their capacity to get along with other people and to fit smoothly into a cooperative relationship. In short the culture now places a premium upon the qualities which will enable the individual to function effectively as a member of a large organizational group. The strategic importance of this institutional factor has been well recognized by William H. Whyte, Jr., in his significantly titled book *The Organization Man* (1956)—for the conformity of Whyte's bureaucratized individual results from the fact that he lives under an imperative to succeed in a situation where promotion and even survival depend upon effective inter-action with others in an hierarchical structure.

Thus, by an argument from logic (always a treacherous substitute for direct observation in historical study), one can make a strong case that the nineteenth-century American should have been (and therefore must have been) an individualist, while the twentieth-century American should be (and therefore is) a conformist. But this formula crashes headlong into the obdurate fact that no Americans have ever been more classically conformist than Tocqueville's Jacksonian democrats—hardy specimens of the frontier breed, far back in the nineteenth century, long before the age of corporate images, peer groups, marginal differentiation, and status frustration. In short, Tocqueville's nineteenth-century American, whether frontiersman or no, was to some extent an other-directed man. Carl N. Degler has pointed out this identity in a very cogent paper not yet published, in which he demonstrates very forcibly that most of our easy assumptions about the immense contrast between the nineteenth-century American and the twentieth-century American are vulnerable indeed.

This conclusion should, perhaps, have been evident from the outset, in view of the fact that it was Tocqueville who, in the nineteenth century, gave us the image which we now frequently identify as the twentieth-century American. But in any case, the fact that he did so means that we can hardly resolve the dilemma of our individualist democrat and our majoritarian democrat by assuming that both are historically valid but that one replaced the other. The problem of determining what use we can make of either of these images, in view of the fact that each casts doubt upon the other, still remains. Is it possible to uncover common factors in these apparently contradictory images, and thus to make use of them both in our quest for a definition of the national character? For no matter whether either of these versions of the American is realistic as a type or image, there is no doubt that both of them reflect fundamental aspects of the American experience.

There is no purpose, at this point in this essay, to execute a neat, prearranged sleight-of-hand by which the individualist democrat and the conformist democrat will cast off their disguises and will reveal themselves as identical twin Yankee Doodle Dandies, both born on the fourth of July. On the contrary, intractable, irresolvable discrepancies exist between the two figures, and it will probably never be possible to go very far in the direction of accepting the one without treating the other as a fictitious image, to be rejected as reflecting an anti-democratic bias and as at odds with the evidence from actual observation of the behavior of *Homo Americanus* in his native haunts. At the same time, however, it is both necessary to probe for the common factors, and legitimate to observe that there is one common factor conspicuous in the extreme—namely the emphasis on equality, so dear both to Jefferson's American and to Tocqueville's. One of these figures, it will be recalled, has held no truth to be more self-evident than that all men are created equal, while the other has made equality his "idol," far more jealously guarded than his liberty.

If the commitment to equality is so dominant a feature in both of these representations of the American, it will perhaps serve as a key to various facets of the national character, even to contradictory aspects of this character. In a society as complex as that of the United States, in fact, it may be that the common factors underlying the various manifestations are all that our quest should seek. For it is evident that American life and American energy have expressed themselves in a great diversity of ways, and any effort to define the American as if nearly two hundred million persons all corresponded to a single type would certainly reduce complex data to a blunt, crude, and oversimplified form. To detect what qualities Americans share in their diversity may be far more revealing than to superimpose the stereotype of a fictitious uniformity. If this is true, it means that our quest must be to discover the varied and dissimilar ways in which the commitment to equality expresses itself— the different forms which it takes in different individuals—rather than to regard it as an undifferentiated component which shows in all individuals in the same way. Figuratively, one might say that in seeking for what is common, one should think of the metal from which Americans are forged, no matter into how many shapes this metal may be cast, rather than thinking of a die with which they all are stamped into an identical shape. If the problem is viewed in this way, it will be readily apparent that Tocqueville made a pregnant statement when he observed that the idea of equality was "the fundamental fact from which all others seem to be derived."

The term "equality" is a loose-fitting garment and it has meant very different things at very different times. It is very frequently used to imply parity or uniformity. The grenadiers in the King of Prussia's guard were equal in that they were all, uniformly, over six feet six inches tall. Particularly, it can mean, and often does mean in some social philosophies, uniformity of material welfare—of income, of medical care, etc. But people are clearly not uniform in strength or intelligence or beauty, and one must ask, therefore, what kind of uniformity Americans believed in. Did they believe in an equal sharing of goods? Tocqueville himself answered this question when he said, "I know of no country . . . where a profounder contempt is expressed for the theory of the permanent equality of property."

At this point in the discussion of equality, someone, and very likely a business man, is always likely to break in with the proposition that Americans believe in equality of opportunity—in giving everyone what is called an equal start, and in removing all handicaps such as illiteracy and all privileges such as monopoly or special priority, which will tend to give one person an advantage over another. But if a person gains the advantage without having society give it to him, by being more clever or more enterprising or even just by being stronger than someone else, he is entitled to enjoy the benefits that accrue from these qualities, particularly in terms of possessing more property or wealth than others.

Historically, equality of opportunity was a particularly apt form of equalitarianism for a new, undeveloped frontier country. In the early stages of American history, the developed resources of the country were so few that an equality in the division of these assets would only have meant an insufficiency for everyone. The best economic benefit which the government could give was to offer a person free access in developing undeveloped resources for his own profit, and this is what America did offer. It was an ideal formula for everyone: for the individual it meant a very real chance to gain more wealth than he would have secured by receiving an equal share of the existing wealth. For the community, it meant that no one could prosper appreciably without activities which would develop undeveloped resources, at a time when society desperately needed rapid economic development. For these reasons, equality of opportunity did become the most highly sanctioned form of equalitarianism in the United States.

Because of this sanction, Americans have indeed been tolerant of great discrepancies in wealth. They have approved of wealth much more readily when they believed that it had been earned—as in the case, for instance, of Henry Ford—than when they thought it had been acquired by some special privilege or monopoly. In general, however, they have not merely condoned great wealth; they have admired it. But to say that the ideal of equality means only equality of opportunity is hardly to tell the whole story. The American faith has also held, with intense conviction, the belief that all men are equal in the sense that they share a common humanity—that all are alike in the eyes of God—and that every person has a certain dignity, no matter how low his circumstances, which no one else, no matter how high *his* circumstances, is entitled to disregard. When this concept of the nature of man was translated into a system of social arrangements, the crucial point on which it came to focus was the question of rank. For the concept of rank essentially denies that all men are equally worthy and argues that some are better than others—that some are born to serve and others born to command. The American creed not only denied this view, but even condemned it and placed a taboo upon it. Some people, according to the American creed, might be more fortunate than others, but they must never regard themselves as better than others. Pulling one's rank has therefore been the unforgivable sin against American democracy, and the American people have, accordingly, reserved their heartiest dislike for the officer class in the military, for people with upstage or condescending manners, and for anyone who tries to convert power or wealth (which are not resented) into overt rank or privilege (which are). Thus it is permissible for an American to have servants (which is a matter of function), but he must not put them in livery (which is a matter of rank); permissible to attend expensive schools, but not to speak with a cultivated accent; permissible to rise in the world, but never to repudiate the origins from which he rose. The most palpable and overt possible claim of rank is, of course, the effort of one individual to assert authority, in a personal sense, over others, and accordingly the rejection of authority is the most pronounced of all the concrete expressions of American beliefs in equality.

In almost any enterprise which involves numbers of people working in conjunction, it is necessary for some people to tell other people what to do. This function cannot be wholly abdicated without violating the taboos against authority. The result is that the American people have developed an arrangement which skillfully combines truth and fiction, and maintains that the top man does not rule, but leads; and does not give orders, but calls signals; while the men in the lower echelons are not underlings, but members of the team. This view of the relationship is truthful in the sense that the man in charge does depend upon his capacity to elicit the voluntary or spontaneous co-operation of the members of his organization, and he regards the naked use of authority to secure compliance as an evidence of failure; also, in many organizations, the members lend their support willingly, and contribute much more on a voluntary basis than authority could ever exact from them. But the element of fiction sometimes enters, in terms of the fact that both sides understand that in many situations authority would have to be invoked if voluntary compliance were not forthcoming. This would be humiliating to all parties—to the top man because it would expose his failure as a leader and to the others because it would force them to recognize the carefully concealed fact that in an ultimate sense they are subject to coercion. To avoid this mutually undesirable exploration of the ultimate implications, both sides recognize that even when an order has to be given, it is better for it to be expressed in the form of a request or a proposal, and when compliance is mandatory, it should be rendered with an appearance of consent.

It is in this way that the anti-authoritarian aspect of the creed of equality leads to the extraordinarily strong emphasis upon permissiveness, either as a reality or as a mere convention in American life. So strong is the taboo against authority that the father, once a paternal authority, is now expected to be a pal to his children, and to persuade rather than to command. The husband, once a lord and master, to be obeyed under the vows of matrimony, is now a partner. And if, perchance, an adult male in command of the family income uses his control to bully his wife and children, he does not avow his desire to make them obey, but insists that he only wants them to be co-operative. The unlimited American faith in the efficacy of discussion as a means of finding solutions for controversies reflects less a faith in the powers of rational persuasion than a supreme reluctance to let anything reach a point where authority will have to be invoked. If hypocrisy is the tribute that vice pays to virtue, permissiveness is, to some extent, the tribute that authority pays to the principle of equality.

When one recognizes some of these varied strands in the fabric of equalitarianism it becomes easier to see how the concept has contributed to the making both of the Jeffersonian American and the Tocquevillian American. For as one picks at the strands they ravel out in quite dissimilar directions. The strand of equality of opportunity, for instance, if followed out, leads to the theme of individualism. It challenged each individual to pit his skill and talents in a competition against the skill and talents of others and to earn the individual rewards which talent and effort might bring. Even more, the imperatives of the competitive race were so compelling that the belief grew up that everyone had a kind of obligation to enter his talents in this competition and to "succeed." It was but a step from the belief that ability and virtue would produce success to the belief that success was produced by—and was therefore an evidence of—ability and virtue. In short, money not only represented power, it also was a sign of the presence of admirable qualities in the man who attained it. Here, certainly, an equalitarian doctrine fostered materialism, and if aggressiveness and competitiveness are individualistic qualities, then it fostered individualism also.

Of course, neither American individualism nor American materialism can be explained entirely in these terms. Individualism must have derived great strength, for instance, from the reflection that if all men are equal, a man might as well form his own convictions as accept the convictions of someone else no better than himself. It must also have been reinforced by the frontier experience, which certainly compelled every man to rely upon himself. But this kind of individualism is not the quality of independent-mindedness, and it is not the quality which Tocqueville was denying when he said that Americans were conformists. A great deal of confusion has resulted, in the discussion of the American character, from the fact that the term individualism is sometimes used (as by Tocqueville) to mean willingness to think and act separately from the majority, and sometimes (as by Turner) to mean capacity to get along without help. It might be supposed that the two would converge, on the theory that a man who can get along by himself without help will soon recognize that he may as well also think for himself without help. But in actuality, this did not necessarily happen. Self-reliance on the frontier was more a matter of courage and of staying power than of intellectual resourcefulness, for the struggle with the wilderness challenged the body rather than the mind, and a man might be supremely effective in fending for himself, and at the same time supremely conventional in his ideas. In this sense, Turner's individualist is not really an antithesis of Tocqueville's conformist at all.

Still, it remains true that Jefferson's idealist and Tocqueville's conformist both require explanation, and that neither can be accounted for in the terms which make Jefferson's individualist and Tocqueville's materialist understandable. As an explanation of these facets of the American character, it would seem that the strand of equalitarianism which stresses the universal dignity of all men, and which hates rank as a violation of dignity, might be found quite pertinent. For it is the concept of the worth of every man which has stimulated a century and a half of reform, designed at every step to realize in practice the ideal that every human possesses potentialities which he should have a chance to fulfill. Whatever has impeded this fulfillment, whether it be lack of education, chattel slavery, the exploitation of the labor of unorganized workers, the hazards of unemployment, or the handicaps of age and infirmity, has been the object, at one time or another, of a major reforming crusade. The whole American commitment to progress would be impossible without a prior belief in the perfectibility of man and in the practicability of steps to bring perfection nearer. In this sense, the American character has been idealistic. And yet its idealism is not entirely irreconcilable with its materialism, for American idealism has often framed its most altruistic goals in materialistic terms—for instance, of raising the standard of living as a means to better life. Moreover, Americans are committed to the view that materialistic means are necessary to idealistic ends. Franklin defined what is necessary to a virtuous life by saying "an empty sack cannot stand upright," and Americans have believed that spiritual and humanitarian goals are best achieved by instrumentalities such as universities and hospitals which carry expensive price tags.

If the belief that all men are equal of worth has contributed to a feature of American life so much cherished as our tradition of humanitarian reform, how could it at the same time have contributed to a feature so much deplored as American conformity? Yet it has done both, for the same respect of the American for his fellow men, which has made many a reformer think that his fellow citizens are worth helping, has also made many another American think that he has no business to question the opinions that his neighbors have sanctioned. True, he says, if all men are equal, each ought to think for himself, but on the other hand, no man should consider himself better than his neighbors, and if the majority have adopted an opinion on a matter, how can one man question their opinion, without setting himself up as being better than they. Moreover, it is understood that the majority are pledged not to force him to adopt their opinion. But it is also understood that in return for this immunity he will voluntarily accept the will of the majority in most things. The absence of a formal compulsion to conform seemingly increases the obligation to conform voluntarily. Thus, the other-directed man is seen to be derived as much from the American tradition of equalitarianism as the rugged individualist, and the compulsive seeker of an unequally large share of wealth as much as the humanitarian reformer striving for the fulfillment of democratic ideals.

To say that they are all derived from the same tradition is by no means to say that they are, in some larger, mystic sense, all the same. They are not, even though the idealism of the reformer may seek materialistic goals, and though men who are individualists in their physical lives may be conformists in their ideas. But all of them, it may be argued, do reflect circumstances which are distinctively American, and all present manifestations of a character which is more convincingly American because of its diversity than any wholly uniform character could possibly be. If Americans have never reached the end of their quest for an image that would represent the American character, it may be not because they failed to find one image but because they failed to recognize the futility of attempting to settle upon one, and the necessity of accepting several.

4

The Search
for Christian America

Mark Noll, George Marsden, and
Nathan Hatch

---

*In 1983, three noted scholars in the field of American religious history,
all evangelical Christians, coauthored a book entitled* The Search for
Christian America, *intending it for an audience of evangelical readers.
Mark Noll, a professor of history at Wheaton College, is best known for*
Christians in the American Revolution *and his 1989 edited collection*
Religion and American Politics. *George Marsden, author of the highly
acclaimed* Fundamentalism and American Culture, *is now teaching
at the Duke University Divinity School. Nathan Hatch, a historian at
Notre Dame, has also written* The Democratization of American
Christianity *(1989).*

*These three men tackled a touchy but important question that
was particularly timely in the early years of the Reagan administration.
Many evangelical Christians enthusiastically supported Reagan's call
for a return to an idealized America of the past, a Christian America.
The authors sought in their book to determine whether the widespread*

This reading is from *The Search for Christian America,* by Mark A. Noll, Nathan O.
Hatch, and George M. Marsden, copyright © 1983, pp. 13–26. Used by permission of
Good News Publishers/Crossway Books, Westchester, IL 60153.

perception of a formerly Christian America overrun by secular human-
ism reflected reality or myth.

Their conclusions, stated in this introductory chapter, are that early
America was not predominantly Christian and that the whole idea of a
"Christian" nation is ambiguous and even harmful to true Christianity. In
terms of the American character, however, the authors note that the
United States has been a uniquely religious, as opposed to a Christian,
nation. Although Christianity has provided the dominant religious influ-
ence, the roots of the American character, like those of American society
generally, are to be found in pluralism rather than in any single source.

At times of crisis it is a natural human reaction to turn to the past
for support. Evangelicals and fundamentalists in modern America are no
different. We have suffered with the nation through the traumas of Vietnam and Watergate. And we continue to share fully in the uncertainties
of a ricocheting economy and nuclear-shrouded international tensions.
But as theologically conservative Christians, evangelicals and fundamentalists are troubled by another dimension of modern American life:
its flight from morality and godliness. The collapse of discipline in the
schools, the spread of pornography, the strident voices proclaiming
"rights" for homosexuals and "freedom" for abortion, along with the
manifest presence of great social injustices, fill us with foreboding. To
resist the evil of our day and to build a healthier society we almost
instinctively turn to those who have gone before for wisdom and practical guidance. At stake is nothing less than what was once widely assumed to be America's Christian heritage.

EVANGELICAL MOBILIZATION

It is undeniable that American evangelicals in recent years have taken a
more fervent interest in public life. Prominent leaders are speaking out
forcefully on issues of government policy like defense and questions
of national morality like abortion. Voters concerned about moral issues,
often urged on by political action committees with ties to evangelicals,
have made their presence felt in elections. They may have played a role
in the election of Ronald Reagan as president in 1980. They certainly
have helped to defeat certain candidates in local and state elections.

Two recent events seem to have stimulated this renewed evangelical involvement in the public sphere. The first was the ruling of the
Supreme Court on abortion in 1973. Its decision in *Roe v. Wade,* which in
effect legalized abortion-on-demand, angered many evangelicals. That
decision sparked active political involvement. And it has led to repeated
calls for defense of Judeo-Christian reverence for life.

The second event was the nation's Bicentennial in 1976. During that year evangelical publishers turned out an array of nationalistic titles, such as *America: God Shed His Grace on Thee; One Nation Under God;* and *Faith, Stars and Stripes.* A host of evangelical magazines extolled America's Christian heritage, the biblical origins of American government, and the spiritual insights of the founding fathers. "America," suggested one in typical fashion, "has a great past, a great present, and a great future, because America has a GREAT GOD."

During the Bicentennial celebrations other leaders evoked powerful religious images concerning the American past, like George Washington kneeling before God at Valley Forge or Benjamin Franklin breaking a deadlock at the Constitutional Convention by calling for prayer. Some speakers also pointed to the central role of Scripture in the creation of the United States. Said one at a "Festival of Faith": "The men who signed the Declaration of Independence were moved by a magnificent dream. . . . And this dream is rooted in the book we call the Bible."

The combination of these two events—the shocking decision of the Supreme Court on abortion and the Bicentennial reminder of the Christian past—led to a new evangelical engagement in public life and fueled actions that were already underway. Protests against abortion-on-demand, opposition to the Equal Rights Amendment, public appeals to save the family, campaigns against pornography, protests against the removal of prayer from public schools, and appeals for national military strength against godless foreign foes have become well-established parts of American evangelical culture.

In addition, several groups with evangelical connections have mounted campaigns with more positive goals. Evangelicals have helped found homes for mothers to bear babies who otherwise might have been aborted, they have taken part in efforts to make the nation's prisons more humane, and they have aided efforts to feed the world's hungry.

Much of the evangelical concern about public life has risen in response to the perception of a spreading "secular humanism." This world view, which to some is the product of a well-organized conspiracy and to others a more general cultural trend, rules God out of the picture, sees the world only in material terms, abandons theistic foundations for traditional freedoms, and treats religion as an illusion. The fight against this secular humanism has been carried into school boards, the courts, and legislative assemblies.

A VISION OF THE PAST

An important part of this concern about "secular humanism" is historical. Many evangelical leaders regard it as a relatively new intrusion into

American life. The adoption and influence of secular humanism is seen as a momentous new development in American history. It is said to represent nothing less than the triumph of atheism and irreligion over the Christian heritage of America.

It follows, then, that one of the calls to reform America in our day becomes an appeal to recover the Christian roots, the Christian heritage, the Christian values of an older America. Our instinctive reaction is to regain what we have lost. To make such a recovery, it is thought, would put modern evangelicals in a place once again to encourage righteousness in the land and overcome the evils of our society.

This view of the past is the one which featured so prominently in celebrations of the Bicentennial. It is one which makes much of the piety of the Pilgrims and of the Puritans. It is one which regards the great revivals of earlier American history as crucial shapers of our culture. And, above all, it is a view which holds the American Revolution and the creation of a new United States in special reverence. The new nation, it is widely felt, emerged from the generally Christian actions of generally Christian people. And these actions bequeathed Christian values, and a Christian heritage, to later American history. But now recent national backsliding has placed that entire Christian heritage in jeopardy.

Such widespread public opinions about the United States' Christian past are, very naturally, of great interest to historians of America who are also Christians. The authors of this book belong to that number. We earn our daily bread by teaching about the past, we regularly read the work of other practitioners in the field, and we spend considerable time in libraries and archives doing our own research. But we are also evangelical Christians who are concerned about the fate of the church in twentieth-century America. We feel, therefore, that we have a special stake in discovering how the activity of Christians shaped the country. It is not surprising that we are very much concerned with the question of whether America's past was really Christian or not.

All three of us have addressed the question of America's Christian character in more technical or specialized studies. We have written for our academic peers about individual Christians, churches, and larger Christian groups from various eras in the nation's history. And for such audiences we have also dealt with questions concerning the way Christianity has influenced American life and how American life has influenced the Christians. We have also tried to share some of the insights of our historical work more broadly by writing popular books and articles for Christian magazines and publishers. Each of us would be pleased for any who are intrigued or disturbed by the conclusions of this book to refer to the other things we have written for a closer look at the research on which this volume's arguments rest. Even more, we would be pleased to have our conclusions checked against other solid studies of American history. . . .

At the present, however, it has seemed useful for us to combine our efforts in order to make a careful search for Christian America. Our purpose is to examine carefully the popular belief that America was once a "Christian nation" which has now been all but overrun by secular humanism. To put it most simply: Is this a factual picture, a mythical picture, or something else altogether?

THE ARGUMENT

We have three general concerns in making this inquiry. The first has to do with the accuracy of our picture of the past. We wish to report as simply as possible what actually happened in early America, with particular reference to the activities and aspirations of Christians. But, secondly, we want to go beyond a concern for setting the historical record straight by also asking how a proper understanding of Scripture should influence our thoughts about the nation. To accomplish this goal it will be necessary to pose careful questions about what we mean when we talk about "a Christian country" and "a Christian heritage." Thirdly, we feel that the historical and theoretical discussion involved in addressing our first two concerns leads to important practical implications. How we regard the past often dramatically shapes our perception of the present. And so we hope that this book about history will leave some positive suggestions about how Christians may responsibly use the past in acting for Christ in the world today.

The argument . . . can be stated quite simply.

1. We feel that a careful study of the facts of history shows that early America does not deserve to be considered uniquely, distinctly or even predominantly Christian, if we mean by the word "Christian" a state of society reflecting the ideals presented in Scripture. There is no lost golden age to which American Christians may return. In addition, a careful study of history will also show that evangelicals themselves were often partly to blame for the spread of secularism in contemporary American life.

2. We feel also that careful examination of Christian teaching on government, the state, and the nature of culture shows that the idea of a "Christian nation" is a very ambiguous concept which is usually harmful to effective Christian action in society.

STRIKING A BALANCE

In making our case, we do not want to contend that Christian values have been absent from American history. On the contrary, we hope to show that there has been much commendable Christian belief, practice, and influence in the history of the United States and the colonies which formed the new country. Christian goals and aspirations certainly had a part in the settlement of North America. It is also indubitable that Christian factors contributed to the struggle for national independence and that Christian principles played a role in the founding documents of the United States. We want to give due recognition to these positive Christian aspects of our history, for they have had a marked influence on the shape of modern America. Their presence, we agree, justifies a picture of the United States as a singularly *religious* country.

Recent polls in America and Western Europe underscore the continuing strength of this religious heritage. Surveys by the Gallup Organization in 1981 revealed that over 40 percent of America's population was likely to attend religious services in any given week. This may not seem impressive, but it is a considerably higher percentage than for the countries of Western Europe. Polls in the late 1970s which asked Americans and Europeans about the personal importance of religious beliefs also yield significant results. In the United States 88 percent of those surveyed responded that religious beliefs were "very" or "fairly" important, while the percentages of those in Europe who responded in this same way ranged downwards from Italy's 75 percent to Scandinavia's 45 percent. Such figures should make any observer cautious about dismissing the importance of religion in America, and especially cautious about dismissing the influence of the Christian faith, since it has been the primary religious expression in our history.

Modern polls and the historical record do not, thus, justify the attitude taken by some in our day who paint the history of America with darkest possible colors. If historians of America used to talk of its past as if it revealed the unalloyed progress of freedom, prosperity, and virtue, others today now speak of it as an unalloyed tale of oppression, exploitation, and alienation. Similarly, while many Christians continue to look upon American history as if it were uniquely Christian, some believers have now come to picture that same history as the epitome of sinful arrogance and callousness.

We do not subscribe to either of these extremes. We feel, rather, that America has had a generally religious past. And we feel that its history is liberally sprinkled with genuine Christian influences radiating from lives of exemplary belief.

As much as we acknowledge Christian influences in United States history, however, we still wish to call into question the assumption that just because many Christians have done many Christian deeds in America, the country enjoys simply a "Christian heritage." There are too many problems with this assumption. . . . It would be appropriate here to state some of them briefly.

CRUCIAL QUESTIONS

One set of questions has to do with how much Christian action is required to make a whole society Christian. Another way of stating the same issue is to pose it negatively—how much evil can a society display before we disqualify it as a Christian society? These kinds of questions are pertinent for all of early American history. When we look at the Puritans of the 1600s, do we emphasize only their sincere desire to establish Christian colonies, and their manifest desire to live by the rule of Scripture? Or do we focus rather on the stealing of Indian lands, and their habit of displacing and murdering these Indians wherever it was convenient? Roger Williams, one of the Puritans himself, asked these very questions and came to much the same conclusion as we have more than 300 years later. Again, do we place more emphasis on the Massachusetts Puritans' desire to worship God freely in the new world or their persecution (and, in four cases, execution) of Quakers who also wished to be free to worship God in Massachusetts?

In the age of the American Revolution the same questions are pertinent. Do we praise American patriots for wanting to be free of Parliament's restraints upon their freedom, or condemn them for taking away freedom of speech and press from their opponents? Likewise, do we praise American patriots for their defense of "natural law" and "unalienable right," or condemn them for failing to heed Paul's injunctions in Romans 13 to honor their legitimate rulers?

The same questions apply to the period between the Revolution and the Civil War. How do we bring together our assessment of the great evangelistic and reform movements, which did so much to spread biblical righteousness in the country, with inhuman treatment of black slaves and Indian outcasts? Obviously, the need in responding to these sorts of considerations is for a balance that can acknowledge both good and evil in our past and come to conclusions that take both sides into account.

Another problem has to do with Christian use of secular thought. Beginning about the middle of the 1700s, at the time of the French and Indian War, many Americans began to mix their politics and their Christian faith thoroughly and often indiscriminately. Some began to talk about resistance to France, and later to England, as if this were resistance to the Antichrist or Satan himself. During the war against Great Britain, American patriots began to speak about the republican political principles of the Revolution as if these had an almost saving power. Many Christian patriots regarded Americans who were loyal to Great Britain or who wanted to stay out of the conflict as much more than just politically mistaken. They were rather "accursed of God." Then in the early years of the United States, most Christian bodies took the basically secular principles of the American Revolution as the guiding light for organizing churches, interpreting the Bible, and expressing the Christian faith. This process of baptizing political philosophies into the Christian faith was a precarious one. Certainly some of the features of the political philosophy of the American Revolution were commendable from a Christian point of view. But just as certainly they did not deserve to be equated with Christianity or permitted to dictate church structure, interpretations of Scripture, or expressions of the Christian faith. How, then, are we as modern Christians to evaluate our predecessors who seemed to have forgotten that Christianity existed before the creation of American democracy?

A third kind of question involves more theological considerations. Is it, after all, ever proper to speak of a Christian nation after the coming of Christ? From Scripture we know that Old Testament Israel enjoyed a special status as a nation under God. Modern evangelicals differ among themselves over whether the modern state of Israel remains special as a nation to God. But regardless of how a Christian feels about the modern Jewish nation, is it proper ever to look upon the American nation as the special agent of God in the world? Many great and godly Americans have done so, including Governor John Winthrop in early Massachusetts and President Abraham Lincoln during the Civil War. But were they correct? And what were the practical effects—for the promotion of the gospel or for its harm—when this assumption was made about the Christian uniqueness of America? . . .

THE PRACTICAL POINT

What is the point, some may ask, in subjecting our ideas about the past to rigorous scrutiny? Even if it turns out that the common picture of an American Christian past is inaccurate, what difference does it make? The difference, we are convinced, is something which profoundly affects the way in which we approach the public arena today. In fact, a true picture of America's past will make Christians today better equipped to speak the gospel in evangelism and to put it to work in social concern.

The Search for Christian America presents in some detail our reasons for questioning whether America has had a predominately Christian past. At the same time, we are convinced that fellow Christians who hold such a view are nevertheless correct in many of their views concerning America's present problems. With them, we deplore abortion-on-demand. We recognize that secular ideas undermine education in public schools. We abhor the ravages of divorce and the weakening of the family. And we feel that American foreign policy should take account of religious persecution in other countries.

We must say also that we share many of the concerns of the smaller number of fellow Christians who have a more negative view of the American past. That is, we also think that American Christians have too often been indifferent to the oppressed and the unrepresented, the very ones to whom the Old Testament prophets, Jesus himself, and the inspired apostles directed our specific attention. We too feel that Americans have trusted far too much in military might and not enough in the strength of the Lord in protecting our property and rights. And we have serious questions about the morality of a defense posture that rests primarily on the threatened use of strategic nuclear arms.

For [our] purposes [here], however, we are not concerned if readers share our own views on Christian social policy. Rather, we are concerned to point out how inaccurate views of the past may hamper Christians from mounting the kind of actions that our country and world needs.

Incorrect views of American history are a stumbling block precisely when Christians advance to address public issues. We are hindered in our contemporary Christian efforts if we consider American history as uniformly pernicious. But only a few evangelicals hold this view. So it is not an opinion that we will address at length. The more serious hindrance to positive Christian action in the present is the distorted and overinflated view of America as a distinctively Christian nation. And so we direct most of what follows to redressing the inadequacies of that view.

The final justification for a book like *The Search for Christian America*, if it is written by Christians, must be to clarify our understanding of the gospel and to advance positive Christian action. A view of American history which gives it a falsely Christian character is a hindrance, first, because it distorts the nature of the past. Positive Christian action does not grow out of distortions or half-truths. Such errors lead rather to false militance, to unrealistic standards for American public life today, and to romanticized visions about the heights from which we have fallen.

But a false estimation of America's history also hinders positive Christian action by discouraging a biblical analysis of our position today. And it can compromise genuinely biblical guidelines for action. If we accept traditional American attitudes toward public life as if these were Christian, when in fact they are not, we do the cause of Christ a disservice. Similarly, if we perpetuate the sinful behavior and the moral blind spots of our predecessors, even if these predecessors were Christians, it keeps us from understanding scriptural mandates for action today.

In addition, responsible historical study should also lead to more careful thinking about aspirations for a "biblical politics." The founding fathers in 1776 were much closer to the religious wars of the sixteenth and seventeenth centuries, when nations with competing "biblical politics" fought it out in bloody battle. The founders sought general principles of public life which adherents of all faiths, and none, could accept.

There are dangers in their approach, but it also contains strengths which a pell-mell pursuit of a uniquely biblical politics can destroy.

Our historical research has convinced us that two contrasting dangers lurk in wait when we attempt to put the past to use for present purposes. The first danger comes as a result of treating the naturalistic political ideals of American history as if they were on a par with scriptural revelation. This leads to idolatry of our nation and an irresistible temptation to national self-righteousness. The second danger comes from the failure to establish an independent scriptural position over against the prominent values of the culture, a position which allows for selective approval and disapproval of the culture's various values. This failure can lead to secularization, if Christians merely tag along when the culture veers away from God, or it can lead to confusion, when Christians are unable to figure out how public institutions that once supported the faith now work against it. Against both dangers we hope to offer a clearer picture of the past and a more mature understanding of contemporary political concerns. . . . We hope to correct the mistaken assumption that the American past offers an adequate Christian blueprint for our lives today, an adequate biblical standard for responding to public issues, or an adequate understanding of the positive value of pluralistic public policy.

BIBLICAL GUIDELINES

. . . [I]t would be well to state positively what we consider proper biblical principles for our attitudes to the American nation and its heritage.

In the first place, we must agree with Roger Williams that no nation since the coming of Christ has been uniquely God's chosen people. The New Testament teaches unmistakably that Christ set aside national and ethnic barriers and that he has chosen to fulfill his central purposes in history through the church, which transcends all such boundaries. Samuel Hopkins, a pupil of Jonathan Edwards, reached a similar conclusion at the time of the American Revolution. Hopkins attacked the idea that since God was blessing America in its struggle for independence against Britain, God was somehow designating the nation as his special people and somehow justifying its continuation of slavery. Israel, Hopkins said, could enslave Canaanites because of God's express permission. But this was one of those "many directions and laws to the Jews which had no respect to mankind in general." Now things are different: "the distinction [of Israel] is . . . at an end, and all nations are put upon a level; and Christ . . . has taught us to look on all nations as our neighbors and brethren."

However much particular nations may be used at particular times to do God's work in the world, they are not the primary tools that he is now using. Similarly, the Lord of history has not aligned his purposes with the particular values of any given country or civilization.

Instead, God calls out his people to be strangers and pilgrims, as many of America's early settlers knew. He calls them to repent of their sins and to avoid conformity with the world. We are to be good citizens, but we must remember that our real home, that city with foundations, is beyond our own culture. Our renderings to Caesar, while they must be taken seriously, are to follow the values of that Kingdom which stands above all earthly authority. These priorities, rather than those of our culture and nation, demand our unfettered loyalty.

A second principle is that God has no interest in religion *per se.* There are strong indications, in fact, that he hates religion that is not truly Christian more than the absence of religion. Christ condemned the Pharisees because not only were they blind, but as religious leaders they misled others. "I hate the sound of your solemn assemblies," the prophet Amos informed religious men and women of the Old Testament, when they used their religion as an excuse not to face the Lord himself. One of the biggest dangers of an awareness of America's religious past is the temptation to condone religion *per se* as the means to the ends of national righteousness.

There is the implicit tendency among uncritically patriotic Christians to confirm any religion that tends to uphold the basic principles of American morality. Where is the prophetic voice that condemns all religion which does not have its ultimate end in the God of our Lord Jesus Christ? We must recognize that the American civic faith constantly repeats the chorus that any religion is good enough and that none should claim exclusive truth. Against this tenet, we must be willing to stand as lonely prophets whose hearts are not glad with mere religiosity. Jehovah demands exclusive loyalty.

A third principle is that God judges people not according to what they say they believe but according to their real faith commitment. God always is very practical in this respect. We are liars, he says, if we claim to love God while we are busy hating our brother. Similarly, when Israel would parade her religiosity, God would remind her people of the social injustice that was everywhere practiced upon the powerless. This is the message of the book of James. Real Christian faith can always be evaluated by the fruit it bears. Real Christian faith will produce works, or it is not genuine faith. According to this principle, we should evaluate the righteousness of any society not merely by the religious professions that people make, but also by the extent to which Christian principles concerning personal morality and justice for the oppressed are realized in the society.

The basis for judging the righteousness of this nation at any point is not solely to examine the membership rolls of the churches. No doubt, professions of faith are important. But we must also look at the extent to which believers are engaged in the task of applying Christian love and justice to every facet of life. What is really important is not the claims about an American Christian heritage, nor an unjustifiable equation of modern America with the "my people" of 2 Chronicles 7:14. What will stand in the final analysis is how believers, who recognize that their final Kingdom is not of this world, prove their faith in God by works of worship and love.

A final word is in order about the polemical nature of *The Search for Christian America*. The views which it presents do, in fact, attempt to rebut some opinions of those who speak much about America's Christian past. Our intent in making this rebuttal, however, is not vindictive. It is meant as a positive contribution to responsible Christian action today. Just as each of us have benefited, either directly or indirectly, from some of those who make such claims about America, so we offer this contribution as a way of helping them to carry on their work for Christ's Kingdom with greater truth and effect.

5

England's Vietnam:
The American Revolution

Richard M. Ketchum

Richard M. Ketchum (1922–   ), a former editor of American Heritage
magazine, has written and edited numerous books, including The American Heritage Picture History of the Civil War *and* The Borrowed
Years: America on the Way to War, 1938–1941 *(1989). His special interest in the Revolution is reflected in* The American Heritage Book of
the Revolution *(1958) and* The Battle for Bunker Hill *(1962).*

*While history never exactly repeats itself, events frequently fol-
low patterns surprisingly close to those of the past. One of the primary
values of the study of history is to make us aware of the parallels between present problems and those of the past. Failure to perceive such
similarities can doom us to repeat past mistakes. In this article Ketchum
notes a number of remarkable parallels between Great Britain's attitudes toward the American Revolution and American attitudes toward
the Vietnam War two hundred years later. He wrote this article in 1971
in hopes of convincing Americans of the error of their involvement in
Vietnam, but he avoided distorting the facts to fit his argument. He*

did not need to: The facts speak eloquently for themselves. If only, he laments, Kennedy, Johnson, and Nixon had paid more attention in class when they were studying the American Revolution . . .

This article, along with observation of the behavior of England and the United States as great powers, suggests that the national character of a country, like the character of a person, is a blend of heredity and environment. Understanding this hereditary similarity should help clarify the way in which the American character was forged.

If it is true that those who cannot remember the past are condemned to repeat it, America's last three Presidents might have profited by examining the ghostly footsteps of America's last king before pursuing their adventure in Vietnam. As the United States concludes a decade of war in Southeast Asia, it is worth recalling the time, two centuries ago, when Britain faced the same agonizing problems in America that we have met in Vietnam. History seldom repeats itself exactly, and it would be a mistake to try to equate the ideologies or the motivating factors involved; but enough disturbing parallels may be drawn between those two distant events to make one wonder if the Messrs. Kennedy, Johnson, and Nixon had their ears closed while the class was studying the American Revolution.

Britain, on the eve of that war, was the greatest empire since Rome. Never before had she known such wealth and power; never had the future seemed so bright, the prospects so glowing. All, that is, except the spreading sore of discontent in the American colonies that, after festering for a decade and more, finally erupted in violence at Lexington and Concord on April 19, 1775. When news of the subsequent battle for Bunker Hill reached England that summer, George III and his ministers concluded that there was no alternative to using force to put down the insurrection. In the King's mind, at least, there was no longer any hope of reconciliation—nor did the idea appeal to him. He was determined to teach the rebellious colonials a lesson, and no doubts troubled him as to the righteousness of the course he had chosen. "I am not sorry that the line of conduct seems now chalked out," he had said even before fighting began; later he told his prime minister, Lord North, "I know I am doing my Duty and I can never wish to retract." And then, making acceptance of the war a matter of personal loyalty, "I wish nothing but good," he said, "therefore anyone who does not agree with me is a traitor and a scoundrel." Filled with high moral purpose and confidence, he was certain that "when once these rebels have felt a smart blow, they will submit . . . "

In British political and military circles there was general agreement that the war would be quickly and easily won. "Shall we be told," asked one of the King's men in Commons, "that (the Americans) can resist the powerful efforts of this nation?" Major John Pitcairn, writing home from

Boston in March, 1775, said, "I am satisfied that one active campaign, a smart action, and burning two or three of the towns, will set everything to rights." The man who would direct the British navy during seven years of war, the unprincipled, inefficient Earl of Sandwich, rose in the House of Lords to express his opinion of the provincial fighting man. "Suppose the Colonies do abound in men," the First Lord of the Admiralty asked, "what does that signify? They are raw, undisciplined, cowardly men. I wish instead of forty or fifty thousand of these *brave* fellows they would produce in the field at least two hundred thousand; the more the better, the easier would be the conquest; if they did not run away, they would starve themselves into compliance with our measures. . . . " And General James Murray, who had succeeded the great Wolfe in 1759 as commander in North America, called the native American "a very effeminate thing, very unfit for and very impatient of war." Between these estimates of the colonial militiaman and a belief that the might of Great Britain was invincible, there was a kind of arrogant optimism in official quarters when the conflict began. "As there is not common sense in protracting a war of this sort," wrote Lord George Germain, the secretary for the American colonies, in September, 1775, "I should be for exerting the utmost force of this Kingdom to finish the rebellion in one campaign."

Optimism bred more optimism, arrogance more arrogance. One armchair strategist in the House of Commons, William Innes, outlined for the other members an elaborate scheme he had devised for the conduct of the war. First, he would remove the British troops from Boston, since that place was poorly situated for defense. Then, while the people of the Massachusetts Bay Colony were treated like the madmen they were and shut up by the navy, the army would move to one of the southern colonies, fortify itself in an impregnable position, and let the provincials attack if they pleased. The British could sally forth from this and other defensive enclaves at will, and eventually "success against one half of America will pave the way to the conquest of the whole. . . . " What was more, Innes went on, it was "more than probable you may find men to recruit your army in America." There was a good possibility, in other words, that the British regulars would be replaced after a while by Americans who were loyal to their king, so that the army fighting the rebels would be Americanized, so to speak, and the Irish and English lads sent home. General James Robertson also believed that success lay in this scheme of Americanizing the combat force: "I never had an idea of subduing the Americans," he said, "I meant to assist the good Americans to subdue the bad."

This notion was important not only from the standpoint of the fighting, but in terms of administering the colonies once they were beaten; loyalists would take over the reins of government when the British pulled out, and loyalist militiamen would preserve order in the pacified colonies. No one knew, of course, how many "good" Americans there were; some thought they might make up half or more of the population. Shortly after arriving in the colonies in 1775, General William Howe, for one, was convinced that "the insurgents are very few, in comparison with the whole of the people."

Before taking the final steps into full-scale war, however, the King and his ministers had to be certain about one vitally important matter: They had to be able to count on the support of the English people. On several occasions in 1775 they were able to read the public pulse (that part of it, at least, that mattered) by observing certain important votes in Parliament. The King's address to both Houses on October 26, in which he announced plans to suppress the uprising in America, was followed by weeks of angry debate; but when the votes were counted, the North ministry's majority was overwhelming. Each vote indicated the full tide of anger that influenced the independent members, the country gentlemen who agreed that the colonials must be put in their place and taught a lesson. A bit out of touch with the news, highly principled, and content in the belief that the King and the ministry must be right, none of them seem to have asked what would be the best for the empire; they simply went along with the vindictive measures that were being set in motion. Eloquent voices—those of Edmund Burke, Charles James Fox, the Earl of Chatham, John Wilkes, among others—were raised in opposition to the policies of the Crown, but as Burke said, " . . . it was almost in vain to contend, for the country gentlemen had abandoned their duty, and placed an implicit confidence in the Minister."

The words of sanity and moderation went unheeded because the men who spoke them were out of power and out of public favor; and each time the votes were tallied, the strong, silent, unquestioning majority prevailed. No one in any position of power in the government proposed, after the Battle of Bunker Hill, to halt the fighting in order to settle the differences; no one seriously contemplated conversations that might have led to peace. Instead the government—like so many governments before and since—took what appeared to be the easy way out and settled for war.

George III was determined to maintain his empire, intact and undiminished, and his greatest fear was that the loss of the American colonies would set off a reaction like a line of dominoes falling. Writing to Lord North in 1779, he called the contest with America "the most serious in which any country was ever engaged. It contains such a train of consequences that they must be examined to feel its real weight. . . . Independence is (the Americans') object, which every man not willing to sacrifice every object to a momentary and inglorious peace must concur with me in thinking this country can never submit to. Should America succeed in that, the West Indies must follow, not in independence, but for their own interest they must become dependent on America. Ireland would soon follow, and this island reduced to itself, would be a poor island indeed."

Despite George's unalterable determination, strengthened by his domino theory; despite the wealth and might of the British empire; despite all the odds favoring a quick triumph, the problems facing the King and his ministers and the armed forces were formidable ones indeed. Surpassing all others in sheer magnitude was the immense distance between the mother country and the rebellious colonies. As Edmund Burke described the situation in his last, most eloquent appeal for the conciliation, "Three thousand miles of ocean lie between you and them. No contrivance can prevent the effect of this distance in weakening government. Seas roll, and months pass, between the order and the execution; and the want of a speedy explanation of a single point is enough to defeat a whole system." Often the westerly passage took three months, and every soldier, every weapon, every button and gaiter and musket ball, every article of clothing and great quantities of food and even fuel, had to be shipped across those three thousand miles of the Atlantic. It was not only immensely costly and time consuming, but there was a terrifying wastefulness to it. Ships sank or were blown hundreds of miles off course, supplies spoiled, animals died en route. Worse yet, men died, and in substantial numbers: Returns from regiments sent from the British Isles to the West Indies between 1776 and 1780 reveal that an average of 11 percent of the troops was lost on these crossings.

Beyond the water lay the North American land mass, and it was an article of faith on the part of many a British military man that certain ruin lay in fighting an enemy on any large scale in that savage wilderness. In the House of Lords in November, 1775, the Duke of Richmond warned the peers to consult their geographies before turning their backs on a peaceful settlement. There was, he said, "one insuperable difficulty with which an army would have to struggle"—America abounded in vast rivers that provided natural barriers to the progress of troops; it was a country in which every bush might conceal an enemy, a land whose cultivated parts would be laid waste, so that "the army (if any army could march or subsist) would be obliged to draw all its provisions from Europe, and all its fresh meat from Smithfield market." The French, the mortal enemies of the Great Britain, who had seen a good deal more of the North American wilds than the English had, were already laying plan to capitalize on the situation when the British army was bogged down there. In Paris, watchfully eyeing his adversary's every move, France's foreign minister, the Comte de Vergennes, predicted in July, 1775, that "it will be vain for the English to multiply their forces" in the colonies; "no longer can they bring that vast continent back to dependence by force of arms." Seven years later, as the war drew to a close, one of Rochambeau's aides told a friend of Charles James Fox: "No opinion was clearer than that though the people of America might be conquered by well-disciplined European troops, the country of America was unconquerable."

Yet even in 1775 some thoughtful Englishmen doubted if the American people or their army could be defeated. Before the news of Bunker Hill arrived in London, the adjutant general declared that a plan to defeat the colonials militarily was "as wild an idea as ever controverted common sense," and the secretary-at-war, Lord Barrington, had similar reservations. As early as 1774 Barrington ventured the opinion that a war in the wilderness of North America would cost Britain far more than she could ever gain from it; that the size of the country and the colonials' familiarity with firearms would make victory questionable—or at best achievable only at the cost of enormous suffering; and finally if Britain would win such a contest, Barrington believed that the cost of maintaining the colonies in any state of subjection would be staggering. John Wilkes, taunting Lord North on this matter of military conquest, suggested that North— even if he rode out at the head of the entire English cavalry—would not venture ten miles into the countryside for fear of guerrilla fighters. "The Americans," Wilkes promised, "will dispute every inch of territory with you, every narrow pass, every strong defile, every Thermopylae, every Bunker's Hill."

It was left to the great William Pitt to provide the most stirring warning against fighting the Americans. Now Earl of Chatham, he was so crippled in mind and body that he rarely appeared in the House of Lords, but in May, 1777, he made the supreme effort, determined to raise his voice once again in behalf of conciliation. Supported on canes, his eyes flashing with the old fire and his beak-like face thrust forward belligerently, he warned the peers: "You cannot conquer the Americans. You talk of your numerous friends to annihilate the Congress, and of your powerful forces to disperse their army, but I might as well talk of driving them before me with this crutch. . . . You have been three years teaching them the art of war, and they are apt scholars. I will venture to tell your lordships that the American gentry will make officers enough fit to command the troops of all the European powers. What you have sent there are too many to make peace, too few to make war. You cannot make them respect you. You cannot make them wear your cloth. You will plant an invincible hatred in their breast against you . . . "

"My lords," he went on, "you have been the aggressors from the beginning. I say again, this country has been the aggressor. You have made descents upon their coasts. You have burnt their towns, plundered their country, made war upon the inhabitants, confiscated their property, proscribed and imprisoned their persons. . . . The people of America look upon Parliament as the authors of their miseries. Their affections are estranged from their sovereign. Let then, reparation come from the hands that inflicted the injuries. Let conciliation succeed chastisement. . . . "

But there was no persuading the majority; Chatham's appeal was rejected and the war went on unabated.

It began to appear, however, that destruction of the Continental Army—even if that goal could be achieved—might not be conclusive. After the disastrous campaign around Manhattan in 1776, George Washington had determined not to risk his army in a major engagement, and he began moving away from the European battle style in which two armies confronted each other head to head. His tactical method became that of the small, outweighed prizefighter who depends on his legs to keep him out of range of his opponent and who, when the bigger man begins to tire, darts in quickly to throw a quick punch, then retreats again. It was an approach to fighting described by Nathanael Greene, writing of the campaign in the South in 1780: "We fight, get beat, rise, and fight again." In fact, between January and September of the following year, Greene, short of money, troops, and supplies, won a major campaign without ever really winning a battle. The battle at Guilford Courthouse, which was won by the British, was typical of the results. As Horace Walpole observed, "Lord Cornwallis has conquered his troops out of shoes and provisions and himself out of troops."

There was, in the colonies, no great political center like Paris or London, whose loss might have been demoralizing to the Americans; indeed, Boston, New York, and Philadelphia, the seat of government, were all held at one time or another by the British without irreparable damage to the rebel cause. The fragmented political and military structure of the colonies was often a help to the rebels, rather than a hindrance, for it meant that there was almost no chance of the enemy striking a single crushing blow. The difficulty, as General Frederick Haldimand, who succeeded Carleton in Canada, saw it, was the seemingly unending availability of colonial militiamen who rose up out of nowhere to fight in support of the nucleus of regular troops called the Continental Army. "It is not the number of troops Mr. Washington can spare from his army that is to be apprehended," Haldimand wrote, "it is the multitude of militia and men in arms ready to turn out at an hour's notice at the shew of a single regiment of Continental Troops. . . . " So long as the British were able to split up their forces and fan out over the countryside in relatively small units, they were fairly successful in putting down the irregulars' activities and cutting off their supplies; but the moment they had to concentrate again to fight the Continentals, guerrilla warfare burst out like so many brush fires on their flank and rear. No British regular could tell if an American was friend or foe, for loyalty to King George was easy to attest; and the man who was a farmer or merchant when a British battalion marched by his home was a militiaman as soon as it had passed by, ready to shoulder his musket when an emergency or an opportunity to confound the enemy arose.

Against an unnumberable supply of irregular forces the British could bring to bear only a fixed quantity of troops—however many, that is, they happened to have on the western side of the Atlantic Ocean at any given moment. Early in the war General James Murray had foreseen the difficulties that would undoubtedly arise. Writing to Lord Barrington, he warned that military conquest was no real answer. If the war proved to be a long one, their advantage in numbers would heavily favor the rebels, who could replace their losses while the British could not. Not only did every musket and grain of powder have to be shipped across the ocean; but if a man was killed or wounded, the only way to replace him was to send another man in full kit across the Atlantic. And troop transports were slow and small: Three or four were required to move a single battalion.

During the summer of 1775 recruiting went badly in England and Ireland, for the war was not popular with a lot of the people who would have to fight it, and there were jobs to be had. It was evident that the only means of assembling a force large enough to suppress the rebellion in the one massive stroke that had been determined upon was to hire foreign troops. And immediately this word was out, the rapacious petty princes of Brunswick, Hesse-Cassel, and Waldeck, and the Margrave of Anspach-Bayreuth, generously offered up a number of their subjects— at a price—fully equipped and ready for duty, to serve His Majesty George III. Frederick the Great of Prussia, seeing the plan for what it was, announced that he would "make all the Hessian troops, marching through his dominions to America, pay the usual cattle tax, because, although human beings, they had been sold as beasts." But George III and the princes regarded it as a business deal, in the manner of such dubious alliances ever since: Each foot soldier and trooper supplied by the Duke of Brunswick, for instance, was to be worth seven pounds, four shillings, fourpence halfpenny in levy money to his Most Serene Highness. Three wounded men were to count as one killed in action, and it was stipulated that a soldier killed in combat would be paid for at the same rate as levy money. In other words the life of a subject was worth precisely seven pounds, four shillings, fourpence halfpenny to the Duke.

As it turned out, the large army that was assembled in 1776 to strike a quick, overpowering blow that would put a sudden end to the rebellion proved—when that decisive victory never came to pass—to be a distinct liability, a hideously expensive and at times vulnerable weapon. In the indecisive hands of men like William Howe and Henry Clinton, who never seemed absolutely certain about what they should do or how they should do it, the great army rarely had an opportunity to realize its potential; yet, it remained a ponderous and insatiable consumer of supplies, food, and money.

The loyalists, on whom many Englishmen had placed such high hopes, proved a will-o'-the-wisp. Largely ignored by the policy makers early in the war despite their pleas for assistance, the loyalists were numerous enough but were neither well organized nor evenly distributed throughout the colonies. Where the optimists in Britain went wrong in thinking that loyalist strength would be an important factor was to imagine that anything like a majority of Americans *could* remain loyal to the Crown if they were not continuously supported and sustained by the mother country. Especially as the war went on, as opinions hardened, and as the possibility increased that the new government in America might actually survive, it was a very difficult matter to retain one's loyalty to the King unless friends and neighbors were of like mind and unless there was British force nearby for the British command to satisfy the loyalists, who were bitterly angry over the persecution and physical violence and robbery they had to endure and who charged constantly that the British generals were too lax in their treatment of rebels.

While the problems of fighting the war in distant America mounted, Britain found herself unhappily confronted with the combination of circumstances the Foreign Office dreaded most: with her armies tied down, the great European maritime powers—France and Spain—vengeful and adventurous and undistracted by war in the Old World, formed a coalition against her. When the American war began, the risk of foreign intervention was regarded as minimal, and the decision to fight was made on the premise that victory would be early and complete and that the armed forces would be released before any threatening European power could take advantage of the situation. But as the war continued without any definite signs of American collapse, France and Spain seized the chance to embarrass and perhaps humiliate their old antagonist. At first they supported the rebels surreptitiously with shipments of weapons and other supplies; then, when the situation appeared more auspicious, France in particular furnished active support in the form of an army and a navy, with catastrophic results for Great Britain.

One fascinating might-have-been is what would have happened had the Opposition in Parliament been more powerful politically. It consisted, after all, of some of the most forceful and eloquent orators imaginable, men whose words still have the power to send shivers up the spine. Not simply vocal, they were highly intelligent men whose concern went beyond the injustice and inhumanity of war. They were quick to see that the personal liberty of the King's subjects was as much an issue in London as it was in the colonies, and they foresaw irreparable damage to the empire if the government followed its unthinking policy of coercion. Given a stronger power base, they might have headed off war or the ultimate disaster; had the government been in the hands of men like Chatham or Burke or their followers, some accommodation with America might conceivably have evolved from the various proposals for reconciliation. But the King and North had the votes in their pockets, and the antiwar Opposition failed because a majority that was largely indifferent to reason supported the North ministry until the bitter end came with Cornwallis' surrender. Time and again a member of the Opposition would rise to speak out against the war for one reason or another: "This country," the Earl of Shelburne protested, "already burdened much beyond its abilities, is now on the eve of groaning under new taxes, for the purpose of carrying on this cruel and destructive war." Or, from Dr. Franklin's friend David Hartley: "Every proposition for reconciliation has so constantly and uniformly been crushed by Administration, that I think they seem not even to wish for the appearance of justice. The law of force is that which they appeal to. . . . " Or, from Sir James Lowther, when he learned that the King had rejected an "Olive Branch Petition" from the provincials: "Why have we not peace with a people who, it is evident, desire peace with us?" Or this, from General Henry Seymour Conway, inviting Lord North to inform members of the House of Commons about his overall program: "I do not desire the detail; let us have general outline, to be able to judge of the probability of its success. It is indecent not to lay before the House some plan, or the outlines of a plan. . . . If (the) plan is conciliation, let us see it, that we may form some opinion of it; if it be hostility and coercion, I do repeat, that we have no cause for a minute's consideration; for I can with confidence pronounce, that the present military armament will never succeed." But all unavailing, deafened by self-righteousness and minds hardened against change.

Although it might be said that the arguments raised by the Opposition did not change the course of the war, they nevertheless affected the manner in which it was conducted, which in turn led to the ultimate British defeat. Whether Lord North was uncertain of that silent majority's loyalty is difficult to determine, but it seems clear that he was sufficiently nervous about public support to decide that a bold policy which risked defeats was not for him. As a result, the war of the American Revolution was a limited war—limited from the standpoint of its objectives and the force with which Britain waged it.

In some respects the aspect of the struggle that may have had the greatest influence on the outcome was an intangible one. Until the outbreak of hostilities in 1775 no more than a small minority of the colonials had seriously contemplated independence, but after a year of war the situation was radically different. Now the mood was reflected in words such as these—instructions prepared by the county of Buckingham, in Virginia, for its delegates to a General Convention in Williamsburg: " . . . as far as your voices are admitted, you (will) cause a free and happy Constitution to be established, with a renunciation of the old, and so much thereof as has been found inconvenient and oppressive." That simple and powerful idea—renunciation of the old and its replacement with something new, independently conceived—was destined to sweep all obstacles before it. In Boston James Warren was writing the news of home to John Adams in Philadelphia and told him: "Your Declaration of Independence came on Saturday and diffused a general joy. Every one of us feels more important than ever; we now congratulate each other as Freemen." Such winds of change were strong, and by contrast all Britain had to offer was a return to the status quo. Indeed, it was difficult for the average Englishman to comprehend the appeal that personal freedom and independence held for a growing number of Americans. As William Innes put it in a debate in Commons, all the government had to do to put an end to the nonsense in the colonies was to "convince the lower class of those infatuated people that the imaginary liberty they are so eagerly pursuing is not by any means to be compared to that which the Constitution of this happy country already permits them to enjoy."

With everything to gain from victory and everything to lose by defeat, the Americans could follow Livy's advice, that "in desperate matters the boldest counsels are the safest." Frequently beaten and disheartened, inadequately trained and fed and clothed, they fought on against unreasonably long odds because of that slim hope of attaining a distant goal. And as they fought on, increasing with each passing year the possibility that independence might be achieved, the people of Britain finally lost the will to keep going.

In England the goal had not been high enough, while the cost was too high. There was nothing compelling about the limited objective of bringing the colonies back into the empire, nothing inspiring about punishing the rebels, nothing noble in proving that retribution awaited those who would change the nature of things.

After the war had been lost and the treaty of peace signed, Lord North looked back on the whole affair and sadly informed the members of the House of Commons where, in his opinion, the fault lay. With a few minor changes, it was a message as appropriate to America in 1971 as to Britain in 1783: "The American war," he said, "has been suggested to have been the war of the Crown, contrary to the wishes of the people. I deny it. It was the war of Parliament. There was not a step in it that had not the sanction of Parliament. It was the war of the people, for it was undertaken for the express purpose of maintaining the just rights of Parliament, or, of the empire. For this reason, it was popular at its commencement, and eagerly embraced by the people and Parliament. . . . Nor did it ever cease to be popular until a series of unparalleled disasters and calamities caused the people, wearied out with almost uninterrupted ill-success and misfortune, to call out as loudly for peace as they had formerly done for war."

6

The Revolutionary Context of the Constitutional Convention

Lance Banning

Lance Banning (1942–   ), awarded his Ph.D. by Washington University in St. Louis in 1971, is a professor of history at the University of Kentucky. A specialist in the revolutionary and early national periods, he wrote this article in 1985 as part of the celebration of the bicentennial of the Constitution. As the title implies, he sees the times as having been revolutionary.

The years 1774 to 1789 encompassed a whirlwind of events, but it is important to keep the Declaration of Independence, the Revolutionary War, the Articles of Confederation, and the Constitution separate in our minds. The revolution is often viewed as conservative because it did not cause immediate social or economic upheaval like the French and Russian models. Banning argues that it was not only radical but that it was generally viewed that way at the time on both sides of the Atlantic. Yet the Articles of Confederation emerged not from careful reflection, but more as a codification of the ad hoc arrangements that had emerged in the post–1774 struggle for survival. The shortcomings of the new

This reading is from the spring, 1985 issue of *This Constitution*. Reprinted by permission of The American Political Science Association.

government seemed likely to result in chaos and a loss of both union and liberty. Out of this morass, once chronicled by John Fiske as "the critical period," came the impetus for the Constitution, the culmination of the revolutionary age.

The political debates of the era reflected the tensions inherent in conflicting perceptions of the American character. On the one hand, a healthy skepticism about human nature (sinfulness in Calvinist terms) led to effective controls on governors to prevent their abuse of power, and then to a Constitution with checks and balances to avert the same. On the other hand, the optimistic view embodied in Jefferson's independent idealists encouraged reductions in property requirements for the vote and started the nation toward a distant day when virtually everyone over the age of eighteen could vote. The egalitarian genie was out of the bottle, and despite persistent resistance, this key aspect of the American character would not be headed.

Most Americans recall our Revolution in decidedly selective ways. As a people, we are not as eager as we used to be to recollect how truly revolutionary are our roots. Our Bicentennial celebration, for example, focused overwhelmingly on independence and the war with Britain, not on the genuinely revolutionary facets of the struggle. Too often, we commemorated even independence with hoary myths about tyrannical King George and clever minutemen who used the woods and fences to defeat the British regulars. Perhaps, then, it is not so inexcusable as it would first appear for some Americans to think that Thomas Jefferson wrote the Constitution as well as the Declaration of Independence in 1776. If we think of the American Revolution as no more than a sudden, brave attempt to shake off English rule, perverse consistency leads easily to a mistake that lumps together all the documents and incidents connected with the Founding. For a better understanding, . . . we would do well to fit the Constitution back into the revolutionary process from which it emerged.

As John Adams said, the American Revolution was not the war against Great Britain; it should not be confused with independence. The Revolution started in the people's minds at least ten years before the famous shots at Lexington and Concord. It was well advanced before the colonies declared their independence. It continued for perhaps a quarter of a century after the fighting came to an end. It dominated the entire life experience of America's greatest generation of public men. And it was fully revolutionary in many of the strictest definitions of that term. The men who made it wanted not just independence, but a change that would transform their own societies and set a new example for mankind. They wanted to create, as they put it on the Great Seal of the United States, "a new order of the ages" which would become a foundation for the happiness of all of their descendants and a model for the other peoples of the world. To their minds, the federal Constitution was a Revolutionary act, an episode in their experimental quest for such an order.

A REPUBLICAN EXPERIMENT

From a twentieth-century perspective, the American Revolution may appear conservative and relatively tame. There were no mass executions. Social relationships and political arrangements were not turned upside down in an upheaval of shattering violence, as they would be later on in France or Russia or any of a dozen other countries we might name. To people living through it, nonetheless—or watching it from overseas— the American Revolution seemed very radical indeed. It was not self-evident in 1776 that all men are created equal, that governments derive their just authority from popular consent, or that good governments exist in order to protect God-given rights. These concepts are not undeniable in any age. From the point of view of eighteenth-century Europeans, they contradicted common sense. The notions that a sound society could operate without the natural subordination customary where men were either commoners or nobles or that a stable government could be based entirely on elections seemed both frightening and ridiculously at odds with the obvious lessons of the past. A republican experiment had been attempted once before on something like this scale—in England during the 1640s and 1650s—and the ultimate result had been a Cromwellian dictatorship and a quick return to the ancient constitution of King, Lords, and Commons.

Nevertheless, the Americans dreamed revolutionary visions of perfection, comparable in many ways to revolutionary visions of later times. They sought a new beginning, a rebirth, in which hereditary privilege would disappear and all political authority would derive exclusively from talent, public service, and the people's choice. And their commitment to the principles of liberty and equal rights did touch and change most aspects of their common life.

No essay of this length can possibly describe all of the ways in which the Revolution altered American society. To understand the Constitution, though, we have to realize, at minimum, that as they fought the War for Independence, Americans were equally involved in a fundamental transformation of political beliefs and thus of political institutions. The decision to separate from England was also a decision that Americans were a people different from the English, a separate nation with a special mission in the world. This people had no way to understand their new identity except in terms of their historical mission, no way to define or perfect their national character except by building their new order. To be an American, by 1776, was to be a republican, and to become consistently republican required a thorough reconstruction of existing institutions.

A republican experiment, in fact, required rebuilding governments afresh. For in the months between the clash at Lexington and the Declaration of Independence, formal governments dissolved in one American colony after another. The people, who had ordinarily elected only one branch of their local governments, simply transferred their allegiance from their legal governmental institutions to extra-legal revolutionary committees, state conventions, and the Continental Congress. Through the first months of the fighting, the conventions and committees managed very well. Power rested with the people in a wholly literal sense, the people followed the directives of these revolutionary bodies, and those bodies turned the popular determination into armies and materials of war.

Some revolutionaries might have been content to see their states continue indefinitely under governmental bodies of this sort. Many patriots were intensely localistic, and they had learned a fierce distrust of any power much beyond the people's easy reach. Other patriots, however, many more of those who exercised great influence, never saw the revolutionary agencies as anything but temporary. A structure that depended so immediately on the people was good enough for an emergency, but hardly suitable for the longer term. For permanence, most patriots admired a governmental structure that balanced and divided power between different and independent parts, not one that concentrated it in single bodies which performed both legislative and executive functions.

The revolutionaries had been reared as Englishmen, in a tradition that instructed them that liberty was incompatible with the unchecked rule of the majority or with a government composed of only a single branch. Proper constitutions, they believed, depended on consent, but governments existed in order to protect the liberties of all. The revolutionaries had decided that good governments should have no place for aristocrats or kings, but they continued to believe that immediate and undiluted rule by the majority could not provide the wisdom and stability that governments require, nor could it offer proper safeguards for the rights of all. Thus, as they moved toward independence, the revolutionaries started a long search for a governmental structure in which liberty and representative democracy could be combined. This was what they meant by a "republic."

Most of the revolutionary states established written constitutions before the end of 1776. Although they differed greatly in details, these constitutions tended to be similar in broader lines. The colonial experience, together with the quarrel with Great Britain, had taught a powerful fear of the executive and of the executive's ability to undermine the independence of the other parts of government by use of patronage or "influence." Accordingly, most states created governors too weak to do such harm. Most stripped the governors of the majority of their traditional powers of appointment and deprived them of the traditional right to veto legislation. Most provided for election of the governors by the legislative branch. Most confined the chief executives, in short, to the job of enforcing the legislatures' wills.

According to these constitutions, the legislative power would remain within the people's hardy grip. The concept of a balance required two legislative houses, but hostility to privilege was far too sharp to let the second house become a bastion for any special group, in imitation of the English House of Lords. Moreover, in societies without hereditary ranks, it was difficult to reach agreement on a genuinely republican method for selecting the few men of talent and leisure whose superior wisdom, lodged in an upper house, was traditionally supposed to check the passions of the multitude. The revolutionary senates differed relatively little in their makeup from the lower houses of assembly. Democratic Pennsylvania did without an upper house at all and placed executive authority in the hands of a council, rather than a single man, though this was such a radical departure from general ideas that it quickly created an anti-constitutional party in that state.

Nearly all the revolutionaries would have failed a modern test of loyalty to democratic standards. Even the most dedicated patriots were eighteenth-century men, and eighteenth-century thinking normally excluded many portions of the people from participation in the politics of a republic: adherents to unpopular religions, women, blacks, and even very poor white males.

Accordingly, not even Pennsylvania departed so far from tradition as to give the vote to every male adult. And yet most states moved noticeably in that direction. Most lowered the amount of property one had to own in order to possess the franchise. Several gave the vote to every man who paid a tax. All the states provided for annual elections of the lower house of legislature and, often, for annual elections of the senate and governor as well. Every part of these new governments would be chosen by the people or by those the people had elected. And the legislatures in particular were filled with men whose modest means and ordinary social rank would have excluded them from higher office in colonial times. In a variety of ways, these governments were far more responsive to the people than the old colonial governments had been. They were also far more closely watched. The revolutionary air was full of popular awareness of the people's rights.

The revolutionary movement disestablished churches, altered attitudes toward slavery, and partly redefined the role of women in American society. Eventually, of course, revolutionary concepts paved the way for an extension of the rights of citizens to all the groups that eighteenth-century patriots excluded. But whatever else the Revolution was or would become, its essence lay originally in these thirteen problematic experiments in constructing republican regimes. It would succeed or fail, in revolutionary minds, according to the success of these regimes in raising the new order and fulfilling expectations that republicanism would defend and perfect this special people and the democratic social structure that they hoped would become the envy of the world.

A PERMANENT CONFEDERATION

Americans did not intend, at the beginning, to extend the revolutionary experiment in republican government from the states to the nation as a whole. Republics were expected to be small. The Revolution had begun as an attempt to protect the old colonial governments from external interference by a distant Parliament and king. Traditional loyalties and revolutionary ideas were both keyed to the states.

Still, the argument with Britain taught Americans to think that they were a single people, and the War for Independence built a growing sense of nationhood. There was a Continental Congress before there were any independent states. *Congress* declared American independence and recommended that new state governments be formed. *Congress* assumed the direction of the war.

The Continental Congress was an extralegal body. It had simply emerged in the course of the imperial quarrel and continued to exert authority with the approval of the people and the states, all of which sent an unspecified number of delegates to help take care of common concerns. As early as June 12, 1776, these delegates initiated consideration of a plan to place their authority on formal grounds. But the experiences that had led to independence made Americans powerfully suspicious of any central government, and there were many disagreements in the Congress. Meanwhile, there was also the necessity of managing a war.

Not until November 17, 1777, did Congress finally present a formal proposal to the states. This plan, the Articles of Confederation, called upon the sovereign states to join in a permanent confederation presided over by a Congress whose authority would be confined to matters of interest to all: war and peace; foreign relations; trade with the Indians; disputes between states; and other common concerns. Each state would continue to have a single vote in Congress. In matters of extreme importance, such as war and peace, Congress would act only when nine of the thirteen states agreed. Since Congress would not directly represent the people, troops or money could be raised only by requisitioning the states.

The Articles of Confederation did not issue from a systematic, theoretical consideration of the problems of confederation government. For the most part, they only codified the structure and procedures that had emerged in practice in the years since 1774. Most of the country scarcely noticed when they finally went into effect, which was not until February 1781—three years after they were first proposed. Maryland, which had a definite western border, refused its consent until Virginia and the other giant states, whose colonial charters gave them boundaries which might stretch from coast to coast, agreed to cede their lands beyond the mountains to the Confederation as a whole. Then, for the most of the rest of the 1780s, Americans lived in a confederation of this sort.

Historians have long since given up the old idea that the Confederation years were a period of governmental folly and unmixed disaster. The Articles established a genuine federal government, not merely a league of states. The union was to be permanent, and Congress was granted many of the usual attributes of sovereign authority. Great things were accomplished. The states secured their independence and won a generous treaty of peace, which placed their western border at the Mississippi River. The country weathered a severe post-war depression. Congress organized the area northwest of the Ohio for settlement and eventual statehood. In fact, the Northwest Ordinance of 1787 established the pattern for all the rest of the continental expansion of the United States, providing that new territories would eventually enter the union on terms of full equality with its original members and thus assuring that America would manage to escape most of the problems usually confronted by an expanding empire. It was not an unimpressive record.

THIRTEEN SQUABBLING STATES

Nevertheless, the Articles of Confederation came under increasing criticism from an influential minority even before they formally went into practice. This minority was centered in the Congress itself and around the powerful executive officials created by the Congress, especially Robert Morris, a Philadelphia merchant was was appointed Superintendent of Finance in 1781. Morris and his allies were necessarily concerned with the Confederation as a whole, and they found it almost impossible to meet their responsibilities under this kind of government. By the time the war was over, the Confederation's paper money was entirely worthless—"not worth a Continental," as the phrase still goes. The Confederation owed huge debts to army veterans, to citizens who had lent supplies or money during the war, and to foreign governments and foreign subjects who had purchased American bonds. Dependent on the states for revenues, Congress could not even pay the interest on these obligations. All the states had war debts of their own, and in the midst of a depression, their citizens were seldom willing or even able to pay taxes high enough to make it possible for the republics to handle their own needs and meet their congressional requisitions as well. By 1783, Morris, Alexander Hamilton, James Madison, and many other continental-minded men were insisting on reform. They demanded, at the very least, that Congress be granted the authority to levy a tax on foreign imports, which might provide it with a steady, independent source of revenue.

The need for revenue, however, was only the most urgent of several concerns. Lacking a direct connection with the people, Congress had to work through and depend on the states for nearly everything. Unable to compel cooperation, its members watched in futile anger as the sovereign republics went their separate ways. Some states quarreled over boundaries. Troubled by the depression, others passed competitive duties on foreign imports. The states ignored Confederation treaties, fought separate wars with Indians, and generally neglected congressional pleas for money.

As this happened, American ambassadors in foreign lands—John Adams in England and Thomas Jefferson in France—discovered that the European nations treated the American confederation with contempt. The European powers refused to make commercial treaties that would lower their barriers to freer trade and ease America's commercial problems. England refused to remove her soldiers from forts in the American northwest, insisting that she would abide by the treaty of peace only when the states began to meet their own obligations to cease persecuting returning loyalists and to open their courts to British creditors who wanted to collect their debts.

Nevertheless, the nationalists in Congress were frustrated in their desire for reform. The Articles of Confederation could be amended only by unanimous consent, but when Congress recommended an amendment that would give it the authority to levy a five percent duty on imports, little Rhode Island refused to agree. When Congress asked for power to retaliate against Great Britain's navigation laws, the states again could not concur.

Repeatedly defeated in their efforts at reform, increasingly alarmed by mutual antagonisms between the states, which had grown serious enough by 1786 to threaten an immediate fragmentation of the union into several smaller confederacies, the men of continental vision turned their thoughts to fundamentals. A much more sweeping change, they now suspected, might be necessary to resolve the pressing problems of the current central government. And if the change went far enough, a few of them began to think, it might accomplish something more. It might restore the Revolution to its proper course.

The Revolution, after all, involved a dream of national greatness; and the dream was going wrong. A people who had hoped to be a model for the world was fragmented into thirteen petty, squabbling states. The states would not—or could not—subordinate their separate interests to the good of the Confederation as a whole. Even worse, too many of the states fell short of fulfilling revolutionary expectations within their individual bounds. The early revolutionary constitutions had delivered overwhelming power to the people's immediate representatives in the lower houses of assembly. As these lower houses struggled to protect the people from hard times, they frequently neglected private rights and seldom seemed to give a due consideration to the long-term good. As clashing groups in different states competed to control their house of representatives, nobody could feel certain what the law might be next year, when one majority replaced another. The lower houses of assembly were essentially unchecked by the other parts of government, and to many revolutionaries it appeared that the assemblies proceeded on their ways with slight regard for justice and little thought about tomorrow. The rule of law appeared to be collapsing into a kind of anarchy in which the liberty and property of everyone might depend on the good will of whichever temporary majority happened to control his state. No one could feel secure in the enjoyment of his rights.

LIBERTY IN PERIL

During the 1780s, in other words, the feeling grew that liberty was once again in peril. Alarm was most intense among the men whose duties, education, or experience encouraged them to pin their patriotic feelings on the continent as a whole: certain members of Congress; most of the best-known revolutionary thinkers; most of the former officers of the continental army; many merchants, public creditors, and other men of wealth. Men of social standing were distressed with the way in which the revolutionary principles of liberty and equality seemed to shade into a popular contempt for talent or distinction. Too often, to their minds, the best men lost elections in the states to self-serving, scrambling demagogues, and the revolutionary constitutions made it far too easy for these demagogues to set an ill-considered course or even to oppress the propertied minority in order to secure the people's favor. Continued confiscations of the property of people who had sympathized with Britain and continued use of paper money, which threatened men's investments and their right to hold their property secure, were grievances of particular importance to those who had investments and positions to defend.

And yet the sense of fading hopes and failing visions was not exclusively confined to men of wealth. Anyone whose life had been immersed in revolutionary expectations might share in the concern. Every state seemed full of quarrels. Every individual seemed to be on the scrape for himself. No one seemed to have a real regard for common interests, a willingness to recognize that selfish interests must be limited by some consideration for the good of all. Public virtue, to use the phrase the revolutionaries used, seemed to be in danger of completely disappearing as every man and every social group sought private goods at the expense of harmony and other people's rights. But virtue, revolutionaries thought, was the indispensable foundation for republics, without which they could not survive. If public virtue was collapsing, then the Revolution was about to fail. It would degenerate into a kind of chaos, from which a tyrant might emerge, or else the people, in disgust, might eventually prefer to return to hereditary rule.

So, at least, did many fear. Guided by the same ideas that had impelled them into independence, they saw a second crisis, as dangerous to liberty as the crisis that had led them into Revolution. As they had done in 1776, they blamed their discontents on governments that lacked the character to mold a virtuous people and fit them for their special role. Once more, they turned to constitutional reform. They saw in the problems of the Confederation government not merely difficulties that would have to be corrected, but an opportunity that might be seized for even greater ends, an opportunity to rescue revolutionary hopes from their decay.

The constitutional reformers of the 1780s had several different motives and several different goals. Some had an economic interest in a constitutional reform that would enable the central government to pay its debts and act to spur the economic revival. All wanted to make the government adequate to its tasks and able to command more respect from the rest of the world. Some wanted more: to reconstruct the central government in such a way that its virtues might override the mistakes that had been made in some of the states. They wanted to redeem the reputation of democracy and save the republican experiment from a process of degeneration which threatened to destroy all that they had struggled for.

Shays's Rebellion handed them their chance. Out in western Massachusetts, hard times, large debts, and the high taxes prompted by the state's attempt to handle its revolutionary debt drove many farmers to distress. They first petitioned for relief, but when the legislature refused to issue paper money or to pass the laws required to protect their property from seizure, petitions gave way to rebellion. Farmers forced the courts to close in several counties, and Daniel Shays, a revolutionary captain, organized an armed resistance. The rebels were defeated with surprising ease. The state called out the militia during the winter of 1786, and Shays' forces disintegrated after a minor fight. The incident was nonetheless, for many, the final straw atop a growing load of fears. Armed resistance to a republican government seemed the ultimate warning of a coming collapse.

Earlier in 1786, delegates from five states had met at Annapolis, Maryland, to consider better means of regulating interstate and international trade. Nationalist sentiment was strong among the delegates. Hamilton and Madison were there. The participants quickly agreed that little could be done about commercial problems without a revision of the Articles of Confederation. They said as much in a report to Congress and their states, and Congress endorsed their recommendation for the meeting of a national convention to consider ways to make the central government "adequate to the exigencies of the union." Badly frightened by events in Massachusetts, whose constitution was widely thought to be among the best, every state except Rhode Island answered the call. From this context and in hope that it might save both liberty and union, the Constitutional Convention emerged.

7

The Frontier and the American Character

Ray Allen Billington

In 1893 historian Frederick Jackson Turner advanced the most famous interpretation of the American character, the "frontier thesis." Dissatisfied with existing theories of the national character, he found in the 1890 census report the clue to a new approach. The census noted that there no longer existed a frontier line, that settlement had (despite large empty areas) reached from coast to coast. Turner argued that the frontier had shaped both American society and the American character from earliest colonial times. Among other characteristics, Turner suggested that the frontier explained American mobility, optimism, openness to innovation, materialism, wastefulness, individualism, nationalism, and faith in democracy. Turner looked ahead with foreboding to a nation without free land in the west to revitalize it. Historians have debated the pros and cons of Turner's arguments ever since.

Ray Allen Billington (1903–1981), a student of Turner's, has been this century's foremost expert on frontier history. His text Westward Expansion, *first published in 1940, was still the standard even after*

This reading is reprinted with permission from *American Heritage*, volume 9, number 3. Copyright 1958 by American Heritage Publishing Company, Inc.

his death. Billington wrote the definitive biography Frederick Jackson Turner: Historian, Scholar, Teacher *(1973), a critical yet sympathetic examination of the influential historian. His obvious mastery of the literature of the field of frontier history makes him the logical choice to sum up the thesis and the debate it has provoked. This article, published in* American Heritage *in 1958, does just that.*

Since the dawn days of historical writing in the United States, historians have labored mightily, and usually in vain, to answer the famous question posed by Hector St. John de Crèvecoeur in the eighteenth century: "What then is the American, this new man?" Was that composite figure actually a "new man" with unique traits that distinguished him from his Old World ancestors? Or was he merely a transplanted European? The most widely accepted—and bitterly disputed—answer was advanced by a young Wisconsin historian named Frederick Jackson Turner in 1893. The American was a new man, he held, who owed his distinctive characteristics and institutions to the unusual New World environment—characterized by the availability of free land and an ever-receding frontier—in which his civilization had grown to maturity. The environmental theory, accepted for a generation after its enunciation, has been vigorously attacked and vehemently defended during the past two decades. How has it fared in this battle of words? Is it still a valid key to the meaning of American history?

Turner's own background provides a clue to the answer. Born in Portage, Wisconsin, in 1861 of pioneer parents from upper New York state, he was reared in a land fringed by the interminable forest and still stamped with the mark of youth. There he mingled with pioneers who had trapped beaver or hunted Indians or cleared the virgin wilderness; from them he learned something of the free and easy democratic values prevailing among those who judged men by their own accomplishments rather than those of their ancestors. At the University of Wisconsin Turner's faith in cultural democracy was deepened, while his intellectual vistas were widened through contact with teachers who led him into that wonderland of adventure where scientific techniques were being applied to social problems, where Darwin's evolutionary hypothesis was awakening scholars to the continuity of progress, and where searchers after truth were beginning to realize the multiplicity of forces responsible for human behavior. The young student showed how well he had learned these lessons in his master's essay on "The Character and Influence of the Fur Trade in Wisconsin"; he emphasized the evolution of institutions from simple to complex forms.

From Wisconsin Turner journeyed to Johns Hopkins University, as did many eager young scholars of that day, only to meet stubborn opposition for the historical theories already taking shape in his mind. His principal professor, Herbert Baxter Adams, viewed mankind's development in evolutionary terms, but held that environment had no place in the equation; American institutions could be understood only as outgrowths of European "germs" that had originated among Teutonic tribes in the forests of medieval Germany. To Turner this explanation was unsatisfactory. The "germ theory" explained the similarities between Europe and America, but what of the many differences? This problem was still much in his mind when he returned to the University of Wisconsin as an instructor in 1889. In two remarkable papers prepared during the next few years he set forth his answer. The first, "The Significance of History," reiterated his belief in what historians call "multiple causation"; to understand man's complex nature, he insisted, one needed not only a knowledge of past politics, but a familiarity with social, economic, and cultural forces as well. The second, "Problems in American History," attempted to isolate those forces most influential in explaining the unique features of American development. Among these Turner believed that the most important was the need for institutions to "adapt themselves to the changes of a remarkably developing, expanding people."

This was the theory that was expanded into a full-blown historical hypothesis in the famous essay on "The Significance of the Frontier in American History," read at a conference of historians held in connection with the World Fair in Chicago in 1893. The differences between European and American civilization, Turner stated in that monumental work, were in part the product of the distinctive environment of the New World. The most unusual features of that environment were "the existence of an area of free land, its continuous recession, and the advance of American settlement westward." This free land served as a magnet to draw men westward, attracted by the hope of economic gain or adventure. They came as Europeans or easterners, but they soon realized that the wilderness environment was ill-adapted to the habits, institutions, and cultural baggage of the stratified societies they had left behind. Complex political institutions were unnecessary in a tiny frontier outpost; traditional economic practices were useless in an isolated community geared to an economy of self-sufficiency; rigid social customs were outmoded in a land where prestige depended on skill with the axe or rifle rather than on hereditary glories; cultural pursuits were unessential in a land where so many material tasks awaited doing. Hence in each pioneer settlement there occurred a rapid reversion to the primitive. What little government was necessary was provided by simple associations of settlers; each man looked after his family without reliance on his fellows; social hierarchies disintegrated, and cultural progress came to a halt. As the newcomers moved backward along the scale of civilization, the habits and customs of their traditional cultures were forgotten.

Gradually, however, newcomers drifted in, and as the man–land ratio increased, the community began a slow climb back toward civilization.

Governmental controls were tightened and extended, economic special-
ization began, social stratification set in, and cultural activities quickened. But the new society that eventually emerged differed from the old
from which it had sprung. The abandonment of cultural baggage during
the migrations, the borrowings from the many cultures represented in
each pioneer settlement, the deviations natural in separate evolutions,
and the impact of the environment all played their parts in creating a
unique social organism similar to but differing from those in the East. An
"Americanization" of men and their institutions had taken place.

Turner believed that many of the characteristics associated with
the American people were traceable to their experience, during the three
centuries required to settle the continent, of constantly "beginning over
again." Their mobility, their optimism, their inventiveness and willingness to accept innovation, their materialism, their exploitive wastefulness—these were frontier traits; for the pioneer, accustomed to repeated
moves as he drifted westward, viewed the world through rose-colored
glasses as he dreamed of a better future, experimented constantly as he
adapted artifacts and customs to his peculiar environment, scorned culture as a deterrent to the practical tasks that bulked so large in his life,
and squandered seemingly inexhaustible natural resources with abandon. Turner also ascribed America's distinctive brand of individualism,
with its dislike of governmental interference in economic functions,
to the experience of pioneers who wanted no hindrance from society as
they exploited nature's riches. Similarly, he traced the exaggerated nationalism of the United States to its roots among frontiersmen who
looked to the national government for land, transportation outlets, and
protection against the Indians. And he believed that America's faith in
democracy had stemmed from a pioneering experience in which the
leveling influence of poverty and the uniqueness of local problems encouraged majority self-rule. He pointed out that these characteristics,
prominent among frontiersmen, had persisted long after the frontier
itself was no more.

This was Turner's famous "frontier hypothesis." For a generation
after its enunciation its persuasive logic won uncritical acceptance
among historians, but beginning in the late 1920s, and increasingly after
Turner's death in 1932, an avalanche of criticism steadily mounted. His
theories, critics said, were contradictory, his generalizations unsup-
ported, his assumptions inadequately based; what empirical proof could
he advance, they asked, to prove that the frontier experience was responsible for American individualism, mobility, or wastefulness? He was
damned as a romanticist for his claim that democracy sprang from the
forest environment of the United States and as an isolationist for failing
to recognize the continuing impact of Europe on America. As the "bait-
Turner" vogue gained popularity among younger scholars of the 1930s

with their international, semi-Marxian views of history, the criticisms of the frontier theory became as irrational as the earlier support given by overenthusiastic advocates.

During the past decade, however, a healthy reaction has slowly and unspectacularly gained momentum. Today's scholars, gradually realizing that Turner was advancing a hypothesis rather than proving a theory, have shown a healthy tendency to abandon fruitless haggling over the meaning of his phrases and to concentrate instead on testing his assumptions. They have directed their efforts primarily toward re-examining his hypothesis in the light of criticisms directed against it and applying it to frontier areas beyond the borders of the United States. Their findings have modified many of the views expressed by Turner but have gone far toward proving that the frontier hypothesis remains one essential tool— albeit not the only one—for interpreting American history.

That Turner was guilty of oversimplifying both the nature and the causes of the migration process was certainly true. He pictured settlers as moving westward in an orderly procession—fur trappers, cattlemen, miners, pioneer farmers, and equipped farmers—with each group playing its part in the transmutation of a wilderness into a civilization. Free land was the magnet that lured them onward, he believed, and this operated most effectively in periods of depression, when the displaced workers of the East sought a refuge from economic storms amidst nature's abundance in the West. "The wilderness ever opened the gate of escape to the poor, the discontented and oppressed," Turner wrote at one time. "If social conditions tended to crystallize in the east, beyond the Alleghenies there was freedom."

No one of these assumptions can be substantiated in the simplified form in which Turner stated it. His vision of an "orderly procession of civilization, marching single file westward" failed to account for deviations that were almost as important as the norm; as essential to the conquest of the forest as trappers or farmers were soldiers, mill operators, distillers, artisans, storekeepers, merchants, lawyers, editors, speculators, and town dwellers. All played their role, and all contributed to a complex frontier social order that bore little resemblance to the primitive societies Turner pictured. This was especially the case with the early town builders. The hamlets that sprang up adjacent to each pioneer settlement were products of the environment as truly as were the cattlemen or Indian fighters; each evolved economic functions geared to the needs of the primitive area surrounding it, and, in the tight public controls maintained over such essential functions as grist-milling or retail selling, each mirrored the frontiersmen's community-oriented views. In these villages, too, the equalitarian influence of the West was reflected in thoroughly democratic governments, with popularly elected councils supreme and the mayor reduced to a mere figurehead.

The pioneers who marched westward in this disorganized procession were not attracted by the magnet of "free land," for Turner's assumption that before 1862 the public domain was open to all who could pay $1.25 an acre, or that acreage was free after the Homestead Act was passed in that year, has been completely disproved. Turner failed to recognize the presence in the procession to the frontier of that omnipresent profit-seeker, the speculator. Jobbers were always ahead of farmers in the advance westward, buying up likely town sites or appropriating the best farm lands, where the soil was good and transportation outlets available. When the settler arrived his choice was between paying the speculator's price or accepting an inferior site. Even the Homestead Act failed to lessen speculative activity. Capitalizing on generous government grants to railroads and state educational institutions (which did not want to be bothered with sales to individuals), or buying bonus script from soldiers, or securing Indian lands as the reservations were contracted, or seizing on faulty features of congressional acts for the disposal of swampland and timberland, jobbers managed to engross most of the Far West's arable acreage; for every newcomer who obtained a homestead from the government, six or seven purchased farms from speculators.

Those who made these purchases were not, as Turner believed, displaced eastern workers fleeing periodic industrial depressions. Few city-dwelling artisans had the skills or inclination, and almost none the capital, to escape to the frontier. Land prices of $1.25 an acre may seem low today, but they were prohibitive for laborers earning only a dollar a day. Moreover, needed farm machinery, animals, and housing added about $1,000 to the cost of starting a farm in the 1850s, while the cheapest travel rate from New York to St. Louis was about $13 a person. Because these sums were always beyond the reach of factory workers (in bad times they deterred migration even from the rural East), the frontier never served as a "safety valve" for laborers in the sense that Turner employed the term. Instead, the American frontiers were pushed westward largely by younger sons from adjacent farm areas who migrated in periods of prosperity. While these generalizations apply to the pre–Civil War era that was Turner's principal interest, they are even more applicable to the late nineteenth century. During that period the major population shifts were from country to city rather than vice versa; for every worker who left the factory to move to the farm, twenty persons moved from farm to factory. If a safety valve did exist at that time, it was a rural safety valve, drawing off surplus farm labor and thus lessening agrarian discontent during the Granger and Populist eras.

Admitting that the procession to the frontier was more complex than Turner realized, that good lands were seldom free, and that a safety valve never operated to drain the dispossessed and the malcontented from industrial centers, does this mean that his conclusions concerning the migration process have been completely discredited? The opposite is emphatically true. A more divergent group than Turner realized felt the frontier's impact, but that does not minimize the extent of the impact. Too, while lands in the West were almost never free, they were relatively cheaper than those in Europe or the East, and this differential did serve as an attracting force. Nor can pages of statistics disprove the fact that, at least until the Civil War, the frontier served as an indirect safety valve by attracting displaced eastern farmers who would otherwise have moved into industrial cities; thousands who left New England or New York for the Old Northwest in the 1830s and 1840s, when the "rural decay" of the Northeast was beginning, would have sought factory jobs had no western outlet existed.

The effect of their exodus is made clear by comparing the political philosophies of the United States with those of another frontier country, Australia. There, lands lying beyond the coastal mountains were closed to pioneers by the aridity of the soil and by great sheep ranchers who were first on the scene. Australia, as a result, developed an urban civilization and an industrialized population relatively sooner than did the United States; and it had labor unions, labor-dominated governments, and political philosophies that would be viewed as radical in America. Without the safety valve of its own West, feeble though it may have been, such a course might have been followed in the United States.

Frederick Jackson Turner's conclusions concerning the influence of the frontier on Americans have also been questioned, debated, and modified since he advanced his hypothesis, but they have not been seriously altered. This is true even of one of his statements that has been more vigorously disputed than any other: "American democracy was born of no theorist's dream; it was not carried in the *Susan Constant* to Virginia, nor in the *Mayflower* to Plymouth. It came out of the American forest, and it gained a new strength each time it touched a new frontier." When he penned those oft-quoted words, Turner wrote as a propagandist against the "germ theory" school of history; in a less emotional and more thoughtful moment, he ascribed America's democratic institutions not to "imitation, or simple borrowing," but to "the evolution and adaptation of organs in response to changed environment." Even this moderate theory has aroused critical venom. Democracy, according to anti-Turnerians, was well advanced in Europe and *was* transported to America on the *Susan Constant* and the *Mayflower;* within this country democratic practices have multiplied most rapidly as a result of eastern lower-class pressures and have only been imitated in the West. If, critics ask, some mystical forest influence was responsible for such practices as manhood suffrage, increased authority for legislatures at the expense of executives, equitable legislative representation, and women's political rights, why did they not evolve in frontier areas outside the United States—in Russia, Latin America, and Canada, for example—exactly as they did here?

The answer, of course, is that democratic theory and institutions were imported from England, but that the frontier environment tended to make them, in practice, even more democratic. Two conditions common in pioneer communities made this inevitable. One was the wide diffusion of land ownership; this created an independent outlook and led to a demand for political participation on the part of those who had a stake in society. The other was the common social and economic level and the absence, characteristic of all primitive communities, of any prior leadership structure. The lack of any national or external controls made self-rule a hard necessity, and the frontiersmen, with their experience in community co-operation at cabin-raisings, logrollings, cornhuskings, and road or school building, accepted simple democratic practices as natural and inevitable. These practices, originating on the grass roots level, were expanded and extended in the recurring process of government-building that marked the westward movement of civilization. Each new territory that was organized—there were 31 in all—required a frame of government; this was drafted by relatively poor recent arrivals or by a minority of upper-class leaders, all of whom were committed to democratic ideals through their frontier community experiences. The result was a constant democratization of institutions and practices as constitution-makers adopted the most liberal features of older frames of government with which they were familiar.

This was true even in frontier lands outside the United States, for wherever there were frontiers, existing practices were modified in the direction of greater equality and a wider popular participation in governmental affairs. The results were never identical, of course, for both the environment and the nature of the imported institutions varied too greatly from country to country. In Russia, for instance, even though it promised no democracy comparable to that of the United States, the eastward-moving Siberian frontier, the haven of some seven million peasants during the nineteenth and early twentieth centuries, was notable for its lack of guilds, authoritarian churches, and all-powerful nobility. An official visiting there in 1910 was alarmed by the "enormous, rudely democratic country" evolving under the influence of the small homesteads that were the normal living units; he feared that czarism and European Russia would soon be "throttled" by the egalitarian currents developing on the frontier.

That the frontier accentuated the spirit of nationalism and individualism in the United States, as Turner maintained, was also true. Every page of the country's history, from the War of 1812 through the era of Manifest Destiny to today's bitter conflicts with Russia, demonstrates that the American attitude toward the world has been far more nationalistic than that of non-frontier countries and that this attitude has been strongest in the newest regions. Similarly, the pioneering experience converted settlers into individualists, although through a somewhat different process than Turner envisaged. His emphasis on a desire for freedom as a primary force luring men westward and his belief that pioneers developed an attitude of self-sufficiency in their lone battle against nature have been questioned, and with justice. Hoped-for gain was the magnet that attracted most migrants to the cheaper lands of the West, while once there they lived in units where co-operative enterprise—for protection against the Indians, for cabin-raising, law enforcement, and the like—was more essential than in the better established towns of the East. Yet the fact remains that the abundant resources and the greater social mobility of frontier areas did instill into frontiersmen a uniquely American form of individualism. Even though they may be sheeplike in following the decrees of social arbiters or fashion dictators, Americans today, like their pioneer ancestors, dislike governmental interference in their affairs. "Rugged individualism" did not originate on the frontier any more than democracy or nationalism did, but each concept was deepened and sharpened by frontier conditions.

His opponents have also cast doubt on Turner's assertion that American inventiveness and willingness to adopt innovations are traits inherited from pioneer ancestors who constantly devised new techniques and artifacts to cope with an unfamiliar environment. The critics insist that each mechanical improvement needed for the conquest of the frontier, from plows to barbed-wire fencing, originated in the East; when frontiersmen faced such an incomprehensible task as conquering the Great Plains they proved so tradition-bound that their advance halted until eastern inventors provided them with the tools needed to subdue grasslands. Unassailable as this argument may be, it ignores the fact that the recurring demand for implements and methods needed in the frontier advance did put a premium on inventiveness by Americans, whether they lived in the East or West. That even today they are less bound by tradition than other peoples is due in part to their pioneer heritage.

The anti-intellectualism and materialism which are national traits can also be traced to the frontier experience. There was little in pioneer life to attract the timid, the cultivated, or the aesthetically sensitive. In the boisterous western borderlands, book learning and intellectual speculation were suspect among those dedicated to the material tasks necessary to subdue a continent. Americans today reflect their background in placing the "intellectual" well below the "practical businessman" in their scale of heroes. Yet the frontiersman, as Turner recognized, was an idealist as well as a materialist. He admired material objects not only as symbols of advancing civilization but as the substance of his hopes for a better future. Given economic success he would be able to afford the aesthetic and intellectual pursuits that he felt were his due, even though he was not quite able to appreciate them. This spirit inspired the cultural activities— literary societies, debating clubs, "thespian groups," libraries, schools, camp meetings—that thrived in the most primitive western communities. It also helped nurture in the pioneers an infinite faith in the future. The belief in progress, both material and intellectual, that is part of modern America's creed was strengthened by the frontier experience.

Frederick Jackson Turner, then, was not far wrong when he maintained that frontiersman did develop unique traits and that these, perpetuated, form the principal distinguishing characteristics of the American people today. To a degree unknown among Europeans, Americans do display a restless energy, a versatility, a practical ingenuity, an earthy practicality. They do squander their natural resources with an abandon unknown elsewhere; they have developed a mobility both social and physical that marks them as a people apart. In few other lands is the democratic ideal worshiped so intensely, or nationalism carried to such extremes of isolationism or international arrogance. Rarely do other peoples display such indifference toward intellectualism or aesthetic values; seldom in comparable cultural areas do they cling so tenaciously to the shibboleth of rugged individualism. Nor do residents of non-frontier lands experience to the same degree the heady optimism, the rosy faith in the future, the belief in the inevitability of progress that form part of the American creed. These are pioneer traits, and they have become a part of the national heritage.

Yet if the frontier wrought such a transformation within the United States, why did it not have a similar effect on other countries with frontiers? If the pioneering experience was responsible for our democracy and nationalism and individualism, why have the peoples of Africa, Latin America, Canada, and Russia failed to develop identical characteristics? The answer is obvious: In few nations of the world has the sort of frontier that Turner described existed. For he saw the frontier not as a borderland between unsettled and settled lands, but as an accessible areas in which a low man-land ratio and abundant natural resources provided an unusual opportunity for the individual to better himself. Where autocratic governments controlled population movements, where resources were lacking, or where conditions prohibited ordinary individuals from exploiting nature's virgin riches, a frontier in the Turnerian sense could not be said to exist.

The areas of the world that have been occupied since the beginning of the age of discovery contain remarkably few frontiers of the American kind. In Africa the few Europeans were so outnumbered by relatively un-civilized native inhabitants that the need for protection transcended any impulses toward democracy or individualism. In Latin America the rugged terrain and steaming jungles restricted areas exploitable by individuals to the Brazilian plains and the Argentine pampas; these did attract frontiersmen, although in Argentina the prior occupation of most good lands by government-favored cattle growers kept small farmers out until railroads penetrated the region. In Canada the path westward was blocked by the Laurentian Shield, a tangled mass of hills and sterile, brush-choked soil covering the country north and west of the St. Lawrence Valley. When railroads finally penetrated this barrier in the late nineteenth century, they carried pioneers directly from the East to the prairie provinces of the West; the newcomers, with no prior pioneering experience, simply adapted to their new situation the eastern institutions with which they were familiar. Among the world's frontier nations only Russia provided a physical environment comparable to that of the United States, and there the pioneers were too accustomed to rigid feudal and monarchic controls to respond as Americans did.

Further proof that the westward expansion of the United States has been a powerful formative force has been provided by the problems facing the nation in the present century. During the past fifty years the American people have been adjusting their lives and institutions to existence in a frontierless land, for while the superintendent of the census was decidedly premature when he announced in 1890 that the country's "unsettled area has been so broken into by isolated bodies of settlement that there can hardly be said to be a frontier line" remaining, the era of cheap land was rapidly drawing to a close. In attempting to adjust the country to its new, expansionless future, statesmen have frequently called upon the frontier hypothesis to justify everything from rugged individualism to the welfare state, and from isolationism to world domination.

Political opinion has divided sharply on the necessity of altering the nation's governmental philosophy and techniques in response to the changed environment. Some statesmen and scholars have rebelled against what they call Turner's "Space Concept of History," with all that it implies concerning the lack of opportunity for the individual in an expansionless land. They insist that modern technology has created a whole host of new "frontiers"—of intensive farming, electronics, mechanics, manufacturing, nuclear fission, and the like—which offer such diverse outlets to individual talents that governmental interference in the nation's economic activities is unjustified. On the other hand, equally competent spokesmen argue that these newer "frontiers" offer little opportunity to the individual—as distinguished from the corporation or the capitalist—and hence cannot duplicate the function of the frontier of free land. The government, they insist, must provide the people with the security and opportunity that vanished when escape to the West became impossible. This school's most eloquent spokesman, Franklin D. Roosevelt, declared: "Our last frontier has long since been reached. . . . Equality of opportunity as we have

known it no longer exists. . . . Our task now is not the discovery or exploitation of natural resources or necessarily producing more goods. It is
the sober, less dramatic business of administering resources and plants
already in hand, of seeking to re-establish foreign markets for our surplus
production, of meeting the problem of under-consumption, of adjusting
production to consumption, of distributing wealth and products more eq-
uitably, of adapting existing economic organizations to the service of the
people. The day of enlightened administration has come." To Roosevelt,
and to thousands like him, the passing of the frontier created a new era in
history which demanded a new philosophy of government.

Diplomats have also found in the frontier hypothesis justification
for many of their moves, from imperialist expansion to the restriction of
immigration. Harking back to Turner's statement that the perennial rebirth of society was necessary to keep alive the democratic spirit, expan-
sionists have argued through the twentieth century for an extension of
American power and territories. During the Spanish–American War im-
perialists preached such a doctrine, adding the argument that Spain's
lands were needed to provide a population outlet for a people who could
no longer escape to their own frontier. Idealists such as Woodrow Wilson
could agree with materialists like J. P. Morgan that the extension of
American authority abroad, either through territorial acquisitions or economic penetration, would be good for both business and democracy.
Later, Franklin D. Roosevelt favored a similar expansion of the American
democratic ideal as a necessary prelude to the better world that he hoped
would emerge from World War II. His successor, Harry Truman, envisaged his "Truman Doctrine" as a device to extend and defend the frontiers of democracy throughout the globe. While popular belief in the
superiority of America's political institutions was far older than Turner,
that belief rested partly on the frontier experience of the United States.

These practical applications of the frontier hypothesis, as well as its
demonstrated influence on the nation's development, suggest that its
critics have been unable to destroy the theory's effectiveness as a key to
understanding American history. The recurring rebirth of society in the
United States over a period of three hundred years did endow the people
with characteristics and institutions that distinguish them from the inhabitants of other nations. It is obviously untrue that the frontier experience alone accounts for the unique features of American civilization; that
civilization can be understood only as the product of the interplay of the
Old World heritage and New World conditions. But among those conditions none has bulked larger than the operation of the frontier process.

8

Tecumseh:
The First Advocate
of Red Power

Raymond Friday Locke

Raymond Friday Locke, the editor for Holloway House Publishing Com pany, has long taken an interest in the history of the American Indian. His Book of the Navajo *(rev. ed., 1986) is his most noteworthy contribution to the field. In this article, Locke paints a colorful portrait of the man many regard as the greatest native American leader in history. Locke's listing of Tecumseh's admirable qualities—leadership, humanitarianism, education, diplomacy, wisdom, and even a romantic nature—give him a universal appeal. The tragic end to Tecumseh's great organization and planning demonstrates that even great men are at times undone by small flaws.*

It is difficult to escape the conviction that the Indians had justice on their side and that, as Oliver LaFarge indicated in his earlier article, they had much to offer the whites who engulfed them. Tecumseh's story also suggests that bigotry, part of the dark side of the American character, has denied the nation the valuable contributions of many people because they didn't happen to be white. Because of whites' failure to absorb much of the native Americans' wisdom, the original inhabitants of the continent have

This reading is from *Mankind* (April 1971). Reprinted by permission of the author.

*been only a small tributary stream in their influence on the American
character rather than a significant part of the mainstream.*

If the present day advocates of Red Power and Pan-Indianism need
an idol they need search no further than the great Shawnee Chief
Tecumseh. Realizing that the contact of white and Indian civilizations
always meant the eventual supremacy of the white, with the decay and
destruction of the Indian, Tecumseh attempted to block the white advance into the old Northwest Territory by forming a federation of Indian
tribes that reached all the way from Alabama to Minnesota and from
Kansas to New England—and almost succeeded.

Born in Ohio in the spring of 1768, Tecumseh was the son of the
Shawnee chief Pucksinwah, head of the Kispolotha sept, or clan. His
mother was named Methotasa (early writers incorrectly referred to her as
a Creek or Cherokee) and at the time of Tecumseh's birth his parents were
on their way to an important council at Chillicothe, located at the present
site of Oldtown, Greene County, Ohio, three miles north of the county
seat, Xenia. For five years the various septs of the Shawnee had been
meeting at Chillicothe at intervals in an effort to determine what the
Shawnee should do, as a nation, about the white who, despite treaties
forbidding it, were crossing the mountains to the east and spilling into
lands used by that tribe.

When Tecumseh was six years of age, his father was killed by a
white hunting party. Thereafter, the young boy was guided and trained
by his older brother, Chiksika. He was taught Shawnee history, traditions and the codes of the tribe. As was the custom, Tecumseh had to
commit these matters to perfect memory and learn to repeat them ver-
batim. From his mother and older sister, Tecumapese, the young Indian
learned the value of patience and the need for pity for those without
power, and that cruelty for the sake of cruelty, whether to animals
or man, degraded a person. By the time he was eight years old, Tecumseh was already exhibiting signs of leadership. By this time the Americans were already establishing settlements in the traditional hunting
grounds of the Shawnee—Cantuc-kee (Kentucky)—and the Shawnee,
like other tribes of the old Northwest, increasingly realized that their
total elimination was not far distant if they did not fight back. The
ever-increasing number of whites were driving off the game and taking
possession of the land. Far away in Washington, the government of the
whites continued to give lip service to the fiction of Indian independence and land ownership, but the Indian was more impressed by the
rapidity with which the whites obtained any area they coveted. No
opposition short of war seemed to have the least chance of damming
the white flood. And in the spring of 1777, the Shawnee, under the
leadership of Tecumseh's godfather, Black Fish, went to war against the

settlers of Kentucky. It was to be a war without end for the Shawnee, who were supported by the British, who desired to retain the lucrative Great Lakes fur trade and were glad to help the Indians keep the aggressive American frontiersmen as far from Canada as possible. The Indians preferred trading with the British to trading with the American and felt no danger from Canadian expansion.

As the Shawnee war waged on, year after year, other tribes occasionally joined them in battle against the Americans. The Indians, even those who had been friendly toward the whites in the beginning, were becoming resentful of the way in which they suffered at the hands of the white men. They were cheated at trading posts after being plied with whiskey until their reasoning powers were gone. An Indian might trade a year's catch of furs for a few trinkets and a little bad whiskey. He gave the trinkets to his wife and drank the whiskey and was left with nothing but a heavy head to show for a year's work. Too, the white man's diseases wrecked havoc among the Indians with whom they came into contact along the advancing frontier. Such was the world in which Tecumseh grew up.

In the spring of 1779, the situation grew so bad for the Shawnees that the nation split up and hundreds of men, women and children left the homeland in Ohio and moved across the Mississippi, hoping to find peace there—and relief from the constant war. But Black Fish, Chiksika, and the white chief, Blue Jacket, remained behind. Of course, Tecumseh and the rest of his family stayed in Ohio with his brother, Chiksika.

In the spring of 1783, Tecumseh took part in his first battle against the whites, and at the age of fifteen, outshone even the ablest warriors of the Shawnee. He killed four men in the fight and helped Chiksika kill another. The most any other Shawnee killed in the battle was two. One white was taken prisoner. Later, at the Shawnee camp he was burned alive. Tecumseh found the torture and burning of the prisoner so revolting that, without any voice in tribal matters as of yet, he protested. In an impassioned speech he pointed out that such cruelty was unworthy of real men, of Shawnees, and swore that never again would he take part in the torture of any living creature, man or animal, nor would he consider as friend any man who allowed himself to take part in anything so degrading. The vigorous manner and eloquence with which he spoke so impressed his companions that they agreed with him not to repeat the act. Tecumseh never altered his resolution. Time and again he protected women and children from his infuriated followers. Years later, at the battle of Fort Meigs, a party of Americans were captured by the British and Indians. Although the Americans had surrendered as prisoners of war, they were herded into an outdoor pen and the British General, Henry A. Procter, gave the Indians leave to select any man each of the prisoners and kill him in any manner desired. The Indians were firing point blank into the huddled Americans, others were being selected and tomahawked in cold blood when Tecumseh arrived on the scene. Slamming to a halt, leaping from his mount and brandishing his war club, he rushed to the aid of an American, Colonel John Dudley. Two Indians had grabbed him, one had jerked his head back by the hair and the other was just about to stab him. Tecumseh knocked the knife-wielder aside and ordered the other to turn the prisoner loose. Instead, the Indian whipped out his knife and cut Dudley's throat, severing the jugular vein. Tecumseh struck the Indian a blow on the head with his club, killing him. Tecumseh then ordered the other Indians to stop the slaughter, which they did, then addressed them scathingly, calling them cowards and saying that he would slay anyone who harmed another prisoner. Turning to Procter, he asked, "Why have you allowed this massacre?"

"Sir," replied Procter, "your Indians cannot be commanded."

"Begone," was the angry reply of the outraged Tecumseh. "You are unfit to command. Go, put on petticoats."

Tecumseh put the remaining prisoners under the guard of four warriors, warning them that if any more were killed or abused, all four would be executed. He then ordered the others to mount up and follow him back to the battle, where brave men, not cowards, were needed.

When Chiksika was killed in battle in April, 1788, there was no question of Tecumseh's taking over the command of the remaining Kispolotha Shawnee who were then fighting against the whites with the Cherokees. The occasion was so automatic that no vote had to be taken. Time and time again the young Tecumseh led his band to victory. He was possessed with an uncanny knack of assessing any situation in an instant and acting immediately in a manner which at once swung the scales in his favor. The Shawnees realized that no one else approached his qualifications for leadership.

Tecumseh watched the advance of the whites and the progressive deterioration of the Indians with an evergrowing surge of anger. He was certain in his own mind that the land belonged to the Indian tribes forever, no matter by what show of legality it might be taken away from them, and that they could cling to their culture and traditions. From the east the tide of whites was ever-increasing, moving toward the lands west of the Ohio river and filling up the Kentucky hunting grounds where the once great herds of buffalo were now becoming scarce. It is not known when the idea of banding the Indians into a vast confederation to drive the white invaders back again beyond the Ohio and the mountains occurred to Tecumseh. But he was still a young man when he concluded that the only possible method of opposing the white advance successfully was to obtain the cooperation of all the Indians and to have them act in concert.

By 1794, Tecumseh found himself with a large number of followers. Tall, handsome and modest, he refrained from boasting of his own prowess, being content to let others boast of him and let his actions speak for themselves. It was in the spring of that year that Tecumseh moved the members of his sept to the banks of Deer Creek in the vicinity of present London, Ohio, and several hundred members of other septs, most of whom were young men, followed him, seeing in Tecumseh the makings of a great new chief. Everything the young chief did turned out well—with two exceptions. One was allowing his younger brother, Lowawluwaysica—who would become known as the Prophet—to assume second in command of his following. Where Tecumseh was tall and perfectly proportioned, his brother was a head shorter and ugly; where Tecumseh was gentle and good-natured, Lowawluwaysica was devious and surly—and would eventually destroy his brother's plans for an Indian confederation.

Tecumseh's second mistake was marrying the Peckuwe maiden, Monetohse. While she was slender and attractive, she was also demanding and found fault in everything her husband did. While Tecumseh was able to overlook her behavior toward himself, he could not overlook the fact that she neglected to care for his son, born two years after the marriage. He invoked an ancient Shawnee marital law and dissolved their marriage, sent Monetohse back to her parents in disgrace, and placed his son in charge of his older sister, Tecumapese.

On August 20, 1794, General Anthony Wayne, commanding an American army, defeated a large Indian force on the banks of the Maumee river in Ohio. In the battle, Tecumseh, leading a party, was with the advance which met the attack of the American infantry. The defeat of the Indians on the Maumee produced an entire change in the relations between the Indians and the Americans and led to treaty negotiations.

Tecumseh refused to have any part of the peace treaty signed at Fort Greenville in August, 1795, between the whites and representatives of various Indian tribes as a result of the defeat administered by Anthony Wayne. The treaty gave the whites twenty-five thousand square miles of Indian territory as well as sixteen tracts *within* lands left to the Indians for government reservations. Representatives of the twelve tribes who attended the treaty conference were given $1,666 for each tribe and promised an annual allowance of $825! As far as Tecumseh was concerned it was out and out thievery of Indians lands and any agreement with the whites was worthless. Upon being told of the terms of the agreement by the white Shawnee chief, Blue Jacket, Tecumseh said: "My heart is a stone: heavy with sadness for my people; cold with the knowledge that no treaty will keep whites out of our lands; hard with the determination to resist as long as I live and breathe. Now we are weak and many of our people are afraid. But hear me; a single twig breaks, but the bundle of twigs is strong. Someday I will embrace our brother tribes and draw them into a bundle and together we will win our country back from the whites."

The Treaty of Greenville brought peace to the Ohio land and the settlement of Ohio by whites began in earnest. William Henry Harrison was given command of Fort Washinton and charged with protecting the new white settlers as the Shawnee land became checkered with new farms.

A short time after the signing of the Greenville Treaty, Tecumseh took a new wife, an older woman named Mamate. Mamate gave birth to a son in the summer of 1796 and died soon afterwards. The new baby was named Nay-tha-way-nah and given to Tecumapese to care for. Perhaps the birth of his second son reminded Tecumseh that the place of his own birth was already the site of a white farm. He became determined to win back the land that rightfully belonged to the Shawnee. Too, the plan of an Indian confederation was never far from his mind and the way to just such a confederation was shown to him when the Delawares, who had been pushed out of lands given to them by treaty time and time again, came to him in 1798. The Delawares had heard much of the young Shawnee chief who was so strong in all ways. Would Tecumseh come and bring his Shawnees to live with the Delawares and lead them too? Tecumseh would and led his followers into Indiana territory to join the Delawares. Within a year other Ohio tribes had come under Tecumseh's sphere of influence, impressed not only with his reputation for fairness and proven ability to lead men, but also with the eloquence with which he held audiences spellbound.

Soon after joining the Delawares, Tecumseh began traveling and addressing councils of various Indian tribes in an effort to bring them into what he saw as a powerful amalgamation of Indian strength and power. He traveled to the council fires of what remained of the Iroquois Confederation in the east; nearer home he spoke to the Wyandots, the Potawatomies and others. The Hurons, Ottawas and Chippewas, Winnebagos, Foxes, Sacs, Menominees of Michigan, Wisconsin, and Canada would hear him, as would the Sioux, Mandans and Cheyennes west of the Mississippi; in the south the Natchez and Choctaws of Mississippi, traditional enemies, sat down together in council with him, as did the Creeks, the Seminoles, Chickasaws, Alabamas, the Biloxis and his old friends, the Cherokees. He urged the Indians to prohibit the consumption of any alcoholic beverages and the smoking of marijuana, to study closely and seriously the ways of the whites, to break all alliances existing between themselves and the whites, and to take no part in the white man's fight with other whites.

Too, he encouraged the Indians to appear weak, to swallow their pride and fall back, and under no pretext take up arms against the whites until the time was ready, the time when all Indians would take up the fight together. For that fight, Tecumseh told them, he would give the sign. It would be a sign that would come to all the tribes on the same day and at the same time. Tecumseh hoped that when the time came the whites would vacate the Indian lands west of the mountains peacefully but if they would not then the great wave of Indians from all tribes, fighting together, would sweep across the land and destroy the whites to the last man.

Meanwhile, William Henry Harrison had pulled political strings to have himself appointed governor of Indiana. He arrived at his new post in early 1801 and soon began new land acquisitions by negotiations with the Indians. In 1802–1803, another million acres were added to lands available for white settlement. Other treaties followed, and the resulting Indian resentment was attributed by Harrison to British influence. Harrison had little sympathy for the Indians and was convinced that the only possible way to deal satisfactorily with them was to destroy them. He had visions of himself as a great conqueror of Indian lands and mapped out grandiose campaigns and felt that all he needed was an opportunity to exhibit his abilities as a strategist. He was not yet aware of Tecumseh, but the Indian leader was very aware of William Henry Harrison.

Tecumseh continued to travel, recruiting tribe after tribe to join his confederation and give their aid when the great sign was given. When he spoke of the great sign he never failed to awe his audience. When the period of waiting was over, he told them, and tribal unification had been completed, he would stamp his foot and the earth would tremble and roar. He promised that great trees would fall, streams would change their courses and run backwards and lakes would be swallowed up into the earth and elsewhere new lakes would appear. The sign would shake men everywhere to their very bones like nothing they had ever known before. But when it came they were told to drop their hunting bows, their hoes, leaving their fields and camps and assemble across the lake from the fort of Detroit. On that day tribes would cease to exist. They would all be Indians, one people united forever for the good of all!

In the summer of 1802, Tecumseh preached his message across the northeast, in Vermont and Massachusetts, two years later he was in Minnesota talking to the Sioux. Everywhere he went he carried the same message and when he left it was with the assurance that another tribe would join him when the time came. In 1805, Tecumseh and Lowawluwaysica, who now called himself the Shawnee Prophet, established a new village near Fort Greenville that was not a Shawnee village but an *Indian* village where all Indians, regardless of tribe, were welcomed. A year later, William Henry Harrison became aware of Tecumseh's activities and wrote a letter to the Delawares in which he accused them of pursuing a "dark, thorny" path by following the "pretended prophet" and asked them to call upon the Shawnee Prophet and demand that he show some sign of his powers. A party of forty Delawares did call upon the Prophet, who, frightened, turned to Tecumseh and asked what he must do. Tecumseh pointed out that he could foretell what would happen just as their brother Chiksika and their father, Pucksinwah, had been able to do. The fact that Tecumseh was the true prophet was known only to himself, his brother and others close to the family. Tecumseh allowed everyone else to think that his younger brother could foretell the future. Tecumseh instructed his brother to tell the Delawares that fifty days from that day the sky would turn black at high noon, the night creatures would stir and the stars would shine. The Shawnee Prophet did as he was told and, of course, was credited with predicting the eclipse. Unfortunately, the Shawnee Prophet forgot that his brother was the true prophet as he enjoyed his new-found fame.

Meanwhile, Tecumseh became friends with a family of whites named Galloway and one of his greatest joys was discussing, at length, matters of politics, religion, ethics and such with James Galloway. Galloway had a fine library with which the Indian chief acquainted himself, *Hamlet* becoming his favorite tale. Tecumseh could speak English quite well, but while he could read and write the white man's language, he was not fluent enough to read the more difficult books in the Galloway library. James Galloway's daughter, Rebecca, offered to help him. She spent many hours teaching the Shawnee chief, who was then thirty-eight years of age. In the spring of 1808, when she turned seventeen, Tecumseh asked for Rebecca's hand in marriage. Rebecca thought over the marriage proposal for a month and then agreed to marry Tecumseh, with whom she was in love, but only if he would adopt her people's mode of life and dress. He thought over her request for a month, then returned and told her that to do as she wanted would lose him the respect and leadership of his people. Rebecca Galloway wept when Tecumseh took leave of her for the last time.

That same year Tecumseh had his first interview with William Henry Harrison. He promised Harrison peace if the United States did not make further treaties involving land cessions and added that if such cessions were made, he would form an alliance with the English and make war on the Americans. Harrison dismissed Tecumseh's request as preposterous. A year later the two men met again but by this time events made peace impossible. Illinois Territory was created, leaving Indiana with its present boundaries. Harrison received permission from the secretary of war to buy more Indian land; the purchase of 2,500,000 acres in the fall of 1809 increased the number and wrath of Indians hostile to the United States. While Tecumseh maintained that the Indians held the land in common, that no one tribe owned this or that territory, Harrison couldn't agree with him less and pointed out that had the Great Spirit intended to make one nation of the Indians, he would not have put different languages into their heads, but would have taught them all to speak alike. Tecumseh replied bitterly that no one tribe had the right to give away or sell what belonged to all and not until the United States agreed to cease purchasing lands from Indians and restored the lands recently bought, would peace be possible. Pointing to the moon that had risen on the council, Governor Harrison said that the moon would sooner fall to the earth than the United States would give up the lands. "Then," said Tecumseh, "I suppose that you and I will have to fight it out."

Another council was held in August, 1810, between Tecumseh and Harrison that was just as fruitless. Describing the arrival of Tecumseh at the conference, Captain George R. Floyd, commanding officer of Fort Knox, wrote: " . . . they were headed by the brother of the Prophet, Tecumseh, who perhaps is one of the finest looking men I ever saw— about six feet high, straight, with large, fine features, and altogether a daring, bold looking fellow."

The next day this "daring, bold looking fellow" let Harrison know for the last time that he meant business. The meeting got started on a bad note when Harrison told Tecumseh that, "Your father wishes you to take a chair." The very idea of the governor calling himself "your father" was repugnant to Tecumseh.

Tecumseh spoke first and pointed out that he felt that the Americans were trying to force the red people to do some injury to the whites so the latter would have an excuse to war on the Indians and that they were "continually driving the red people; when, at last, you will drive them into the Great Lakes, where they can't either stand or walk." The Shawnee chief ended with a threat: "We shall have a great council, at which all the tribes will be present, when we shall show to those who sold that they had no right to the claim that they set up; and we will see what will be done to those chiefs that did sell the land to you. I am not alone in this determination; it is the determination of all the warriors and red people who listen to me. I now wish *you* to listen to me. If you do not, it will appear as if you wished me to kill all the chiefs that sold you the land. I tell you so because I am authorized by all the tribes to do so. I am the head of them all! I am a warrior and all the warriors will meet together in two or three moons from this. Then I will call for those chiefs that sold you the land and shall know what to do with them. If you do not restore the land, you will have a hand in killing them.'

As for confidence in yet another treaty with the whites, Tecumseh asked: "How can we have confidence in the white people? When Jesus Christ came on earth, you killed him and nailed him to a cross . . . "

Harrison's reply was as highhanded as ever and caused the followers of Tecumseh to bring out their arms. They were stilled by the chief and left the council. Another council in July of the next year ended much the same way.

Autumn of 1811 found Tecumseh in the south addressing councils of Cherokees, Seminoles, Choctaws and Chickasaws; autumn of 1811 found William Henry Harrison planning to attack Tecumseh's Tippecanoe village in his absence. Harrison gathered 1,000 men, mostly volunteers, and with a well-planned campaign already formulated, prepared to annihilate his unsuspecting enemies—an act that he forgot to report to the president. He left Vincennes on September 26, 1811, and moved directly up the Wabash, paused long enough to build Fort Harrison on the present site of Terre Haute, and on the night of November 6, encamped on Tippecanoe Creek. Before leaving, Tecumseh had warned his followers, and especially his brother, the Shawnee Prophet, to avoid battle with the whites at all costs. At long last he could see the fulfillment of his years of work: The Indian confederation now actually existed and the time for war was almost at hand.

That night the Prophet sent a deputation of three men to Harrison and it was settled that the terms of peace were to be arranged the next day. But the next morning, under orders from the Prophet, who told them that they would not only be victorious but that he had rendered the bullets of the white men to be harmless when fired against them, the Indians treacherously attacked the Americans. The conflict was fierce and bloody, with the Indians rushing boldly and openly to clinch with the enemy. The Prophet perched himself on a hill nearby and chanted a war song—but not for long. When messengers raced to him to say that the Indians were dying in a most natural way, he urged them on, then deserted them. When the warriors saw that the fire of the whites was just as lethal as ever and that the Prophet had fled, they became demoralized and retreated. The white casualties were 61 killed and 127 wounded; the Indian losses were unknown. Harrison immediately dispatched messengers to the East with reports of an overwhelming defeat of the Indians. In later years there was much controversy as to whether or not Harrison had actually won. He had avoided rout and repulsed the Indians, but he also found it necessary to retreat almost immediately. But the fact that the Indians had fought and had not won an overwhelming victory all but ruined Tecumseh and dashed the Indian confederation on the very eve of its birth.

Tecumseh arrived back at Tippecanoe only four days after the fateful battle, his face as frozen as stone. Shaking his brother, fallen and disgraced, by the hair until his nose began to bleed, he told him that death was too good, too easy, for him. In a day he had destroyed what it had taken Tecumseh a decade to build. The Prophet was drummed out of the camp. He was no longer an Indian, he no longer existed.

As Tecumseh had predicted, the earth did shake. On December 16, 1811, a deep, terrifying rumble was felt in the south of Canada. Trees fell and huge rocks toppled. Lake Michigan and Lake Erie trembled and great waves broke on the shores, though the day was windless. In the west the earth shuddered so fiercely that great herds of bison staggered to their feet and stampeded, and in the south whole forests fell. In Missouri the town of New Madrid was destroyed, the Mississippi River turned and flowed backwards. The earthquake lasted for two days and filled the atmosphere with choking dust. A second struck on January 23 and a third hit four days later. The fourth and worst quake came on February 13 and lasted for an hour. It did more damage than the other three combined. Many of those that had deserted Tecumseh's cause reconsidered, for this was very strong medicine, but it was too late. The defeat at Tippecanoe had taken the ardor for war out of too many of his followers.

Those that remained faithful followed Tecumseh into the British service in the War of 1812, which broke out immediately. But Tecumseh, commissioned as a major-general, was doomed to continued disaster. The English commander, General Henry Procter, was incompetent, and in all the qualities of real manhood, the inferior to his Indian ally. After the Battle of Put-in-Bay, on Lake Erie, he started to retreat. Tecumseh protested and was induced to go on only by the promise that winter supplies would be delivered a few miles up the Thames. It was on this stream that Procter finally determined to make a stand, but at the onset of the action he retreated with his red coats, leaving the Indians to bear the brunt of the battle. On October 5, 1813, as he had predicted before the battle, Tecumseh was killed. Only one person at the site of the battle could identify the Shawnee chief and that was the Kentucky frontiersman, Simon Kenton. While at least four Americans claimed the honor of having killed Tecumseh, as far as is known Kenton never identified his body.

But there on the banks of a quiet Canadian stream, thirty-five miles from Detroit, the great Tecumseh, statesman, diplomat, a man devoted to the cause of his people and yet a humble and modest intellectual, found an unmarked grave. The Indians lost their greatest leader, the whites won the West.

9

The Legacy of Slavery and the Roots of Black Nationalism

Eugene Genovese

Why has there never been a black revolution in the United States? How is it that a people as oppressed as blacks have been throughout their sojourn in this country have never risen up to cast off their oppressors? Eugene Genovese (1930–   ), a Marxist historian and one of the white world's foremost scholars on American slavery, raises these questions from a radical perspective and offers some profound insights into the nature of the character of black Americans.

Genovese has written two masterful books on slavery. The Political Economy of Slavery *(1965) relates economic questions to class structure, social institutions, ideology, and politics.* Roll Jordan Roll: The World the Slaves Made *(1974) explores their lives and concludes that the quality of their existence was suffused with religion. The book has been called the religious history of a people.*

This article, first published in Studies on the Left *in 1966, was revised in 1970. Those dates indicate its timeliness, for black nationalism, growing out of the civil rights movement, had won widespread support among blacks. Slavery, Genovese contends, prevented any sense of group political consciousness, an essential ingredient for a revolutionary tradition. The environment of American slavery turned black leaders into accommodationists rather than rebels, as they became in the Caribbean. Even during the Civil War, when white society broke down, there was not a single widespread slave rebellion. Reconstruction reinforced black dependence on whites —this time Union soldiers rather than their old masters. Booker T. Washington, perceiving his people's unpreparedness for political leadership, backed off on political demands to focus on economic development. The National Association for the Advancement of Colored People (NAACP), ostensibly more radical, also relied heavily on white leaders and money. Marcus Garvey's black nationalist movement in the 1920s embodied a new theme—separatism. Ever since, there has been a conflict between integrationists and separatists over the best way for blacks to achieve maximum dignity. Genovese suggests that nationalism has much to commend it from a radical perspective, but he indicates that it is not consistent with blacks' traditional character and therefore not likely to triumph.*

American Radicals have long been imprisoned by the pernicious notion that the masses are necessarily both good and revolutionary, and by the even more pernicious notion that if they are not, they should be. The principal responsibility of radical historians, therefore, has too often been to provide the masses with historical heroes, to make them aware of their glorious tradition of resistance to oppression, and to portray them as having been implacably hostile to the social order in which they have been held. This viewpoint now dominates the black liberation movement, which for all its rhetoric about "thinking black," has merely followed a romantic line long ago laid out by radical and liberal white historians. It has become virtually sacrilege, if not blatant white racism, to suggest that slavery was a social system within which whites and blacks lived in harmony as well as antagonism, that there is little evidence of massive, organized opposition to the regime, that the blacks did not establish a revolutionary tradition of much significance, and that our main problem is to discover the reasons for the widespread accommodation and, perhaps more important, the long-term effects both of the accommodation and of that resistance which did occur.

In 1831 Nat Turner led a slave revolt on which has hung most of the legend of armed resistance to slavery. Of the 250 or so revolts chronicled and analyzed in Herbert Aptheker's *American Negro Slave Revolts,* Turner's has pride of place and was described by Aptheker as a "cataclysm." Yet, when we look closely, this revolt, like the total history of such revolts, recedes in magnitude and actual intensity. As many of Aptheker's critics have pointed out, most of the 250 revolts probably never happened, being the imagination of hysterical, self-serving whites, minor plots that never matured, or mere local disturbances of a questionable nature. Of the four major revolts, two were crushed before the damage was done, although both (Gabriel Prosser's in 1800 and Denmark Vesey's in 1822) badly frightened the white South. During the nineteenth century only the big rising in Louisiana in 1811, about which we know almost nothing, and Turner's in 1831 came to fruition and reached impressive proportions. Even so painstaking and thorough a scholar as Aptheker has been unable to discover firm evidence of a major revolt between 1831 and 1865.

As for Turner's, less than one hundred slaves joined. A revolt of this size would rate little more than a page or two in a comprehensive study of slave revolts in Brazil and the Caribbean. To cite only two outstanding examples from Brazil, runaway slaves in the northeast of Brazil organized their own colony, Palmares, and waged an almost-century-long struggle for autonomy against both the Dutch and Portuguese. The history of Palmares stretches across the seventeenth century and culminates in the defeat of a regime that embraced twenty thousand black people. During the first four decades of the nineteenth century there was a series of violent and extensive risings in Bahia, which culminated in the dramatic, Muslim-led, and almost successful attempt of the blacks to take the city in 1835. We need not review the story of Haiti, and the record of revolt in Jamaica, Cuba, the Guianas, and other slave countries is also impressive and unmatched in the United States. Even if, as Aptheker suggests, news of smaller risings was suppressed, the effect would have been to prevent the accumulation of a tradition to encourage and sustain revolt-prone slaves. On the balance, we find the absence or extreme weakness of such a tradition in the United States.

There were many reasons for this extreme weakness, a few of which should be noted briefly. The slave trade ended in 1808, although illegal importations continued to trickle in; in contrast, the trade to Cuba and Brazil remained open until the middle of the nineteenth century, and the trade to the Anglo-French Caribbean closed only a few decades before the fall of the slave regimes. The presence of a large number of newly imported Africans can generally be correlated with the incidence of revolt. In the United States the overwhelming majority of the slaves during the ante-bellum period had been born and raised on Southern plantations. Their ranks received little reinforcement from newly enslaved and aggressive Africans.

A review of the history of Brazil and the Caribbean suggests that an important ingredient in the development of revolts out of local disturbances was the division of the whites into warring factions and the general weakness of the state apparatus. Together with these conditions went the general influence of geography in relation to state power.

Where suitable terrain was combined with a weak state, runaway slaves could and did found maroon colonies, which directly fomented revolts and kept alive a tradition of armed resistance. With minor qualifications, these conditions did not exist in the United States.

A substantial revolt presupposed the formation of ideology and leadership. In Brazil and the Caribbean two circumstances combined to encourage both: the cultivation of sugar led to the establishment of plantations averaging more than 150 slaves, and the size of the white population was small. As a result, the blacks could keep alive much of their African culture or could develop a syncretized Afro-Brazilian or Afro-Cuban culture, which militated against the loss of identity and which, under proper conditions, could nurture resistance movements. Apart from Islam, non-Christian religious cults, generally of a syncretized type, played a great role in hemispheric slave revolts. In the United States an imposed Protestant Christianity was used to keep the slaves docile. The slaves, for their part, shaped that Christianity to their own needs and often turned it into a weapon of resistance. But there were two limitations. First, Southern slaves shared their religion with their masters; no matter how distinct their own Christianity, it was a religion that bound them to their masters on some important levels of thought and feeling. It could not, then, create the sharp distinction that separated the religion of the *vaudoun* priests of Saint-Domingue from the Catholic priests of the master class. Slave revolt in the United States could not so easily emerge as a holy war, as it did so often elsewhere in the hemisphere. Second, the religious efforts of the slaves could provide them with tools for survival and even an important degree of cultural autonomy, but in the context of Southern military and political relations it could rarely serve as a rallying point for total or armed resistance. If religion was one of the ingredients in the genesis of slave revolts, the complex of all those ingredients set limits to the subversive force of the religion itself.

Half the slaves in the United States lived on units of twenty or less; most of the others lived on plantations of not much more than fifty. Although blacks heavily outnumbered whites in large areas of the South—generally the areas of the most serious slave revolts the blacks were, in general, floating in a white sea. The white planters were residents, not absentees; the non-slaveholders were loyal, armed, and disciplined; the country immediately beyond the plantation areas was inhabited by armed whites completely hostile to the slaves. Despite an occasional exception in the Dismal Swamps or Florida, death not refuge lay beyond the plantation. For this reason, among others, blacks often had to look to their masters to protect them against the depredations and viciousness of the poorer whites.

The residency of the planters and their hegemony across the South gave American slavery its particular quality and especially set it off from

Caribbean slavery. Between the Revolution and the War for Southern Independence the treatment of slaves, defined as day-to-day conditions of life (food, housing, rigor of work routine, leisure time, incidence and character of corporal punishment) improved steadily and perceptibly. Although manumission was made increasingly difficult and escape from the system was sealed off, the harsh slave codes were steadily tempered by community sentiment and the interpretations of the state supreme courts. During the late ante-bellum period, steady pressure built up to reform the slave codes in order to protect slave family life and to check the more glaring abuses of the slave's person. The purpose and effect of these halting attempts and of the actual amelioration in practice and at law were not to pave the way to freedom, but to consolidate the system from within and without. Like all liberal reformism, it aimed to strengthen the social system.

For the planters these trends formed part of a developing world view within which paternalism became the specific manifestation of class consciousness. Paternalism did not mean kindness or generosity or love, although it embraced some of each; essentially it meant a special notion of duty and responsibility toward one's charges. Arbitrary power, harshness toward disobedience, even sadism, constituted its other side. For immediate purposes paternalism and the trend of treatment are especially noteworthy in confronting the slave with a world in which resistance could be quickly, severely, and legitimately punished whereas obedience placed him in a position to benefit from the favor of a master who more often than not had a genuine interest in his welfare. The picture of the docile, infantilized Sambo, drawn and analyzed so brilliantly by Stanley Elkins, is one-sided, but Elkins is not far from the mark when he argues that the Southern regime greatly encouraged acceptance of and dependence on despotic authority. Elkins errs in thinking that the Sambo personality arose only in the United States, for it arose wherever slavery existed. He does not err in thinking that it was especially marked and extensive in the United States where recourse to armed resistance was minimal and the tradition of paternalism took such firm root.

To say that slaves generally accommodated is not to say that they were dehumanized or failed to protest their condition. Historians have been quick to claim rebelliousness every time a slave broke a plow or stole a hog, but at least some room might be left for lack of initiative, thoughtlessness, stupidity, and venality. Yet, we do know of enough instances of deliberate sabotage to permit us to speak of a strong undercurrent of dissatisfaction and hostility, the manifestations of which require analysis. And we need to remember, apart from these, or rather side by side with them, that the pattern of behavior we call accommodation (for want of a better word) itself represented a struggle for cultural autonomy and unity and as such had its own positive value for black people beyond the terrible and basic question of staying alive.

One of the more prominent and irritating habits of recalcitrant slaves was stealing. Plundering the hog pen and the smokehouse was an especially happy pastime. Radical and liberal historians have taken particular delight in picking up the slaves' own shrewd suggestion that they might steal from each other but could only "take" from the master. The slaves reasoned that since they were chattel they could not steal a hog from the master because by eating it they merely transformed his property from one form to another. The trouble with being too quick to take delight in these charming stories of the Good Soldier Sambo is that they had their ominous side. Too often the masters enjoyed being outwitted in the same way that a tyrannical father sometimes enjoys being outwitted by a child. Every contortion necessary to do the job implied for the slave his own inferiority—certainly as understood by the whites and sometimes as perceived by the slaves themselves. Pilfering, lying, dissembling—these and other ways of warding off blows, settling scores, getting something extra to eat—helped keep the slaves sane and resilient, but they also provided a poor preparation for life in freedom. It is one thing to admire the slaves' resourcefulness, cunning, and toughness; it is another to pretend that a high, long-term price was not being paid in the process.

Arson and the mishandling of tools stand out as more positively rebellious acts. As expressions of frustration and resentment they might have, in a more explosively revolutionary context, constituted important political actions. As it was, they usually amounted to individual protests that often exposed all the slaves to terror and retaliation. It is not surprising that the slaves themselves often helped to put down such behavior and even cooperated to punish offenders. When they did so, they may simply have been playing the Tom, but in many cases they may have been protecting themselves collectively against having to take responsibility for individual actions that could in no way strengthen their position. If slaves generally sympathized with the outburst of a particular slave who could no longer stand his condition, they also understood how dangerous his behavior could be to the group and how futile it was. With luck a few slaves might do enough damage to ruin a planter, in which case he would be forced to sell out and probably to separate families and friends. Advocates of the philosophy of burn-baby-burn, whether on a Mississippi plantation in the 1850s or in a Northern ghetto in the 1970s, must surely know that, of necessity, it is the blacks who usually get burned most severely. On occasion a slave took direct action against a particularly unpleasant master or, more often, overseer, and killed him. For that manly act he would, if lucky, be hanged.

As we review these actions, which by no means exhaust the range, we find the formation of a tradition of recalcitrance but not revolution; individual protest but not collective political action; awareness of oppression but not cumulative ideological growth. Thus, whereas many, and possibly even most, slaves came out of slavery with a psychology of dependence conditioned by paternalism, the most active spirits came out having learned little more than that they could get away with individual acts of undirected, misdirected, or naively directed violence (when they could get away with them at all). On other important levels of existence, they hammered out a rich culture in the slave quarters and guaranteed their survival as a community of individuals capable of resisting the worst of the pressures for infantilization and dehumanization. Important as this achievement was and remains, in combination with their more specifically political behavior it evoked its own high price. What was missing was that sense of group political consciousness and collective responsibility in political effort which form the essence of a revolutionary tradition. The slaves learned well how to defend themselves by collective effort; they had little chance to learn how to use that collective effort to counterattack.

The formation of class leadership presents another side of this development. Legend has it that house slaves and drivers, by virtue of their special positions, arrayed themselves on the side of the master against the field hands, who as the most oppressed were of course the most revolutionary and pure. Examination of plantation documents casts grave doubts on this legend. The range of behavior was wide, but there were many instances of identification and sympathy. The drivers, or slave foremen, present an even clearer case. In general, they compromised as best they could between the master to whom they had pledged loyalty and to whom they were indebted for special favors, and the slaves who constituted their everyday fellows. Often the driver stood as a protector or interpreter between slave and master or overseer. Drivers and house slaves often, although certainly not always, comprised a leading stratum in the eyes of the blacks as well as in the eyes of the whites.

In the Caribbean these privileged slaves led revolts; in the United States they served as agents of accommodation. Toussaint L'Ouverture was only the most prominent of insurrectionary leaders who had been trained to leadership within the system. The problem in the United States was not that the system did not create such privileged strata, nor that these strata were more docile or less courageous than those in the Caribbean. The problem was that the total environment reduced the possibilities for successful insurrection virtually to zero and therefore made accommodationists out of the most high-spirited slave leaders. When the mass exodus from the plantations took place during the War for Southern Independence, drivers and house slaves often led their people to the Union lines. Not docility but lack of a tradition of armed resistance conditioned their leadership.

Potential recruitment of insurrectionary leaders was hampered by many other circumstances, of which two are especially noteworthy. A group of potential leaders recruited from all strata were those who had sufficient strength, daring and resourcefulness to flee. The runaways are black folk heroes, with good reason, but they also drained the best elements out of the slave class. In much of Brazil and the Caribbean, runaways had nowhere to go except into the back country to form maroon colonies, the existence of which encouraged slave disorder and resistance. Then, too, the free blacks and mulattoes in the United States had little opportunity for self-development and rarely could or would provide leadership to slaves. Elsewhere in the hemisphere, where whites were relatively few, these free blacks and mulattoes were needed to fill a wide variety of social and economic functions. Often they prospered as a middle class. In some cases, feelings of racial solidarity or, as in Haiti, the racist stupidity of the whites, led them into partial identification with the cause of black freedom. Thus, with the exception of a rare Nat Turner, black leadership fell to those whose position within the plantation itself encouraged accommodation and negated the possibilities of effective political organization.

The War for Southern Independence brought these tendencies to a head. The staggering truth is that not one full-scale slave revolt broke out during a war in which local white police power had been drastically reduced. In only a few isolated cases did slaves drive off their masters and divide the land among themselves. Many, perhaps most, struck for freedom by fleeing to Union lines at the first opportunity. The attitude of the slaves toward the Federals varied, but the great majority welcomed them with an adulation, trust and dependence that suggests the full force of the old paternalism. Many blacks, free and slaves, Northern and Southern, entered the Union army, where despite humiliating discrimination they gave a creditable account of themselves in action.

For all that, the record of the slaves and ex-slaves during the war constituted a disaster. Having relied previously on the protection and guidance of their masters, they now threw themselves on the mercies of the Union army. As might be expected, untold thousands died in and out of virtual concentration camps, countless women were raped by Union troops, black soldiers generally found themselves used as menials and had to suffer insult and discrimination. Many decent and selfless white and black abolitionists accompanied the Union army south and earnestly worked to educate and organize the freedmen; they deserve all the praise and attention historians are now heaping on them. The fact remains that no black movement and only a weak black leadership emerged from the war.

As the war years passed into the period of Reconstruction, these patterns were reinforced. The blacks could and did fight for their rights, but rarely under their own leadership. When they offered armed resistance under competent leadership they did well enough, but mostly they relied on the leadership of white politicians, or on the protection of Federal troops, or on the advice of their own inexperienced leaders who in turn relied on whites. As Vernon Lane Wharton has observed, "The lesson learned was that the Negroes, largely unarmed, economically dependent, and timid and unresourceful after generations of servitude, would offer no effective resistance to violence." When Whitelaw Reid asked black school children what they would do if someone tried to re-enslave them, most responded that the troops would not permit it. No wonder Northern public opinion asked contemptuously in 1875 why a black majority in Mississippi constantly had to call for outside help.

The blacks sealed their own fate by relying on the protection of others, although they hardly had much choice. The Republican party, the Union army and the Freedmen's Bureau all took on the role of protectors, but, if anything, the new paternalism proved much more flimsy and more insincere than the old. The best illustration may be found in the history of the Republican-sponsored, largely black militias. Ex-slaves responded to the calls of Republican governors and filled the ranks of state militias, which were put to effective use in guaranteeing Republican electoral victories. In several instances, especially toward the end of Reconstruction, militia units opposed each other on behalf of rival Republican factions. In the most appalling of these instances, the so-called Brooks–Baxter War in Arkansas in 1874, the Republican machine so discredited itself that the Democrats soon rode back to power. As Otis A. Singletary has sardonically observed, "The Negroes had been called to arms to fight in behalf of two white claimants for the governorship, as a consequence of which the Negro was eliminated as a political factor in Arkansas." In Mississippi the radical governor, Adelbert Ames, called the blacks to arms in 1875 to counter Democratic violence and then lost his nerve and disarmed them in return for a worthless pledge from the opposition. Significantly the black politicians in his party almost unanimously opposed using the black troops in a showdown. The militia movement failed because it faced greater force, but no less because its leaders were never willing to see it steeled in battle, especially in defense of specifically black interests.

In other respects the Reconstruction experience followed parallel lines. In the famous Sea Island experiment the blacks placed their trust in white generals, some of whom meant well and tried hard but could not prevail in the face of Washington's duplicity. When the old plantation owners returned with Federal support, the blacks protested but ultimately accepted defeat without recourse to arms. Here, as with the militias, the masses seem to have been well ahead of their leaders. Demands for resistance were heard, antiwhite feeling was manifest and the desire for land grew apace, but the leadership proved timid or mortgaged, and action independent of whites was deemed impractical. Black congressmen and state legislators rarely fought for basic black interests and even opposed disfranchisement of ex-Confederate whites. With no powerful separate organizations and paramilitary units, without experience in leading their masses, they temporized and collapsed. Their fault did not lie in having coalesced with Northern whites, but in having coalesced from a position of weakness, without independent demands, organization and force. The masses moved sharply to the left and expressed an intense desire for land, but the old pattern persisted; they could not cut loose from accommodating leaders and from dependence on the ultimate authority of the whites. They did not so much demand, much less fight for, land, as they hoped it would be given them.

The black leaders saw the duplicity of their white Republican allies, but had nowhere to go. Many had been Northerners or privileged Southern mulattoes; their links with the masses had never been firm. When election time arrived they swallowed their doubts and frustrations and, with the best of intentions, lied to their people. Without adequate traditions and without confidence in their masses they made the best deals they could. This lying carried on an old habit. Every slave, at some time or other, would outwit the white folks by pretending to be stupid or docile; unfortunately too often he simultaneously outwitted himself. When carried into slave leadership, it was generally impossible to outwit the whites without also outwitting the blacks. During the war, for example, the respected black pastor of the Baptist church in Virginia offered a prayer for the victory of the Confederate army. Subsequently, he was berated by his deacons for betraying the cause of the slaves, but he pacified them by saying, "Don't worry children; the Lord knew what I was talking about." Undoubtedly, the Lord did, but the good pastor apparently never wondered whether or not his flock did also. If they did, the deacons would have no reason to be upset in the first place.

Some of the Reconstruction leaders simply sold out. As a distinguished South Carolina planter noted, they promised their people land and mules at every election but delivered only offices and jobs for themselves and their friends. (Any resemblance to the War on Poverty is not of my making.)

Slavery and its aftermath left the blacks in a state of acute economic and cultural backwardness. They also left a tradition of accommodation to paternalistic authority on the one hand, and a tradition of nihilistic violence on the other. Not docility or infantilization, but innocence of organized effort and political consciousness plagued the black masses and kept plaguing them well into the twentieth century. As a direct result of these effects and of the virtually unchallenged hegemony of the slave-holders, the blacks had little opportunity to develop a sense of their own worth and had every opportunity to learn to despise themselves. The inability of the men during and after slavery to support their families adequately, and especially to protect their women from rape or abuse without forfeiting their own lives, reproduced those psychological deformities against which they had long had to struggle.

The remarkable ascendancy of Booker T. Washington after the post-Reconstruction reaction must be understood against this background. We need especially to account for his enormous influence over the black nationalists who came after him. Washington tried to meet the legacy of slavery on its own terms. He knew that slavery had ill-prepared his people for political leadership; he therefore retreated from political demands. He knew that slavery had rendered manual labor degrading; he therefore preached the gospel of hard work. He knew that slavery had circumscribed the family and weakened elementary moral standards; he therefore preached the whole gamut of middle-class virtues and manners. He knew his people had never been able to stand on their own feet and face the whites as equals; he therefore preached self-reliance and self-help. Unhappily, apart from other ideological sins, he saw no way to establish self-reliance and self-respect except under the financial and social hegemony of the white upper classes. Somehow he meant to destroy the effects of paternalism in the long run by strengthening paternalism in the short run. It would be easy to say that he failed because of this tactic, but there is no way to be sure that the tactic was wrong in principle. He failed for other reasons, one of which was his reliance on the paternalistic, conservative classes at a time when they were rapidly losing power in the South to racist agrarian demagogues.

Washington's rivals did not, in this respect, do much better. The leaders of the NAACP repeatedly returned to a fundamental reliance on white leadership and money. Even Du Bois, in his classic critique of Washington, argued:

> While it is a great truth to say that the Negro must strive and strive mightily to help himself, it is equally true that unless his striving be not simply seconded, but rather aroused and encouraged by the initiative of the richer and wiser environing group, he cannot hope for great success.

The differences between these militants and Washington's conservatives concerned emphases, tactics and public stance much more than ideological fundamentals. The differences were important, but their modest extent was no less so. The juxtaposition of the two tendencies reveals how little could be done even by the most militant without white encouragement and support. The wonder is that black Americans survived the ghastly years between 1890 and 1920 at all. Survival—

and more impressive, growing resistance to oppression—came at the price of continuing many phases of a paternalistic tradition that had already sapped the strength of the masses.

The conflict between Washington and Du Bois recalled many earlier battles between two tendencies that are still with us. The first has accepted segregation at least temporarily, has stressed the economic development of the black community, and has advocated self-help. This tendency generally prevailed during periods of retrogression in race relations until the upsurge of nationalism in our own day. Washington was its prophet; black nationalism has been its outcome. The second had demanded integration, has stressed political action and has demanded that whites recognize their primary responsibility. Frederick Douglass was its prophet; the civil rights movement has been its outcome. Yet, the lines have generally been blurred. Du Bois often sounded like a nationalist, and Washington probably would have thought Malcolm X a madman. This blurring reflects the dilemma of the black community as a whole and of its bourgeoisie in particular: How do you integrate into a nation that does not want you? How do you separate from a nation that finds you too profitable to release?

To probe the relationship between this past and the recent upsurge of the black masses requires more speculation and tentative judgment than one would like, but they cannot be avoided. Let us, at the risk of being schematic and one-sided, select several features of the developments of the last few decades and especially of the recent crisis for such analysis. In doing so let us bear in mind that the majority of blacks today live outside the South; that they are primarily urban, not rural, in all parts of the country; that whole cities are on the way to becoming black enclaves; that the problem increasingly centers on the urban North and West. Let us bear in mind also that the only large-scale, organized black mass movements until recently have been nationalist. Garvey commanded an organization of hundreds of thousands; the Muslims have tens of thousands and influence many more. No integrationist organization has ever acquired such numerical strength; none has ever struck such deep roots in the black ghettos.

Garvey's movement emphasized blackness as a thing of beauty, and struggled to convince the black masses to repudiate white leadership and paternalism. The pompous titles, offices, uniforms and parades did and do evoke ridicule, but their importance lay, as Edmund David Cronon says, "in restoring the all but shattered Negro self-confidence." There was enormous ideological significance in Garvey's delightful description of a light-skinned mulatto opponent as "a white man passing for Negro."

A decisive break with the white man's church, if not wholly with his religion, has formed a major part of black nationalist thinking. In view of the central role of anti-Christian ideology in the slave risings

of Brazil and the Caribbean, and the generally accommodationist character of American Christianity, this has been a rational response to a difficult problem. Garvey tried to organize his own African Orthodox
church. The Islamic tendency, including that of Elijah Muhammed's
Nation of Islam, has followed the maxim of Noble Drew Ali's earlier
black-nationalist Islamic movement: "Before you can have a God, you
must have a nationality." Garvey's Black Jesus and Muhammed's Allah
have had many attributes of a tribal deity. Of special importance in
Muhammed's teaching is his decidedly un-Islamic denial of an afterlife.
In this way Black Muslim eschatology embodies a sharp reaction against
accommodationist ideology. The tendency to turn away from the white
man's religion has taken many forms, including conversion to Catholicism ostensibly because of its lack of a color line. In Catholic Brazil, on
the other hand, an equivalent reason is given by blacks who embrace
Protestantism.

The first Black Protestants in the United States have largely attended self-
segregated churches since Reconstruction. With the collapse of Reconstruction these churches, especially in the South, played an increasingly
accommodationist role, but they also served as community centers, protective agencies, marriage counseling committees and leadership training
schools. As objective conditions changed, so did many ministers, especially the younger ones. One of the great ironies of the current struggle for
integration has been the leading role played by ministers whose training
and following have been made possible by segregated organizations. The
experience of the Protestant churches and their anti-Christian rivals
brings us back to slavery's legacy of accommodationist, but by no means
necessarily treasonable, leadership, of an absence of collective political
effort, of paternalistically induced dependence and of the constant threat
of emasculation. Theoretically, a militant mass leadership could have
arisen from sources other than enforced segregation; historically there
seems to have been no other way.

The first difficulty with the integrationist movement arises not
from its ultimate commitment, which may or may not be desirable,
but from the determined opposition of the whites, whose hostility to
close association with blacks recedes slowly if at all. Integration may
mean only desegregation, and outstanding black intellectuals insist that
that is all they want it to mean; it need not mean assimilation. In fact,
however, the line is difficult to hold, and segregationists probably do not
err in regarding one as the prelude to the other. In any case, de facto
segregation in education and housing is growing worse, and many of the
professed goals of the civil rights movement look further away than ever.
Communities like Harlem face substantially the same social problems
today as they did forty years ago. We need not dwell on the worsening
problem of black unemployment and its implications.

Even where progress, however defined, occurs, the frustration of the black masses deepens. The prosperity of recent decades has widened the gap between blacks and whites, even of the same class. The rise of the African peoples has inspired blacks here, but has also threatened to open a gap in political power and dignity between Africans and Afro-Americans.

The resistance of whites and the inflexibility of the social system constitute only half the problem. A. James Gregor, in an article published in *Science & Society* in 1963, analyzes an impressive body of sociological and psychological literature to demonstrate that integration under the disorderly conditions of American capitalist life more often than not undermines the development and dignity of the participating blacks. He shows that the problems of the black masses, in contradistinction to those of the bourgeoisie, become intensified by an integration which, in the nature of things, must pass them by. As Gregor demonstrates, black nationalism has been the political reply of these masses and especially of the working class. Similarly, in his honest and thoughtful book, *Crisis in Black and White,* Charles E. Silberman analyzes cases such as that in New Rochelle, in which poor black and rich white children had the wonderful experience of integrating in school. Why should anyone be surprised that the experiment proved a catastrophe for the black children, who promptly lost whatever ambition they might have had?

When liberals and academics speak of a "crisis of identity," they may sometimes merely wish to divert attention from the prior fact of oppression, but, by whatever name, that crisis exists. Slavery and its aftermath severely damaged the black masses; they remain today profoundly shaken. It does us no good to observe, with Kardiner and Ovesey, that a psychology of oppression can disappear only when the oppression has disappeared. It does us no good to admit that the sickness of white racism is more dangerous than the sickness it has engendered. We face an aroused, militant black community that has no intention of waiting for others to heal themselves. Those who believe that this disorder, suggestively but dangerously miscalled emasculation, is the figment of the liberal imagination ought to read the words of any militant leader from David Walker to W. E. B. Du Bois, from Frederick Douglass to Martin Luther King, from Robert F. Williams to Malcolm X. The cry has been to assert manhood and renounce servility. Black intellectuals today—Killens, Baldwin, Ellison—make the point in one way or another. Let me quote only one, Ossie Davis, on the death of Malcolm X:

> Negroes knew that Malcolm—whatever else he was or was not—*Malcolm was a man!*
> White folks do not need anybody to remind them that they are men. We do! This was his one incontrovertible benefit to his people. Protocol and common sense require that Negroes stand back and let the white man speak up

for us, defend us, and lead us from behind the scene in our fight. This is
the essence of Negro politics. But Malcolm said to hell with that! Get up
off your knees and fight your own battles. That's the way to win back
your self-respect. That's the way to make the white man respect you. And
if he won't let you live like a man, he certainly can't keep you from dying
like one.

Is it any wonder, then, that Dr. King could write, almost as a matter of
course, that the blacks in Birmingham during the summer of 1963 shook
off three hundred years of psychological slavery and found out their
own worth? It is no less instructive that his aide, the Reverend Wyatt T.
Walker, denounced as "hoodlums" and "winos" those who responded to
the attempt on King's life by attacking the white racists. King himself put
it bluntly when he pleaded that the black militant be allowed to march
and sit-in. "If his repressed emotions do not come out in these nonviolent
ways, they will come out in ominous expressions of violence."

King and his followers apparently have believed that concerted
action for integration can cure the ills engendered by slavery and subsequent oppression and break down discrimination at the same time. In
one sense he was right. His greatest achievement was to bring order and
collective political effort to a people who had learned little of the necessity for either. But King's followers must deliver victory or face grave
consequences. As we have seen, not all slaves and freedmen yielded
meekly to the oppressor. Many fought, sometimes with great ferocity,
but they generally fought by lashing out individually rather than by
organized revolutionary effort. It would be the crowning irony if the civil
rights movement has taught just enough of the lesson of collective political effort to guarantee greater and more widespread nihilism in the wake
of its inability to realize its program.

More and more young black radicals are currently pouring over
Frantz Fanon's psychopathic panegyric to violence. Fanon argues that
violence frees the oppressor from his inferiority complex and restores his
self-respect. Perhaps; but it is also the worst way to do either. Black
Americans, like colonials, have always resorted to violence without ac-
complishing those goals. A slave who killed his overseer did not establish his manhood thereby—any wild animal can kill—he merely denied
his docility. Violence can serve Fanon's purpose only when it is collective; but then, it is precisely the collective effort, not the violence, that
does the healing.

The legend of black docility threatens to betray those who perpetuate it. They are ill-prepared for the yielding of one part of the slave
tradition—accommodation and servility—to another part—antisocial
and nihilistic action. The failure of integration and the lawlessness to
which the blacks have for so long been subjected combine to produce
that result. James Baldwin, and especially Malcolm X in his remarks on

the prestige of the ghetto hustler, have each warned of this danger. Bayard Rustin has made a similar point with gentle irony:

> From the point of view of motivation, some of the healthiest Negro youngsters I know are juvenile delinquents: vigorously pursuing the American Dream of material acquisition and status, yet finding the conventional means of attaining it blocked off, they do not yield to defeatism but resort to illegal (and sometimes ingenious) methods. They are not alien to American culture.

Those historians who so uncritically admire the stealing of hogs and smashing of plows by slaves might consider its modern equivalent. In the words of Silberman:

> There are other means of protest, of course: misbehaving in school, or dropping out of school altogether; not showing up for work on time, or not showing up at all (and lying about the reason); breaking school windows or ripping telephone receivers out of outdoor phone booths; or the oldest form of protest of all, apathy—a flat refusal to cooperate with the oppressor or to accept his moral code.

Black nationalism, in its various manifestations, constitutes a necessary response on the part of the black masses. The Muslims, for example, have understood the inner needs of the working-class blacks who have filled their ranks and have understood the futility—for these people at least—of integrationist hopes. Their insistence on the forcible assertion of a dignified, disciplined, collectively responsible black community represents a rational response to a harsh reality. We need waste little time on what is unrealistic, romantic or even reactionary in the Nation of Islam or other nationalist groups; they are easy to see. Ralph Bunche, in his radical days, Gunnar Myrdal, and many others have for years pointed out that the idea of a separate black economy is a will-o'-the-wisp and that the idea of a separate territory is less than that. Yet I am not sure how to answer Marc Schleifer, who in 1963 asked whether these goals were less realistic than those of equality under capitalism or a socialist revolution in the foreseeable future. I am not sure, either, that Malcolm X, Harold W. Cruse, and others have not been wiser than their Marxist critics in demanding black ownership of everything in Harlem. Such ownership will do little toward the creation of a black economy, but many of its advocates are easily bright enough to know as much. The point is that it may, as Malcolm X suggested, play a decisive role in the establishment of community stability and self-respect.

The black struggle for equality in America has always had two tendencies—integrationist and separatist—and it is likely to retain both. Since a separate economy and national territory are not serious possibilities, the struggle for economic integration will undoubtedly be pressed forward. For this reason alone some degree of unity between the civil rights and nationalist tendencies may be expected. The black bourgeoisie and its allied stratum of skilled and government clerical workers will certainly continue its fight for integration, but the interest of the black workers in this fight is, at bottom, even greater. At the same time, clearly there will be serious defeats, as well as some victories, and the slogan "Freedom Now!" is now turning to ashes.

The cumulative problems of past and present nonetheless demand urgent action. The assertion of black hegemony in specific cities and districts—nationalism if you will—offers the only politically realistic hope of transcending the slave heritage. First, it seems the only way for black communities to police themselves, to curb antisocial elements and to enforce adequate health and housing standards, and yet break with paternalism and instill pride and a sense of worth. Second, it seems the best way to build a position of strength from which to fight for a proper share of jobs and federal funds as a matter of right not privilege. Black nationalism may yet prove to be the only force capable of building upon the genuine achievements of Afro-American culture, as well as of restraining the impulse to violence, of disciplining black rebelliousness and of absorbing the nihilistic tradition into a socially constructive movement. If this seems like a conservative rendering of an ostensibly revolutionary movement, I can only answer that there are no ingredients for a successful, independent black revolution, and that black nationalism can ultimately go only a few steps further toward the left than the white masses. The rise of specifically black cities, countries and districts with high-quality black schools, well-paid teachers, as well as political leaders, churches and community centers, could and should uproot the negative features of the slave tradition once and for all, could and should act as a powerful lever for structural reform of the American economy and society.

I do not offer these remarks as a program for a black movement, for the time is past when white men can offer programs to black militants. They are, happily, no longer listening. But I do submit that they are relevant to the formation of a program for ourselves—for the American Left. If this analysis has merit, the demands of the black community will increasingly swing away from the traditional appeal to federal power and toward the assertion of local and regional autonomy. Even now Bayard Rustin and others warn that federal troops can only preserve the status quo. I should observe, further, that the appeals to Washington reflect the convergence of two powerful and debilitating traditions: slave-engendered paternalistic dependence and the growing state paternalism of white America. Let us admit that the naive fascination of leftists for centralized power has, since the 1930s, greatly strengthened this tendency. With such labels as "progressive" and even "socialist," corporate liberalism has been building what

William Appleman Williams has aptly called a nonterroristic totalitarian society. Yet American socialism has never even posed a theoretical alternative. When Professor Williams called for a program of regional and local reassertion and opposition to centralization, he was dismissed by most radicals as a utopian of doubtful mental competence. We may now rephrase his question: How do we propose to support an increasingly nationalistic black radicalism, with its demands for local hegemony, unless we have an ideology and program of opposition to the centralization of state power?

The possible courses for the black liberation movement include a total defeat in an orgy of violence (we ought to remember that there is nothing inevitable in its or our victory), a compromise with imperialism in return for some degree of local rule or the integration of its bourgeois strata, and the establishment of black power on the basis of a developing opposition to American capitalism. Since its future depends to a great extent on the progress of its integrationist struggle for a place in the economy, the black community must for a while remain well to the left of the current liberal consensus by its demands for public works and structural reform. But reform could occur under the auspices of an expansion rather than a contraction of state centralization, and the most militant of the black leaders may have to settle for jobs and local political control in return for allegiance to a consolidating national and international empire. The final result will be decided by the struggle within white America, with the blacks playing the role of an increasingly independent ally for one or another tendency. Notwithstanding some offensive and pretentious rhetoric, the advocates of black power have judged their position correctly. They are determined to win control of the ghettoes, and we would be foolish not to bet on them. The use to which they put that power, however, depends neither on our good wishes nor on their good intentions, but on what they are offered as a *quid pro quo*. For American socialism the black revolt opens an opportunity for relevance that has been missing for decades. What we do with that opportunity is our problem, not theirs.

10

The Mountain Man
as Jacksonian Man

William Goetzmann

William Goetzmann (1930–   ) received his Ph.D. in American Studies from Yale University in 1957. He specializes in American cultural history and the history of the American West. Among his many books is The Mountain Man *(1978), a fuller treatment of this 1963 article. At present Goetzmann is director of the American Studies program at the University of Texas.*

Goetzmann argues that the conventional image of the uncivilized mountain man seeking to escape encroaching civilization is wide of the mark. Instead, the mountain man was a typical Jacksonian man pursuing traditional conservative goals. Despite his alleged disregard for civilization, he consciously promoted American acquisition and development of the West to ensure the future he envisioned for the region, a future strikingly similar to that pursued by other Jacksonian "venturous conservatives."

      How does this article affect your perception of the independent,

This reading is from *American Quarterly,* (Washington, D.C.: American Studies Association), volume 15 (1963), pp. 402–15. Copyright © 1963, by American Studies Association. Reprinted by permission of William Goetzmann.

self-directed figure Jefferson idealized (as presented in David Potter's
article)? Was Jefferson's or de Tocqueville's portrait of the American
character more accurate in depicting the mountain man? If the moun-
tain man was not the ultimate independent, self-directed man, who
was? In Volume II, David Brion Davis will consider the cowboy, another
candidate, and see how he fits the stereotype.

One of the most often studied and least understood figures in American history has been the Mountain Man. Remote, so it would seem, as
Neanderthal, and according to some almost as inarticulate, the Mountain
Man exists as a figure of American mythology rather than history. As such
he has presented at least two vivid stereotypes to the public imagination.
From the first he has been the very symbol for the romantic banditti of the
forest, freed of the artificial restrictions of civilization—a picturesque
wanderer in the wilderness whose very life is a constant and direct association with Nature.

> There is perhaps, no class of men on the face of the earth," said Captain
> Bonneville (and through him Washington Irving), "who lead a life of more
> continued exertion, peril, and excitement, and who are more enamoured of
> their occupations, than the free trappers of the west. No toil, no danger, no
> privation can turn the trapper from his pursuit. His passionate excitement
> at times resembles a mania. In vain may the most vigilant and cruel savages
> beset his path; in vain may rocks, and precipices, and wintry torrents
> oppose his progress; let but a single track of a beaver meet his eye, and he
> forgets all dangers and defies all difficulties. At times, he may be seen
> with his traps on his shoulder, buffeting his way across rapid streams
> amidst floating blocks of ice: at other times, he is to be found with his traps
> on his back clambering the most rugged mountains, scaling or descending
> the most frightening precipices, searching by routes inaccessible to the
> horse, and never before trodden by white man, for springs and lakes
> unknown to his comrades, and where he may meet with his favorite game.
> Such is the mountaineer, the hardy trapper of the west; and such as we
> have slightly sketched it, is the wild, Robin Hood kind of life, with all its
> strange and motley populace, now existing in full vigor among the Rocky
> mountains."

To Irving in the nineteenth century the Mountain Man was Robin
Hood, a European literary convention. By the twentieth century the
image was still literary and romantic but somewhat less precise. According to Bernard De Voto, "For a few years Odysseus Jed Smith and
Siegfried Carson and the wing-shod Fitzpatrick actually drew breath in
this province of fable," and Jim Beckwourth "went among the Rockies as
Theseus dared the wine-dark seas. Skirting the rise of a hill, he saw the
willows stirring; he charged down upon them, while despairing Blackfeet sang the death-song—and lo, to the clear music of a horn, Roland
had met the pagan hordes. . . . "

On the other hand, to perhaps more discerning eyes in his own day and down through the years, the Mountain Man presented another image—one that was far less exalted. Set off from the ordinary man by his costume of greasy buckskins, coonskin cap and Indian finery, not to mention the distinctive odor that went with bear grease and the habitual failure to bathe between one yearly rendezvous and the next, the Mountain Man seemed a forlorn and pathetic primitive out of the past. "They are stared at as though they were bears," wrote Rudolph F. Kurz, a Swiss artist who traveled the Upper Missouri.

The Mountain Man, so it was said, was out of touch with conventional civilization and hence not quite acceptable. Instead in his own time and even more today he has been viewed as a purely hedonistic character who lived for the year's end rendezvous where he got gloriously drunk on diluted rotgut company alcohol, gave his beaver away for wildly inflated company trade goods and crawled off into the underbrush for a delirious orgy with some unenthusiastic Indian squaw. In this view the romantic rendezvous was nothing more than a modern company picnic, the object of which was to keep the employees docile, happy and ready for the coming year's task.

Pacified, satisfied, cheated, impoverished, and probably mortified the next day, the Mountain Man, be he free trapper or not, went back to his dangerous work when the rendezvous was over. He was thus to many shrewd observers not a hero at all but a docile and obedient slave of the company. By a stretch of the imagination he might have seemed heroic, but because of the contrast between his daring deeds and his degraded status he seemed one of the saddest heroes in all history. Out of date before his time was up, he was a wild free spirit who after all was not free. He was instead an adventurer who was bringing about his own destruction even as he succeeded in his quest to search out the beaver in all of the secret places of the mountain West. A dependent of the London dandy and his foppish taste in hats, the Mountain Man was Caliban. He was a member of a picturesque lower class fast vanishing from the face of America. Like the Mohican Indian and quaint old Leatherstocking he was a vanishing breed, forlorn and permanently classbound in spite of all his heroics.

Both of these stereotypes embody, as do most effective stereotypes, more than a measure of reality. The Mountain Man traveled far out ahead of the march of conventional civilization, and the job he did required him to be as tough, primitive and close to nature as an Indian. Moreover, it was an out-of-doors life of the hunt and the chase that he often grew to like. By the same token because he spent much of his time in primitive isolation in the mountains, he very often proved to be a poor businessman ignorant of current prices and sharp company practices. Even if aware of his disadvantageous position he could do nothing to free himself until he had made his stake.

The fact is, however, that many Mountain Men lived for the chance to exchange their dangerous mountain careers for an advantageous start in civilized life. If one examines their lives and their stated aspirations one discovers that the Mountain Men, for all their eccentricities, were astonishingly similar to the common men of their time-plain republican citizens of the Jacksonian era.

Jacksonian Man, according to Richard Hofstadter, "was an expectant capitalist, a hardworking ambitious person for whom enterprise was a kind of religion." He was "the master mechanic who aspired to open his own shop, the planter, or farmer who speculated in land, the lawyer who hoped to be a judge, the local politician who wanted to go to Congress, the grocer who would be a merchant. . . . " To this list one might well add, the trapper who hoped some day, if he hit it lucky and avoided the scalping knife, to be one or all of these, or perhaps better still, a landed gentleman of wealth and prestige.

"Everywhere," writes Hofstadter, the Jacksonian expectant capitalist "found conditions that encouraged him to extend himself." And there were many like William Ashley or Thomas James who out of encouragement or desperation looked away to the Rocky Mountains, teeming with beaver and other hidden resources, and saw a path to economic success and rapid upward mobility. In short, when he went out West and became a Mountain Man the Jacksonian Man did so as a prospector. He too was an expectant capitalist.

Marvin Meyers has added a further characterization of Jacksonian Man. He was, according to Meyers, the "venturous conservative," the man who desired relative freedom from restraint so that he might risk his life and his fortune, if not his sacred honor, on what appeared to be a long-term, continent-wide boom. Yet at the same time he wished to pyramid his fortune within the limits of the familiar American social and economic system, and likewise to derive his status therefrom. Wherever he went, and especially on the frontier, Jacksonian Man did not wish to change the system. He merely wished to throw it open as much as possible to opportunity, with the hope that by so doing he could place himself at the top instead of at the bottom of the conventional social and economic ladder. "They love change," wrote Tocqueville, "but they dread revolutions." Instead of a new world the Jacksonian Man wished to restore the old where the greatest man was the independent man—yeoman or mechanic, trader or ranchero—the man who basked in comfort and sturdy security under his own "vine and fig tree."

The structure of the Rocky Mountain fur trade itself, the life stories of the trappers and on rare occasions their stated or implied aspirations all make it clear that if he was not precisely the Meyers–Hofstadter Jacksonian Man, the Mountain Man was most certainly his cousin once removed, and a clearly recognizable member of the family.

It is a truism, of course, to state that the Rocky Mountain fur trade was a business, though writers in the Mountain Man's day since have sometimes made it seem more like a sporting event. The Mountain Man himself often put such an ambiguous face on what he was doing.

"Westward! Ho!" wrote Warren Ferris, an American Fur Company trapper. "It is the sixteenth of the second month A.D. 1830, and I have joined a trapping, trading, hunting expedition to the Rocky Mountains. Why, I scarcely know, for the motives that induced me to this step were of a mixed complexion,—something like the pepper and salt population of this city of St. Louis. Curiosity, a love of wild adventure, and perhaps also a hope of profit,—for times *are* hard, and my best coat has a sort of sheepish hang-dog hesitation to encounter fashionable folk—combined to make me look upon the project with an eye of favor. The party consists of some thirty men, mostly Canadian; but a few there are, like myself, from various parts of the Union. Each has some plausible excuse for joining, and the aggregate of disinterestedness would delight the most ghostly saint in the Roman calendar. Engage for money! no, not they;—health, and the strong desire of seeing strange lands, of beholding nature in the savage grandeur of her primeval state,—these are the only arguments that *could* have persuaded such independent and high-minded young fellows to adventure with the American Fur Company in a trip to the mountain wilds of the great west."

Ambiguous though the Mountain Man's approach to it may have been, it is abundantly clear that the Rocky Mountain fur trade was indeed a *business,* and not an invariably individualistic enterprise at that. The unit of operation was the company, usually a partnership for the sake of capital, risk and year-round efficiency. Examples of the company are The Missouri Fur Company, Gantt and Blackwell, Stone and Bostwick, Bean and Sinclair, and most famous of all, the Rocky Mountain Fur Company and its successors, Smith Jackson, and Sublette, Sublette & Campbell, and Sublette, Fitzpatrick, Bridger, Gervais and Fraeb. These were the average company units in the Rocky Mountain trade and much of the story of their existence in analogous to Jackson's war on the "Monster Bank" for they were all forced to contend against John Jacob Astor's "Monster Monopoly," the American Fur Co., which was controlled and financed by eastern capitalists.

Perhaps the most interesting aspect of the independent fur companies was their fluid structure of leadership. There was indeed, "a baton in every knapsack" or more accurately, perhaps, in every "possibles" bag. William Ashley, owner of a gun powder factory and Andrew Henry, a former Lisa lieutenant, and lead miner, founded the Rocky Mountain Fur Company. After a few years of overwhelming success, first Henry, and then Ashley, retired, and they were succeeded by their lieutenants, Jedediah Smith, David Jackson and William Sublette, three of the "enterprising young men" who had answered Ashley's advertisement in the St. Louis *Gazette and Public Advertiser* in 1823. When Smith and Jackson moved on to more attractive endeavors, first William Sublette and Robert Campbell, then Tom "Broken Hand" Fitzpatrick, James "Old Gabe" Bridger, Henry Fraeb, Milton "Thunderbolt" Sublette and Jean Baptiste Gervais moved up to fill their entrepreneurial role.

In another example Etienne Provost was successively an employee of Auguste Chouteau, partner with LeClair and leader of his own Green River brigade, and servant of American Fur. Sylvestre Pattie became a Santa Fe trader, then an independent trapper, then manager of the Santa Rita (New Mexico) Copper Mines and ultimately leader of an independent trapping venture into the Gila River country of the far Southwest—a venture that ended in disaster when he was thrown into a Mexican prison in California and there left to die. Most significant is the fact that few of the trappers declined the responsibility of entrepreneurial leadership when it was offered them. On the contrary, the usual practice was to indenture oneself to an established company for a period of time, during which it was possible to acquire the limited capital in the way of traps, rifles, trade goods, etc., that was needed to become independent and a potential brigade leader. Referring to his arrangement with the old Missouri Fur Company in 1809, Thomas James wrote,

> We Americans were all private adventurers, each on his own hook, and were led into the enterprise by the promises of the Company, who agreed to subsist us to the trapping grounds, we helping to navigate the boats, and on our arrival there they were to furnish us each with a rifle and sufficient ammunition, six good beaver traps and also four men of their hired French, to be under our individual commands for a period of three years.
>
> By the terms of the contract each of us was to divide one-fourth of the profits of our joint labor with the four men thus to be appointed to us.

James himself retired when he could from the upper Missouri trade and eventually became an unsuccessful storekeeper in Harrisonville, Illinois.

In addition to the fact of rapid entrepreneurial succession within the structure of the independent fur companies, a study of 446 Mountain Men (perhaps 45 percent of the total engaged in this pursuit between 1805 and 1845) indicates that their life-patterns could be extremely varied. One hundred seventeen Mountain Men definitely turned to occupations other than trapping subsequent to their entering the mountain trade. Of this number, 39 followed more than one pursuit. As such they often worked at as many as four or five different callings.

Moreover, beyond the 117 definite cases of alternative callings, 32 others were found to have indeterminate occupations that were almost certainly not connected with the fur trade, making a total of 149 out of 154 men for whom some occupational data exists who had turned away

Table 1

Total Number of Cases	446
Persons whose other occupations are known	117
Persons whose other occupations are probable	32
Persons with more than one other occupation	39
Persons who stayed on as trappers	5
Persons whose status is unknown	110
Persons killed in the fur trade	182

from the trapping fraternity before 1845. Of the remaining men in the study, 110 men yielded nothing to investigation beyond the fact that they had once been trappers, 182 can be listed as killed in the line of duty and only five men out of the total stayed with the great out-of-doors life of the free trapper that according to the myth they were all supposed to love.

The list of alternative callings pursued by the trappers is also revealing. Twenty-one became ranchers, fifteen farmers, seventeen traders (at stationary trading posts), eight miners, seven politicians, six distillers, five each storekeepers and army scouts, four United States Indian agents, three carpenters, two each bankers, drovers and hatters and at least one pursued each of the following occupations: sheepherder, postman, miller, medium, ice dealer, real estate specualtor, newspaper editor, lawyer, lumberman, superintendent of schools, tailor, blacksmith, and supercargo of trading schooner. Moreover, many of these same individuals pursued secondary occupations such as that of hotel keeper, gambler, soldier, health resort proprietor, coal mine owner, tanner, sea captain, horse thief and opera house impresario.

From this it seems clear that, statistically at least, the Mountain Man was hardly the simple-minded primitive that mythology has made him out to be. Indeed it appears that whenever he had the chance, he exchanged the joys of the rendezvous and the wilderness life for the more civilized excitement of "getting ahead." In many cases he achieved this aim, and on a frontier where able men were scarce he very often became a pillar of the community, and even of the nation. From the beginning, as Ashley's famous advertisement implied, the Mountain Men were men of "enterprise" who risked their lives for something more than pure romance and a misanthropic desire to evade civilization. The picturesqueness and the quaintness were largely the creation of what was the literary mentality of an age of artistic romanticism. For every "Cannibal Phil" or Robert Meldrum or "Peg-Leg" Smith there was a Sarchel Wolfskill (vintner), a George Yount (rancher) and a William Sublette (banker–politician).

Two further facts emerge in part from this data. First, it is clear that though the Jeffersonian agrarian dream of "Arcadia" bulked large in the Mountain Man's choice of occupations, it by no means obscured the whole

Table 2.   List of Occupations

A. Primary

1. Farmer	15	17. Blacksmith	1
2. Rancher	21	18. Tailor	1
3. Politician	7	19. Supercargo	1
4. Sheepherder	1	20. Superintendent of Schools	1
5. Scout (for govt.)	5	21. Lumberman	2
6. Trader	17	22. Newspaper Editor	1
7. Miner	8	23. Carpenter	3
8. Postman	1	24. Cattle Buyer	1
9. Distiller	6	25. Clockmaker	1
10. Miller	1	26. Saloon Keeper	1
11. Storekeeper	5	27. Baker	1
12. Medium	1	28. Fruit Grower	1
13. Banker	2	29. Vintner	1
14. Drover	2	30. Ice Dealer	1
15. Hatter	2	31. Real Estate Speculator	1
16. Indian Agent	4	32. Lawyer	1

B. Secondary

1. Trader	4	12. Lumberman	2
2. Transportation	2	13. Gambler	3
3. Scout	5	14. Blacksmith	1
4. Hotel Keeper	1	15. Soldier	1
5. Miner	2	16. Spa Keeper	1
6. Farmer	5	17. Coal Mine Operator	1
7. Politician	3	18. Tanner	1
8. Rancher	5	19. Opera House Impresario	1
9. Storekeeper	4	20. Sea Captain	1
10. Miller	3	21. Carpenter	1
11. Real Estate	3	22. Horse Thief	1

range of "mechanical" or mercantile pursuits that offered the chance for success on the frontier. Indeed, if it suggests anything a statistical view of the Mountain Man's "other life" suggests that almost from the beginning the Far Western frontier took on the decided aspect of an urban or semiurban "industrial" civilization. Secondly, though it is not immediately apparent from the above statistics, a closer look indicates that a surprising number of the Mountain Men succeeded at their "other" tasks to the extent that they became regionally and even nationally prominent.

William H. Ashley became Congressman from Missouri and a spokesman for the West, Charles Bent an ill-fated though famed governor of New Mexico. "Doc" Newell was a prominent figure in the organization of Oregon Territory. Elbridge Gerry, William McGaa and John Simpson Smith were the founders and incorporators of Denver. Lucien Maxwell held the largest land grant in the whole history of the United States.

Joshua Pilcher was a famous superintendent of Indian affairs. William Sublette, pursuing a hard money policy, saved the Bank of

Missouri in the panic of 1837 and went on to be Democratic elector for "young hickory" James K. Polk in 1844. Benjamin Wilson was elected first mayor of Los Angeles. James Clyman and his Napa Valley estate were famous in California as were the ranches of George Yount and J. J. Warner, while Sarchel Wolfskill was a co-founder of the modern California wine industry. James Waters built the first opera house in Southern California, and Kit Carson, in his later years a silver miner, received the supreme tribute of finding a dime novel dedicated to his exploits in plunder captured from marauding Apache Indians who had recently attacked and massacred a wagon train.

Many of the Mountain Men achieved fame and national status through works that they published themselves, or, as in the case of Carson, through works that immortalized correctly, or as was more usual, incorrectly, their exploits. Here one need only mention Kit Carson's *Autobiography* and his favorable treatment at the hands of Jessie Benton Fremont, T. D. Bonner's *Life and Adventures of James Beckwourth*, Francis Fuller Victor's *River of the West* (about Joe Meek), James Ohio Pattie's *Personal Narrative*, Thomas James' *Three Years Among the Indians and Mexicans*, H. L. Conard's *Uncle Dick Wooton*, David Coyner's *The Lost Trappers* (about Ezekial Williams), Irving's portrait of Joseph Reddeford Walker in *The Adventures of Captain Bonneville*, Zenas Leonard's *Narrative*, Peg-Leg Smith's "as told to" exploits in *Hutchings' California Magazine*, Stephen Meek's *Autobiography*, Warren Ferris' letters to the Buffalo, New York, *Western Literary Messenger*, John Hatcher's yarns in Lewis H. Garrard's *Wah to Yah and the Taos Trail* and perhaps most interesting of all, trapper John Brown's pseudoscientific *Mediumistic Experiences*, to realize the extent and range of the Mountain Man's communication with the outside world in his own day. Not only was he a typical man of his time, he was often a conspicuous success and not bashful about communicating the fact in somewhat exaggerated terms to his fellow countrymen.

Direct evidence of the Mountain Men's motives is scarce, but it is clear their intentions were complex.

"Tell them that I have no heirs and that I hope to make a fortune," wrote Louis Vasquez ("Old Vaskiss" to Bernard De Voto) in 1834 from "Fort Convenience" somewhere in the Rockies. Later as he set out on one last expedition in 1842 he added somewhat melodramatically, "I leave to make money or die." And finally Colonel A. G. Brackett, who visited Fort Bridger (jointly owned by Bridger and Vasquez), described him as "a Mexican, who put on a great deal of style, and used to ride about the country in a coach and four."

"It is, that I may be able to help those who stand in need, that I face every danger," wrote Jedediah Smith from the Wind River Mountains in 1829, "most of all, it is for this, that I deprive myself of the privilege of Society and the satisfaction of the Converse of My Friends! but I shall count all this pleasure, if I am allowed by the Alwise Ruler the privilege of Joining my Friends. . . . "

And he added, "Let it be the greatest pleasure that we can enjoy, the height of our ambition, now, when our Parents are in the decline of Life, to smooth the Pillow of their age, and as much as in us lies, take from them all cause of Trouble." So spoke Jedediah Smith of his hopes and ambitions upon pursuing the fur trade. No sooner had he left the mountains, however, than he was killed by Plains Indians before he could settle down in business with his brothers as he had intended. Noble and ignoble were the motives of the Mountain Men. Colonel John Shaw, starting across the southern plains and into the Rockies in search of gold; Thomas James, desperate to recoup his failing fortunes; the Little Rock *Gazette* of 1829 "confidently" believing "that this enterprise affords a prospect of great profit to all who may engage in it"; the St. Louis *Enquirer* in 1822 labeling the Rocky Mountains "the Shining Mountains," and innocently declaring, "A hunter pursuing his game found the silver mines of Potosi, and many others have been discovered by the like accidents, and there is no reason to suppose that other valuable discoveries may not be made"; Ashley calling clearly and unmistakably for men of "enterprise," all added up to the fact that the Mountain Man when he went West was a complex character. But in his complexity was a clearly discernible pattern—the pattern of Jacksonian Man in search of respectability and success in terms recognized by the society he had left behind. His goal was, of course, the pursuit of happiness. But happiness, contrary to Rousseauistic expectations, was not found in the wilderness; it was an integral product of society and civilization.

If the Mountain Man was indeed Jacksonian Man, then there are at least three senses in which this concept has importance. First, more clearly than anything else a statistical and occupational view of the various callings of the Mountain Man tentatively indicates the incredible rate and the surprising *nature* of social and economic change in the West. In little more than two decades most of the surviving enterprising men had left the fur trade for more lucrative and presumably more useful occupations. And by their choice of occupations it is clear that in the Far West a whole step in the settlement process had been virtually skipped. They may have dreamed of "Arcadia," but when they turned to the task of settling the West as fast as possible, the former Mountain Men and perhaps others like them brought with them all the aspects of an "industrial," mercantile and quasi-urban society. The opera house went up almost simultaneously with the ranch, and the Bank of Missouri was secured before the land was properly put into hay.

Secondly, as explorers—men who searched out the hidden places in the western wilderness—the Mountain Men as Jacksonian Men looked with a flexible eye upon the new land. Unlike the Hudson's Bay explorer who looked only for beaver and immediate profit, the Mountain Man looked to the future and the development of the West, not as a vast game preserve, but as a land like the one he had back home.

"Much of this vast waste of territory belongs to the Republic of the United States," wrote Zenas Leonard from San Francisco Bay in 1833. "What a theme to contemplate its settlement and civilization. Will the jurisdiction of the federal government ever succeed in civilizing the thousands of savages now roaming over these plains, and her hardy freeborn population here plant their homes, build their towns and cities, and say here shall the arts and sciences of civilization take root and flourish? Yes, here, even in this remote part of the Great West before many years will these hills and valleys be greeted with the enlivening sound of the workman's hammer, and the merry whistle of the ploughboy . . . we have good reason to suppose that the territory *west* of the mountains will some day be equally as important to the nation as that on the east."

In 1830 in a famous letter to John H. Eaton, the Secretary of War, Jedediah S. Smith, David E. Jackson and William L. Sublette aired their views on the possibilities of the West. Smith made clear that a wagon road route suitable for settlers existed all the way to Oregon, and Sublette dramatized the point when he brought ten wagons and two dearborns and even a milch cow over the mountains as far as the Wind River rendezvous. Their report made abundantly clear that in their opinion the future of the West lay with settlers rather than trappers. Indeed they were worried that the English at Fort Vancouver might grasp this fact before the American government. In short, as explorers and trappers theirs was a broad-ranging, flexible, settler-oriented, public view of the Far West.

Tied in with this and of the greatest significance is a third and final point. Not only did they *see* a settler's future in the West, but at least some of the Mountain Men were most eager to see to it that such a future was *guaranteed* by the institutions of the United States Government which must be brought West and extended over all the wild new land to protect the settler in the enjoyment of his own "vine and fig tree." The Mexican Government, unstable, and blown by whim or caprice, could not secure the future, and the British Government, at least in North America, was under the heel of monopoly. France was frivolous and decadent. Russia was a sinister and backward despotism. Only the free institutions of Jacksonian America would make the West safe for enterprise. So strongly did he feel about this that in 1841 the Mountain Man Moses "Black" Harris sent a letter to one Thornton Grimsley offering him the command of 700 men, of which he was one, who were eager to "join the standard of their country, and make a clean sweep of what is called the Origon [sic] Territory; that is clear it of British and Indians." Outraged not only at British encroachments, he was also prepared to "march through to California" as well. It may well have been this spirit that settled the Oregon question and brought on the Mexican War.

Settlement, security, stability, enterprise, free enterprise, a government of laws which, in the words of Jackson himself, confines "itself to equal *protection,* and as Heaven does its rains, showers its favors alike on the high and the low, the rich and the poor," all of these shaped the Mountain Man's vision of the West and his role in its development. It was called Manifest Destiny. But long before John L. O'Sullivan nicely turned the phrase in the *Democratic Review,* the Mountain Man as Jacksonian Man—a "venturous conservative"—was out in the west doing his utmost to lend the Almighty a helping hand. James Clyman perhaps put it most simply:

> Here lies the bones of old Black Harris
> who often traveled beyond the far west
> and for the freedom of Equal rights
> He crossed the snowy mountain Hights
> Especially with a Belly full.

11

The Cult
of True Womanhood
1820–1860

Barbara Welter

Barbara Welter is a professor at Hunter College of the City University of New York. She compiled an excellent early collection of articles on women in American history in 1973 (The Woman Question in American History) *and wrote* Dimity Convictions: The American Woman in the Nineteenth Century *(1976).*

Living in an age when many groups view confrontation as the most effective way of achieving progress, we must not read into the past a sense of conflict that was not there. However committed we may be to equal rights for women, we must realize that a major reason for the slow progress toward equal rights has been that the majority of women, perhaps even today, did not wish to change the system. Thus women activists had the disconcerting need to heighten women's conciousness before they would have enough strength to assault the bastions of male supremacy. Welter notes that in an age of rapid social change like that before the Civil War, men saw women as a crucial force

This reading is from American Quarterly, (Washington, D.C.: American Studies Association), volume 18 (1966), pp. 151–74. Copyright © 1966 by American Studies Association. Reprinted by permission from Barbara Welter.

for stability—and women accepted, and even embraced, that role. She concludes, however, that placing women on a pedestal carried the seeds of its own downfall: if women were so close to the angels, then they were logical choices to take active roles in the reform movements of the period—and that activism inexorably challenged their domesticity. Nevertheless, even today the "new woman" is torn by a culturally preserved allegiance to the "true womanhood" of the nineteenth century as she works for an egalitarian twenty-first.

It is important to keep in mind that this article deals primarily with "prescriptive" literature—that is, literature that tells how things are supposed to be. Often such prescriptive literature becomes increasingly rigid and defensive as the behavior it seeks to prescribe changes. A useful parallel for women would come in the 1950s when the "feminine mystique," in essence a revival of "true womanhood," was insistently preached even as women moved out of the home and into the job market. In other words, remember that prescription is not the same as description.

The nineteenth-century American man was a busy builder of bridges and railroads, at work long hours in a materialistic society. The religious values of his forebears were neglected in practice if not in intent, and he occasionally felt some guilt that he had turned this new land, this temple of the chosen people, into one vast countinghouse. But he could salve his conscience by reflecting that he had left behind a hostage, not only to fortune, but to all the values which he held so dear and treated so lightly. Woman, in the cult of True Womanhood presented by the women's magazines, gift annuals and religious literature of the nineteenth century, was the hostage in the home. In a society where values changed frequently, where fortunes rose and fell with frightening rapidity, where social and economic mobility provided instability as well as hope, one thing at least remained the same—a true woman was a true woman, wherever she was found. If anyone, male or female, dared to tamper with the complex of virtues which made up True Womanhood, he was damned immediately as an enemy of God, of civilization and of the Republic. It was a fearful obligation, a solemn responsibility, which the nineteenth-century American woman had—to uphold the pillars of the temple with her frail white hand.

The attributes of True Womanhood, by which a woman judged herself and was judged by her husband, her neighbors and society, could be divided into four cardinal virtues—piety, purity, submissiveness and domesticity. Put them all together and they spelled mother, daughter, sister, wife—woman. Without them, no matter whether there was fame, achievement or wealth, all was ashes. With them she was promised happiness and power.

Religion or piety was the core of woman's virtue, the source of her strength. Young men looking for a mate were cautioned to search first for piety, for if that were there, all else would follow. Religion belonged to woman by divine right, a gift of God and nature. This "peculiar susceptibility" to religion was given her for a reason: "the vestal flame of piety, lighted up by Heaven in the breast of woman," would throw its beams into the naughty world of men. So far would its candle power reach that the "Universe might be Enlightened, Improved, and Harmonized by WOMAN!!" She would be another, better Eve, working in cooperation with the Redeemer, bringing the world back "from its revolt and sin." The world would be reclaimed for God through her suffering, for "God increased the cares and sorrows of woman, that she might be sooner constrained to accept the terms of salvation." A popular poem by Mrs. Frances Osgood, "The Triumph of the Spiritual Over the Sensual," expressed just this sentiment, woman's purifying passionless love bringing an erring man back to Christ.

Dr. Charles Meigs, explaining to a graduating class of medical students why women were naturally religious, said that "hers is a pious mind. Her confiding nature leads her more readily than men to accept the proffered grace of the Gospel." Caleb Atwater, Esq., writing in *The Ladies' Repository,* saw the hand of the Lord in female piety: "Religion is exactly what a woman needs, for it gives her that dignity that best suits her dependence." And Mrs. John Sandford, who had no very high opinion of her sex, agreed thoroughly: "Religion is just what woman needs. Without it she is ever restless or unhappy. . . ." Mrs. Sandford and the others did not speak only of that restlessness of the human heart, which St. Augustine notes, that can only find its peace in God. They spoke rather of religion as a kind of tranquilizer for the many undefined longings which swept even the most pious young girl, and about which it was better to pray than to think.

One reason religion was valued was that it did not take a woman away from her "proper sphere," her home. Unlike participation in other societies or movement, church work would not make her less domestic or submissive, less a True Woman. In religious vineyards, said the *Young Ladies' Literary and Missionary Report,* "you may labor without the apprehension of detracting from the charms of feminine delicacy." Mrs. S. L. Dagg, writing from her chapter of the Society in Tuscaloosa, Alabama, was equally reassuring: "As no sensible woman will suffer her intellectual pursuits to clash with her domestic duties," she would concentrate on religious work "which promotes these very duties."

The women's seminaries aimed at aiding women to be religious, as well as accomplished. Mt. Holyoke's catalogue promised to make female education "a handmaid to the Gospel and an efficient auxiliary in the great task of renovating the world." The Young Ladies' Seminary at

Bordentown, New Jersey, declared its most important function to be "the forming of a sound and virtuous character." In Keene, New Hampshire, the Seminary tried to instill a "consistent and useful character" in its students, to enable them in this life to be "a good friend, wife and mother" but more important, to qualify them for "the enjoyment of Celestial Happiness in the life to come." And Joseph M. D. Mathews, Principal of Oakland Female Seminary in Hillsborough, Ohio, believed that "female education should be preeminently religious."

If religion was so vital to a woman, irreligion was almost too awful to contemplate. Women were warned not to let their literary or intellectual pursuits take them away from God. Sarah Josepha Hale spoke darkly of those who, like Margaret Fuller, threw away the "One True Book" for others, open to error. Mrs. Hale used the unfortunate Miss Fuller as fateful proof that "the greater the intellectual force, the greater and more fatal the errors into which women fall who wander from the Rock of Salvation, Christ the Saviour. . . ."

One gentleman, writing on "Female Irreligion," reminded his readers that "Man may make himself a brute, and does so very often, but can woman brutify herself to his level—the lowest level of human nature—without exerting special wonder?" Fanny Wright, because she was godless, "was no woman, mother though she be." A few years ago, he recalls, such women would have been whipped. In any case, "woman never looks lovelier than in her reverence for religion" and, conversely, "female irreligion is the most revolting feature in human character."

Purity was as essential as piety to a young woman, its absence as unnatural and unfeminine. Without it she was, in fact, no woman at all, but a member of some lower order. A "fallen woman" was a "fallen angel," unworthy of the celestial company of her sex. To contemplate the loss of purity brought tears; to be guilty of such a crime, in the women's magazines at least, brought madness or death. Even the language of the flowers had bitter words for it: a dried white rose symbolized "Death Preferable to Loss of Innocence." The marriage night was the single great event of a woman's life, when she bestowed her greatest treasure upon her husband, and from that time on was completely dependent upon him, an empty vessel, without legal or emotional existence of her own.

Therefore all True Women were urged, in the strongest possible terms, to maintain their virtue, although men, being by nature more sensual than they, would try to assault it. Thomas Branagan admitted in *The Excellency of the Female Character Vindicated* that his sex would sin and sin again, they could not help it, but woman, stronger and purer, must not give in and let man "take liberties incompatible with her delicacy." "If you do," Branagan addressed his gentle reader, "You will be left in silent sadness to bewail your credulity, imbecility, duplicity, and premature prostitution."

Mrs. Eliza Farrar, in *The Young Lady's Friend*, gave practical logistics to avoid trouble: "Sit not with another in a place that is too narrow; read not out of the same book; let not your eagerness to see anything induce you to place your head close to another person's."

If such good advice was ignored the consequences were terrible and inexorable. In *Girlhood and Womanhood: or, Sketches of My Schoolmates*, by Mrs. A. J. Graves (a kind of mid-nineteenth-century *The Group*), the bad ends of a boarding school class of girls are scrupulously recorded. The worst end of all is reserved for "Amelia Dorrington: The Lost One." Amelia died in the almshouse "the wretched victim of depravity and intemperance" and all because her mother had let her be "high-spirited not prudent." These girlish high spirits had been misinterpreted by a young man, with disastrous results. Amelia's "thoughtless levity" was "followed by a total loss of virtuous principle" and Mrs. Graves editorializes that "the coldest reserve is more admirable in a woman a man wishes to make his wife, than the least approach to undue familiarity."

A popular and often-reprinted story by Fanny Forester told the sad tale of "Lucy Dutton." Lucy "with the seal of innocence upon her heart, and a roseleaf on her cheek" came out of her vine-covered cottage and ran into a city slicker. "And Lucy was beautiful and trusting, and thoughtless, and he was gay, selfish and profligate. Needs the story to be told? . . . Nay, censor, Lucy was a child—consider how young, how very untaught—oh! her innocence was no match for the sophistry of a gay, city youth! Spring came and shame was stamped upon the cottage at the foot of the hill." The baby died; Lucy went mad at the funeral and finally died herself. "Poor, poor Lucy Dutton! The grave is a blessed couch and pillow to the wretched. Rest thee there, poor Lucy!" The frequency with which derangement follows loss of virtue suggests the exquisite sensibility of woman, and the possibility that, in the women's magazines at least, her intellect was geared to her hymen, not her brain.

If, however, a woman managed to withstand man's assaults on her virtue, she demonstrated her superiority and her power over him. Eliza Farnham, trying to prove this female superiority, concluded smugly that "the purity of women is the everlasting barrier against which the tides of man's sensual nature surge."

A story in *The Lady's Amaranth* illustrates this dominance. It is set, improbably, in Sicily, where two lovers, Bianca and Tebaldo, have been separated because her family insisted she marry a rich old man. By some strange circumstance the two are in a shipwreck and cast on a desert island, the only survivors. Even here, however, the rigid standards of True Womanhood prevail. Tebaldo unfortunately forgets himself slightly, so that Bianca must warn him: "We may not indeed gratify our fondness by caresses, but it is still something to bestow our kindest language, and looks and prayers, and all lawful and honest attentions on each other."

Something, perhaps, but not enough, and Bianca must further remonstrate: "It is true that another man is my husband, but you are my guardian angel." When even that does not work she says in a voice of sweet reason, passive and proper to the end, that she wishes he wouldn't but "still, if you insist, I will become what you wish; but I beseech you to consider, ere that decision, that debasement which I must suffer in your esteem." This appeal to his own double standards holds the beast in him at bay. They are rescued, discover that the old husband is dead, and after "mourning a decent season" Bianca finally gives in, legally.

Men could be counted on to be grateful when women thus saved them from themselves. William Alcott, guiding young men in their relations with the opposite sex, told them that "Nothing is better calculated to preserve a young man from contamination of low pleasures and pursuits than frequent intercourse with the more refined and virtuous of the other sex." And he added, one assumes in equal innocence, that youths should "observe and learn to admire, that purity and ignorance of evil which is the characteristic of well-educated young ladies, and which, when we are near them, raises us over men in their intercourse with each other."

The Rev. Jonathan F. Stearns was also impressed by female chastity in the face of male passion, and warned women never to compromise the source of her power: "Let her lay aside delicacy, and her influence over our sex is gone."

Women themselves accepted, with pride but suitable modesty, this priceless virtue. *The Ladies' Wreath*, in "Woman the Creature of God and the Manufacturer of Society," saw purity as her greatest gift and chief means of discharging her duty to save the world: "Purity is the highest beauty—the true pole-star which is to guide humanity aright in its long, varied, and perilous voyage."

Sometimes, however, a woman did not see the dangers to her treasure. In that case, they must be pointed out to her, usually by a male. In the nineteenth century any form of social change was tantamount to an attack on woman's virtue, if only it was correctly understood. For example, dress reform seemed innocuous enough and the bloomers worn by the lady of that name and her followers were certainly modest attire. Such was the reasoning only of the ignorant. In another issue of *The Ladies' Wreath* a young lady is represented in dialogue with her "Professor." The girl expresses admiration for the bloomer costume—it gives freedom of motion, is healthful and attractive. The "Professor" sets her straight. Trousers, he explains, are "only one of the many manifestations of that wild spirit of socialism and agrarian radicalism which is at present so rife in our land." The young lady recants immediately: "If this dress has any connection with Fourierism or Socialism, or fanaticism in any shape whatever, I have no disposition to wear it at all . . . no true woman would so far compromise her delicacy as to espouse, however unwittingly, such a cause."

America could boast that her daughters were particularly innocent. In a poem on "The American Girl" the author wrote proudly:

> Her eye of light is the diamond bright,
> Her innocence the pearl,
> And these are ever the bridal gems
> That are worn by the American girl.

Lydia Maria Child, giving advice to mothers, aimed at preserving that spirit of innocence. She regretted that "want of confidence between mothers and daughters on delicate subjects" and suggested a woman tell her daughter a few facts when she reached the age of twelve to "set her mind at rest." Then Mrs. Child confidently hoped that a young lady's "instinctive modesty" would "prevent her from dwelling on the information until she was called upon to use it." In the same vein, a book of advice to the newly married was titled *Whisper to a Bride*. As far as intimate information was concerned, there was no need to whisper, since the book contained none at all.

A masculine summary of this virtue was expressed in a poem "Female Charms":

> I would have her as pure as the snow on the mount—
>   As true as the smile that to infamy's given—
> As pure as the wave of the crystalline fount,
>   Yet as warm in the heart as the sunlight of heaven.
> With a mind cultivated, not boastingly wise,
>   I could gaze on such beauty, with exquisite bliss;
> With her heart on her lips and her soul in her eyes—
>   What more could I wish in dear woman than this.

Man might, in fact, ask no more than this in woman; but she was beginning to ask more of herself, and in the asking was threatening the third powerful and necessary virtue, submission. Purity, considered as a moral imperative, set up a dilemma which was hard to resolve. Woman must preserve her virtue until marriage and marriage was necessary for her happiness. Yet marriage was, literally, an end to innocence. She was told not to question this dilemma, but simply to accept it.

Submission was perhaps the most feminine virtue expected of women. Men were supposed to be religious, although they rarely had time for it, and supposed to be pure, although it came awfully hard to them, but men were the movers, the doers, the actors. Women were the passive, submissive responders. The order of dialogue was, of course, fixed in Heaven. Man was "woman's superior by God's appointment, if not in intellectual dowry, at least by official decree." Therefore, as Charles Elliott argued in *The Ladies' Repository,* she should submit to him "for the sake of good order at least." In *The Ladies Companion* a young wife was quoted approvingly as saying that she did not think woman should "feel and act for herself" because "When, next to God, her husband is not the tribunal to which her heart and intellect appeals—the golden bowl of affection is broken." Women were warned that if they tampered with this equality they tampered with the order of the Universe.

The Young Lady's Book summarized the necessity of the passive virtues in its readers' lives: "It is, however, certain, that in whatever situation of life a woman is placed from her cradle to her grave, a spirit of obedience and submission, pliability of temper, and humility of mind, are required from her."

Woman understood her position if she was the right kind of woman, a true woman. "She feels herself weak and timid. She needs a protector," declared George Burnap, in his lectures on *The Sphere and Duties of Woman.*

> She is in a measure dependent. She asks for wisdom, constancy, firmness, perseverance, and she is willing to repay it all by the surrender of the full treasure of her affections. Woman despises in man every thing like herself except a tender heart. It is enough that she is effeminate and weak; she does not want another like herself.

Or put even more strongly by Mrs. Sandford: "A really sensible woman feels her dependence. She does what she can, but she is conscious of inferiority, and therefore grateful for support."

Mrs. Sigourney, however, assured young ladies that although they were separate, they were equal. This difference of the sexes did not imply inferiority, for it was part of that same order of Nature established by Him "who bids the oak brave the fury of the tempest, and the alpine flower lean its cheek on the bosom of eternal snows." Dr. Meigs had a different analogy to make the same point, contrasting the anatomy of the Apollo of the Belvedere (illustrating the male principle) with the Venus de Medici (illustrating the female principle). "Woman," said the physician, with a kind of clinical gallantry, "has a head almost too small for intellect but just big enough for love."

This love itself was to be passive and responsive. "Love, in the heart of a woman," wrote Mrs. Farrar, "should partake largely of the nature of gratitude. She should love, because she is already loved by one deserving her regard."

Woman was to work in silence, unseen, like Wordsworth's Lucy. Yet, "working like nature, in secret" her love goes forth to the world "to regulate its pulsation, and send forth from its heart, in pure and temperate flow, the life-giving current." She was to work only for pure affection, without thought of money or ambition. A poem, "Woman and Fame," by Felicia Hemans, widely quoted in many of the gift books, concludes with a spirited renunciation of the gift of fame:

> Away! to me, a woman, bring
> Sweet flowers from affection's spring.

"True feminine genius," said Grace Greenwood (Sara Jane Clarke) "is ever timid, doubtful, and clingingly dependent; a perpetual childhood." And she advised literary ladies in an essay on "The Intellectual Woman"—"Don't trample on the flowers while longing for the stars." A wife who submerged her own talents to work for her husband was extolled as an example of a true woman. In *Women of Worth: A Book for Girls,* Mrs. Ann Flaxman, an artist of promise herself, was praised because she "devoted herself to sustain her husband's genius and aid him in his arduous career."

Caroline Gilman's advice to the bride aimed at establishing this proper order from the beginning of a marriage: "Oh, young and lovely bride, watch well the first moments when your will conflicts with his to whom God and society have given the control. Reverence his *wishes* even when you do not his *opinions.*"

Mrs. Gilman's perfect wife in *Recollections of a Southern Matron* realizes that "the three golden threads with which domestic happiness is woven" are "to repress a harsh answer, to confess a fault, and to stop (right or wrong) in the midst of self-defense, in gentle submission." Woman could do this, hard though it was, because in her heart she knew she was right and so could afford to be forgiving, even a trifle condescending. "Men are not unreasonable," averred Mrs. Gilman. "Their difficulties lie in not understanding the moral and physical nature of our sex. They often wound through ignorance, and are surprised at having offended." Wives were advised to do their best to reform men, but if they couldn't, to give up gracefully. "If any habit of his annoyed me, I spoke of it once or twice, calmly, then bore it quietly."

A wife should occupy herself "only with domestic affairs—wait till your husband confides to you those of a high importance—and do not give your advice until he asks for it," advised the *Lady's Token.* At all times she should behave in a manner becoming a woman, who had "no arms other than gentleness." Thus "if he is abusive, never retort," *A Young Lady's Guide to the Harmonious Development of a Christian Character* suggested that females should "become as little children" and "avoid a controversial spirit." *The Mother's Assistant and Young Lady's Friend* listed "Always Conciliate" as its first commandment in "Rules for Conjugal and Domestic Happiness." Small wonder that these same rules ended with succinct maxim: "Do not expect too much."

As mother, as well as wife, woman was required to submit to fortune. In *Letters to Mothers* Mrs. Sigourney sighed: "To bear the evils and sorrows which may be appointed us, with a patient mind, should be the continual effort of our sex. . . . It seems, indeed, to be expected of us; since the passive and enduring virtues are more immediately within our province." Of these trials "the hardest was to bear the loss of children with submission," but the indomitable Mrs. Sigourney found strength to murmur to the bereaved mother: "The Lord loveth a cheerful giver." *The Ladies' Parlor Companion* agreed thoroughly in "A Submissive Mother," in which a mother who had already buried two children and was nursing a dying baby saw her sole remaining child "probably scalded to death. Handing over the infant to die in the arms of a friend, she bowed in sweet submission to the double stroke." But the child "through the goodness of God survived, and the mother learned to say "Thy will be done."

Woman then, in all her roles, accepted submission as her lot. It was a lot she had not chosen or deserved. As *Godey's* said, "the lesson submission is forced upon woman." Without comment or criticism the writer affirms that "To suffer and to be silent under suffering seems the great command she has to obey." George Burnap referred to a woman's life as "a series of suppressed emotions." She was, as Emerson said, "more vulnerable, more infirm, more mortal than man." The death of a beautiful woman, cherished in fiction, represented woman as the innocent victim, suffering without sin, too pure and good for this world but too weak and passive to resist its evil forces. The best refuge for such a delicate creature was the warmth and safety of her home.

The true woman's place was unquestionably by her own fireside—as daughter, sister, but most of all as wife and mother. Therefore domesticity was among the virtues most prized by the women's magazines. "As society is constituted," wrote Mrs. S. E. Farley, on the "Domestic and Social Claims on Woman," "the true dignity and beauty of the female character seem to consist in a right understanding and faithful and cheerful performance of social and family duties." Sacred Scripture re-enforced social pressure: "St. Paul knew what was best for women when he advised them to be domestic," said Mrs. Sandford. "There is composure at home; there is something sedative in the duties which home involves. It affords security not only from the world, but from delusions and errors of every kind."

From her home woman performed her great task of bringing men back to God. *The Young Ladies' Class Book* was sure that "the domestic fireside is the great guardian of society against the excesses of human passions." *The Lady at Home* expressed its convictions in its very title and concluded that "even if we cannot reform the world in a moment, we can begin the work by reforming ourselves and our households—It is woman's mission. Let her not look away from her own little family circle for the means of producing moral and social reforms, but begin at home."

Home was supposed to be a cheerful place, so that brothers, husbands and sons would not go elsewhere in search of a good time. Woman was expected to dispense comfort and cheer. In writing the biography of Margaret Mercer (every inch a true woman) her biographer (male) notes: "She never forgot that it is the peculiar province of woman to minister to the comfort, and promote the happiness, first, of those most nearly allied to her, and then of those, who by the Providence of God are placed in a state of dependence upon her." Many other essays in the women's journals showed woman as comforter: "Woman, Man's Best Friend," "Woman, the Greatest Social Benefit," "Woman, A Being to Come Home To," "The Wife: Source of Comfort and the Spring of Joy."

One of the most important functions of woman as comforter was her role as nurse. Her own health was probably, although regrettably, delicate. Many homes had "little sufferers," those pale children who wasted away to saintly deaths. And there were enough other illnesses of youth and age, major and minor, to give the nineteenth-century American woman nursing experience. The sickroom called for the exercise of her higher qualities of patience, mercy and gentleness as well as for her housewifely arts. She could thus fulfill her dual feminine function—beauty and usefulness.

The cookbooks of the period offer formulas for gout cordials, ointment for sore nipples, hiccough and cough remedies, opening pills and refreshing drinks for fever, along with recipes for pound cake, jumbles, stewed calves head and currant wine. *The Ladies' New Book of Cookery* believed that "food prepared by the kind hand of a wife, mother, sister, friend" tasted better and had a "restorative power which money cannot purchase."

A chapter of *The Young Lady's Friend* was devoted to woman's privilege as "ministering spirit at the couch of the sick." Mrs. Farrar advised a soft voice, gentle and clean hands, and a cheerful smile. She also cautioned against an excess of female delicacy. That was all right for a young lady in the parlor, but not for bedside manners. Leeches, for example, were to be regarded as "a curious piece of mechanism . . . their ornamental stripes should recommend them even to the eye, and their valuable services to our feelings." And she went on calmly to discuss their use. Nor were women to shrink from medical terminology, since "If you cultivate right views of the wonderful structure of the body, you will be as willing to speak to a physician of the bowels as the brains of your patient."

Nursing the sick, particularly sick males, not only made a woman feel useful and accomplished, but increased her influence. In a piece of heavy-handed humor in *Godey's* a man confessed that some women were only happy when their husbands were ailing that they might have the joy of nursing him to recovery, "thus gratifying their medical vanity and their love of power by making him more dependent upon them." In a similar vein a husband sometimes suspected his wife "almost wishes me dead—for the pleasure of being utterly inconsolable."

In the home women were not only the highest adornment of civilization, but they were supposed to keep busy at morally uplifting tasks. Fortunately most of housework, if looked at in true womanly fashion, could be regarded as uplifting. Mrs. Sigourney extolled its virtues: "The science of housekeeping affords exercise for the judgment and energy, ready recollection, and patient self-possession, that are the characteristics of a superior mind." According to Mrs. Farrar, making beds was good exercise, the repetitiveness of routine tasks inculcated patience and perseverance, and proper management of the home was a surprisingly complex art: "There is more to be learned about pouring out tea and coffee, than most young ladies are willing to believe." *Godey's* went so far as to suggest coyly, in "Learning vs. Housewifery" that the two were complementary, not opposed: chemistry could be utilized in cooking, geometry in dividing cloth, and phrenology in discovering talent in children.

Women were to master every variety of needlework, for, as Mrs. Sigourney pointed out, "Needlework, in all its forms of use, elegance, and ornament, has ever been the appropriate occupation of woman." Embroidery improved taste; knitting promoted serenity and economy. Other forms of artsy-craftsy activity for her leisure moments included painting on glass or velvet, poonah work, tussy-mussy frames for her own needlepoint or water colors, stands for hyacinths, hair bracelets or baskets of feathers.

She was expected to have a special affinity for flowers. To the editors of *The Lady's Token*, "A Woman never appears more truly in her sphere, than when she divides her time between her domestic avocations and the culture of flowers." She could write letters, an activity particularly feminine since it had to do with the outpourings of the heart, or practice her drawingroom skills of singing and playing an instrument. She might even read.

Here she faced a bewildering array of advice. The female was dangerously addicted to novels, according to the literature of the period. She should avoid them, since they interfered with "serious piety." If she simply couldn't help herself and read them anyway, she should choose edifying ones from lists of morally acceptable authors. She should study history since it "showed the depravity of the human heart and the evil nature of sin." On the whole, "religious biography was best."

The women's magazines themselves could be read without any loss of concern for the home. *Godey's* promised the husband that he would find his wife "no less assiduous for his reception, or less sincere in welcoming his return" as a result of reading their magazine. *The Lily of the Valley* won its right to be admitted to the boudoir by confessing that it was "like its namesake humble and unostentatious, but it is yet pure, and, we trust, free from moral imperfections."

No matter what later authorities claimed, the nineteenth century knew that girls *could* be ruined by a book. The seduction stories regard "exciting and dangerous books" as contributory causes of disaster. The man without honorable intentions always provides the innocent maiden with such books as a prelude to his assault on her virtue. Books which attacked or seemed to attack woman's accepted place in society were regarded as equally dangerous. A reviewer of Harriet Martineau's *Society in America* wanted it kept out of the hands of American women. They were so susceptible to persuasion, with their "gentle yielding natures," that they might listen to "the bold ravings of the hard-featured of their own sex." The frightening result: "such reading will unsettle them for their true station and pursuits, and they will throw the world back again into confusion."

The debate over women's education posed the question of whether a "finished" education detracted from the practice of housewifely arts. Again it proved to be a case of semantics, for a true woman's education was never "finished" until she was instructed in the gentle science of homemaking. Helen Irving, writing on "Literary Women," made it very clear that if women invoked the muse, it was a genie of the household lamp. "If the necessities of her position require these duties at her hands, she will perform them nonetheless cheerfully, that she knows herself capable of higher things." The literary woman must conform to the same standards as any other woman: "That her home shall be made a loving place of rest and joy and comfort for those who are dear to her, will be the first wish of every true woman's heart." Mrs. Ann Stephens told women who wrote to make sure they did not sacrifice one domestic duty. "As for genius, make it a domestic plant. Let its roots strike deep in your home. . . ."

The fear of "blue stockings" (the eighteenth-century male's term of derision for educated or literary women) need not persist for nineteenth-century American men. The magazines presented spurious dialogues in which bachelors were convinced of their fallacy in fearing educated wives. One such dialogue took place between a young man and his female cousin. Ernest deprecates learned ladies ("A *Woman* is far more lovable than a *philosopher*") but Alice refutes him with the beautiful example of their Aunt Barbara who "although she *has* perpetrated the heinous crime of writing some half dozen folios" is still a model of "the spirit of feminine gentleness." His memory prodded, Ernest concedes that, by George, there was a woman: "When I last had a cold she not only made me a bottle of cough syrup, but when I complained of nothing new to read, set to work and wrote some twenty stanzas on consumption."

The magazines were filled with domestic tragedies in which spoiled young girls learned that when there was a hungry man to feed

French and china painting were not helpful. According to these stories many a marriage is jeopardized because the wife has not learned to keep house. Harriet Beecher Stowe wrote a sprightly piece of personal experience for *Godey's*, ridiculing her own bad housekeeping as a bride. She used the same theme in a story, "The Only Daughter," in which the pampered beauty learns the facts of domestic life from a rather difficult source, her mother-in-law. Mrs. Hamilton tells Caroline in the sweetest way possible to shape up in the kitchen, reserving her rebuke for her son: "You are her husband—her guide—her protector—now see what you can do," she admonishes him. "Give her credit for every effort; treat her faults with tenderness; encourage and praise whenever you can, and depend upon it, you will see another woman in her." He is properly masterful, she properly domestic and in a few months Caroline is making lumpless gravy and keeping up with the darning. Domestic tranquility has been restored and the young wife moralizes: "Bring up a girl to feel that she has a responsible part to bear in promoting the happiness of the family, and you make a reflecting being of her at once, and remove that lightness and frivolity of character which makes her shrink from graver studies." These stories end with the heroine drying her hands on her apron and vowing that *her* daughter will be properly educated, in piecrust as well as Poonah work.

The female seminaries were quick to defend themselves against any suspicion of interfering with the role which nature's God had assigned to women. They hoped to enlarge and deepen that role, but not to change its setting. At the Young Ladies' Seminary and Collegiate Institute in Monroe City, Michigan, the catalogue admitted few of its graduates would be likely "to fill the learned professions." Still, they were called to "other scenes of usefulness and honor." The average woman is to be "the presiding genius of love" in the home, where she is to "give a correct and elevated literary taste to her children, and to assume that influential station that she ought to possess as the companion of an educated man."

At Miss Pierce's famous school in Litchfield, the students were taught that they had "attained the perfection of their characters when they could combine their elegant accomplishments with a turn for solid domestic virtues." Mt. Holyoke paid pious tribute to domestic skills: "Let a young lady despise this branch of the duties of woman, and she despises the appointments of her existence." God, nature and the Bible "enjoin these duties on the sex, and she cannot violate them with impunity." Thus warned, the young lady would have to seek knowledge of these duties elsewhere, since it was not in the curriculum at Mt. Holyoke. "We would not take this privilege from the mother."

One reason for knowing her way around a kitchen was that America was "a land of precarious fortunes," as Lydia Maria Child pointed out in her book *The Frugal Housewife: Dedicated to Those Who Are Not Ashamed of*

Economy. Mrs. Child's chapter "How To Endure Poverty" prescribed a combination of piety and knowledge—the kind of knowledge found in a true woman's education, "a thorough religious *useful* education." The woman who had servants today, might tomorrow, because of a depression or panic, be forced to do her own work. If that happened she knew how to act, for she was to be the same cheerful consoler of her husband in their cottage as in their mansion.

An essay by Washington Irving, much quoted in the gift annuals, discussed the value of a wife in case of business reverses:

> I have observed that a married man falling into misfortune is more apt to achieve his situation in the world than a single one . . . it is beautifully ordained by providence that woman, who is the ornament of man in his happier hours, should be his stay and solace when smitten with sudden calamity.

A story titled simply but eloquently "The Wife" dealt with the quiet heroism of Ellen Graham during her husband's plunge from fortune to poverty. Ned Graham said of her: "Words are too poor to tell you what I owe to that noble woman. In our darkest seasons of adversity, she has been an angel of consolation—utterly forgetful of self and anxious only to comfort and sustain me." Of course she had a little help from "faithful Dinah who absolutely refused to leave her beloved mistress," but even so Ellen did no more than would be expected of any true woman.

Most of this advice was directed to woman as wife. Marriage was the proper state for the exercise of the domestic virtues. "True Love and a Happy Home," an essay in *The Young Ladies' Oasis,* might have been carved on every girl's hope chest. But although marriage was best, it was not absolutely necessary. The women's magazines tried to remove the stigma from being an "Old Maid." They advised no marriage at all rather than an unhappy one contracted out of selfish motives. Their stories showed maiden ladies as unselfish ministers to the sick, teachers of the young, or moral preceptors with their pens, beloved of the entire village. Usually the life of single blessedness resulted from the premature death of a fiance, or was chosen through fidelity to some high mission. For example, in "Two Sisters," Mary devotes herself to Ellen and her abandoned children, giving up her own chance for marriage. "Her devotion to her sister's happiness has met its reward in the consciousness of having fulfilled a sacred duty." Very rarely, a "woman of genius" was absolved from the necessity of marriage, being so extraordinary that she did not need the security or status of being a wife. Most often, however, if girls proved "difficult," marriage and a family were regarded as a cure. The "sedative quality" of a home could be counted on to subdue even the most restless spirits.

George Burnap saw marriage as "that sphere for which woman was originally intended, and to which she is so exactly fitted to adorn and bless, as the wife, the mistress of a home, the solace, the aid, and the counsellor of the ONE, for whose sake alone the world is of any consequence to her." Samuel Miller preached a sermon on women:

> How interesting and important are the duties on devolved on females as WIVES . . . the counsellor and friend of the husband; who makes it her daily study to lighten his cares, to soothe his sorrows, and to augment his joys; who, like a guardian angel, watches over his interests, warns him against dangers, comforts him under trials; and by her pious, assiduous, and attractive deportment, constantly endeavors to render him more virtuous, more useful, more honourable, and more happy.

A woman's whole interest should be focused on her husband, paying him "those numberless attentions to which the French give the title of *Petits soins* and which the woman who loves knows so well how to pay . . . she should consider nothing as trivial which could win a smile of approbation from him."

Marriage was seen not only in terms of service but as an increase in authority for woman. Burnap concluded that marriage improves the female character "not only because it puts her under the best possible tuition, that of the affections, and affords scope to her active energies, but because it gives her higher aims, and a more dignified position." *The Lady's Amaranth* saw it as a balance of power: "The man bears rule over his wife's person and conduct. She bears rule over his inclinations: he governs by law; she by persuasion. . . . The empire of the woman is an empire of softness . . . her commands are caresses, her menaces are tears."

Woman should marry, but not for money. She should choose only the high road of true love and not truckle to the values of a materialistic society. A story "Marrying for Money" (subtlety was not the strong point of the ladies' magazines) depicts Gertrude, the heroine, rueing the day she made her crass choice: "It is a terrible thing to live without love . . . A woman who dares marry for aught but the purest affection, calls down the just judgments of heaven upon her head."

The corollary to marriage, with or without true love, was motherhood, which added another dimension to her usefulness and her prestige. It also anchored her even more firmly to the home. "My Friend," wrote Mrs. Sigourney, "If in becoming a mother, you have reached the climax of your happiness, you have also taken a higher place in the scale of being . . . you have gained an increase in power." The Rev. J. N. Danforth pleaded in *The Ladies' Casket*, "Oh, mother, acquit thyself well in they humble sphere, for thou mayest affect the world." A true woman naturally loved her children; to suggest otherwise was monstrous.

America depended upon her mothers to raise up a whole generation of Christian statesmen who could say "all that I am I owe to my angel mother." The mothers must do the inculcating of virtue since the fathers, alas, were too busy chasing the dollar. Or as *The Ladies' Companion* put it more effusively, the father, "weary with the heat and burden of life's summer day, or trampling with unwilling foot the decaying leaves of life's autumn, has forgotten the sympathies of life's joyous spring-time. . . . The acquisition of wealth, the advancement of his children in worldly honor—these are his self-imposed tasks." It was his wife who formed "the infant mind as yet untainted by contact with evil . . . like was beneath the plastic hand of the mother."

The Ladies' Wreath offered a fifty-dollar prize to the woman who submitted the most convincing essay on "How May An American Woman Best Show Her Patriotism." The winner was Miss Elizabeth Wetherell, who provided herself with a husband in her answer. The wife in the essay of course asked her husband's opinion. He tried a few jokes first— "Call her eldest son George Washington," "Don't speak French, speak American"—but then got down to telling her in sober prize-winning truth what women could do for their country. Voting was no asset, since that would result only in "a vast increase of confusion and expense without in the smallest degree affecting the result." Besides, continued this oracle, "looking down at their child," if "we were to go a step further and let the children vote, their first act would be to vote their mothers at home." There is no comment on this devastating male logic and he con-tinues: "Most women would follow the lead of their fathers and hus-bands," and the few who would "fly off on a tangent from the circle of home influence would cancel each other out."

The wife responds dutifully: "I see all that. I never understood so well before." Encouraged by her quick womanly perception, the master of the house resolves the question—an American woman best shows her patriotism by staying at home, where she brings her influence to bear "upon the right side for the country's weal." That woman will in-stinctively choose the side of right he has no doubt. Beside her "natural refinement and closeness to God" she has the "blessed advantage of a quiet life" while man is exposed to conflict and evil. She stays home with "her Bible and a well-balanced mind" and raises her sons to be good Americans. The judges rejoiced in this conclusion and paid the prize money cheerfully, remarking "they deemed it cheap at the price."

If any woman asked for greater scope for her gifts the magazines were sharply critical. Such women were tampering with society, under-mining civilization. Mary Wollstonecraft, Frances Wright and Harriet Martineau were condemned in the strongest possible language—they were read out of the sex. "They are only semi-women, mental hermaph-rodites." The Rev. Harrington knew the women of America could not possibly approve of such perversions and went to some wives and moth-ers to ask if they did want a "wider sphere of interest" as these nonwomen claimed. The answer was reassuring. "'No!' they cried simultaneously, 'Let the men take care of politics, *we will take care of the children!*'" Again female discontent resulted only from a lack of understanding: women were not subservient, they were rather "chosen vessels." Looked at in this light the conclusion was inescapable: "Noble, sublime is the task of the American mother."

"Women's Rights" meant one thing to reformers, but quite another to the True Woman. She knew her rights,

> The right to love whom others scorn,
> The right to comfort and to mourn,
> The right to shed new joy on earth,
> The right to feel the soul's high worth . . .
> Such women's rights, and God will bless
> And crown their champions with success.

The American woman had her choice—she could define her rights in the way of the women's magazines and insure them by the practice of the requisite virtues, or she could go outside the home, seeking other rewards than love. It was a decision on which she was told, everything in her world depended. "Yours it is to determine," the Rev. Mr. Stearns solemnly warned from the pulpit, "whether the beautiful order of society . . . shall continue as it has been" or whether "society shall break up and become a chaos of disjointed and unsightly elements." If she chose to listen to other voices than those of her proper mentors, sought other rooms than those of her home, she lost both her happiness and her power—"that almost magic power, which, in her proper sphere, she now wields over the destinies of the world."

But even while the women's magazines and related literature encouraged this ideal of the perfect woman, forces were at work in the nineteenth century which impelled woman herself to change, to play a more creative role in society. The movements for social reform, westward migration, missionary activity, utopian communities, industrialism, the Civil War—all called forth responses from woman which differed from those she was trained to believe were hers by nature and divine decree. The very perfection of True Womanhood, moreover, carried within itself the seeds of its own destruction. For if woman was so very little less than the angels, she should surely take a more active part in running the world, especially since men were making such a hash of things.

Real women often felt they did not live up to the ideal of True Womanhood: some of them blamed themselves, some challenged the standard, some tried to keep the virtues and enlarge the scope of womanhood. Somehow through this mixture of challenge and acceptance, of change and continuity, the True Woman evolved into the New Woman—a transformation as startling in its way as the abolition of slavery or the coming of the machine age. And yet, the stereotype, the "mystique" if you will, of what woman was and ought to be persisted, bringing guilt and confusion in the midst of opportunity.

The women's magazines and related literature had feared this very dislocation of values and blurring of roles. By careful manipulation and interpretation they sought to convince woman that she had the best of both worlds—power and virtue—and that a stable order of society depended upon her maintaining her traditional place in it. To that end she identified with everything that was beautiful and holy.

"Who Can Find a Valiant Woman?" was asked frequently from the pulpit and the editorial pages. There was only one place to look for her—at home. Clearly and confidently these authorities proclaimed the True Woman of the nineteenth century to be the Valiant Woman of the Bible, in whom the heart of her husband rejoiced and whose price was above rubies.

12

Men and Women in the Rural American West

John Mack Faragher

John Mack Faragher (1945   ), a professor of history at Mt. Holyoke College, earned his bachelor's degree at the University of California, Riverside, and his doctorate from Yale. His areas of research interest are sex and gender in history and midwestern American society and culture. He combined those two topics in his insightful book Women and Men on the Overland Trail *(1979).*

Faragher disputes the widely held theory that rural women, working side by side with their husbands and struggling with them to succeed economically, achieved both a greater sense of self-worth and the reality of equality. Drawing upon the writings of frontier women (and particularly those who went, almost all reluctantly, on the great trek to the West Coast), Faragher finds that the inequality of the sexes in social relations (women bound to the home and the children, men free to work or wander) formed the foundation of patriarchy and masculine power. When eastern ideologies of "true womanhood" did make it west, they simply reinforced existing and traditional roles. The coming of a

This reading, "Men and Women in the Rural American West," by John Mack Faragher, is published by Yale University Press. Reprinted by permission.

commercial farming economy after the Civil War made matters worse, further separating earning power (and resultant freedom) from the household. Indeed, the "frontier" of opportunity for women, with all due respect to Frederick Jackson Turner, was the city, where women would finally have the opportunity to earn their own money outside the home.

In terms of shaping the feminine American character, preurban changes in society afforded precious little opportunity for women outside the parameters of "true womanhood." Only in the twentieth century would women be able to begin to forge an independent character of their own.

From one perspective all marriages can be viewed as practical relationships for performing the domestic labor of society. The relationships of these midwestern men and women, however, had this practical function at their centers: they were partnerships in production, processing, and consumption. The economic relations of family members to one another held families together and rooted them in the social order.

Until the Civil War the working lives of most midwesterners were shaped by two preeminent facts: first, the relative isolation of their homesteads from markets and their households from neighbors; and second, the dependence of farm labor on hand-tool technology. These two factors meant that most production was for use and that most families were oriented to internal economic processes. A revolution in midwestern agriculture began in the years just preceding the Civil War, was greatly accelerated by wartime demand, and was consolidated by massive movements of people and capital during the postbellum period. But in the meantime most midwestern families lived on a level where the economics of subsistence, not the demands of the market, set the structure of relations among men, women, and children.

In this context the familial division of labor by sex was the basic social division of labor as well; the overall differences between men's and women's work were greater than the differences among the work of all midwestern men. Women worked in domestic space but in addition performed from a third to a half of the productive work of the farm. Farm wives were responsible for the dairy (milk, butter, and cheese), the henhouse (eggs and roasters), the garden (all the fresh vegetables for table and many of those preserved for cold months), and in the earlier years for a textile crop of cotton or flax. Until mid-century, midwestern women spun those fibers into yarn, wove the yarn into cloth, and cut the cloth for home-sewn family clothing. Beginning in the fifties homespun was gradually replaced by store-bought calico and gingham, but clothes were still tailored at home by skillful feminine hands. Men controlled the surrounding homestead, produced an essential corn crop for consumption and as large a marketable grain crop as possible, raised a herd of hogs and some sheep, tended the farm stock, cleared and plowed the land, built, repaired, and decided when to leave it all for a new location.

Corresponding with these economic realities and work relationships, people viewed marriage as the central relationship of a happy homestead. The culture decreed women to be helping wives and loving mothers, men productive farmers and protective husbands and fathers. The reciprocity of the homestead portrayed the kind of marriage to which men and women aspired: a dutiful and responsible partnership of labor, from which grew feelings of connection and affection.

But there was little sense of marriage as life's grand companionship. Indeed, there seems to have been little appreciation of companionate values. Men and women tended to see romance as a dangerous basis for a stable relationship; passion they judged obstructive to the practical tasks of building a solid marriage. And for both men and women, the strongest and most significant social connections, that is, those connections linking them with social units larger than the family, were accomplished not by couples, but by same-sex groupings: in male gatherings from working bees to local elections, and in female communications at quiltings or around the delivery bed.

Nonetheless, the family was the most critical social unit for men and women alike. Without marriages there could be no homesteads, no family to cook and sew for, no family to raise a house for. The first step in coming to terms with adult identity was facing marriage and the family. Those who failed in marriage failed in life.

Having paid our kudos to family values, however, we must immediately recognize the inequity of men's and women's situation in marriage. The spaces of the sexes were not only separate but intrinsically unequal. Men enjoyed the means for wide social communication; it was their responsibility to use that means in their capacity as heads of household in a patriarchal society ostensibly governed by heads of household. Women, on the other hand, as one woman's song lamented, were

> always controlled, they're always confined.
> Controlled by their family until they are wives,
> Then slaves to their husbands the rest of their lives.

Women played no public roles but remained in their domestic spaces, in a mild kind of rural American purdah.

The relative inequality of the sexes in their social relations was the foundation of patriarchy, of masculine power and prerogatives. Even under conditions of the simplest agricultural economy, even under conditions of pure subsistence, the division of labor which confined women to the household implied an unequal division of power and authority. In all agricultural societies, women are more or less excluded from the public world. "The overall status of women in agriculture or peasant society is one of institutionalized dependency, subordination and political immaturity." In its unequal division of power between men and women, then, the Midwest was typical of settled agricultural societies.

To be sure, farm women's ills were exacerbated by the growth of the market, for under commercial pressures gender divisions were widened, men's economic activity was further divorced from the household, and family economic unity shattered; for farm women there was, in consequence, a further devaluation of their already questionable status. But let there be no mistake, male privilege was an aspect of the cultural heritage of the land, expanded, not created, by the growth of capitalist market forces. Lacking in public roles, women were dependent upon men, while men enjoyed considerable responsibility and latitude in their social relations. The presence of children placed the imprimatur of biology on the arrangement and provided male privilege with a natural cover: women were viewed as inherently responsible for domestic society, while men were free to work or wander.

The gender cultures of man to man and woman to woman must be interpreted in the light of these family matters. Woman-to-woman contacts stressed empathy and support, for farm women perceived their life stations as hard ones to be endured, but endured best with the sympathy of sisters. Abigail Scott Duniway remembered her mother, Ann Scott, whispering painfully at the birth of yet another daughter (her ninth child, her twelfth delivery): "Poor baby! She'll be a woman someday! Poor baby! A woman's lot is so hard!" Needing support but lacking social contacts, women clung to their feminine kin and neighbors. Lacking time to socialize, women developed the power of language; they communicated a feminine lore rich with sayings and aphorisms which conveyed the power of feminine support in the loneliest of isolated hours.

There was, as well, an ideal of women's behavior and belief which corresponded with women's social situation. Women were to be sensitive to manners, morals, and the feelings of others. Western women's actual social roles as mothers, wives, and sisters were sufficient to justify the cultural production of these models. Eastern ideologies of femininity certainly filtered into the West, but they simply reinforced the existing traditional roles.

Men's contacts with one another were more communal, open, and exaggerated. Men's character types corresponded: they were rough, aggressive, and egotistic. Occasions of male solidarity included celebratory spectacles of masculine power. Men's relations with one another, however, were double-faced; behind the hail-fellow engagement lurked a competitive spirit that proffered a willingness and desire to succeed, even at the expense of others. Moreover, through the mechanism of the market men conceived a way to realize their longed-for success. The competitive spirit of frontier masculinity was only a railroad and a reaper away from the competitive economy of small capitalist farmers.

Masculine culture fostered the growth of another kind of spirit. Men took as their models the Indian-fighting frontiersmen they imagined their fathers and grandfathers to have been. They longed for a similar test of their own masculinity. Thus they were driven to experiences such as the overland emigration, for on the trail they would be following, as it were, the blazes of previous masculine generations.

In the emigration to the Far West we see some of these factors working in consort—and in conflict. Oregon was a place to take families, because Oregon was a place for homesteading. California, of course, offered gold and prompted a mass male movement otherwise seen only during wars or revolutions. But the miners went as sojourners, not as emigrants; the mining population was transient, and in nonmining areas a more normal sex ratio recurred within ten years of the rush. California, too, was largely a place men went with families—or wished they had.

Men took their families to claim new, richer farmlands, to raise cash crops, and to exploit new markets (the mines, the Orient, or the ports of the world). These were men with dreams of success, but most were not yet successful. They left the isolated Midwest, as their forebears had left the Atlantic, just before their former homes were entangled by commercial connections. But these emigrant men also took their families because they were in part living out a continuing male adventure of life on the wild fringes of society, an adventure entirely masculine. In short, for men, the overland emigration was an archetypal nineteenth-century event, for it was conceived in the spirit of progress, publicly designated to fulfill economic goals, yet infused and overlaid with male projections and identifications.

Most women, for their part, only reluctantly participated in these male fantasies. They went because of the terms of obedience which marriage had imposed and which they had accepted. Their presence and work, however, made the emigration a family matter, and unattached men applied for the privilege of accompanying every family. Women on the trail were a source of great strength to the parties.

Some have suggested that women's working roles on the trail and, in general, women's productive roles on their frontier farms contributed to a relative equality between sexes. "Generally speaking," Caroline Bird writes, "frontier conditions . . . have motivated men and women to similar or androgynous goals." "When Eastern ladies were fainting at a coarse word or vulgar sight," Page Smith offers, "their Western sisters fought off Indians, ran cattle, made homes and raised children in the wilderness. It was in the West, in consequence, that women had the greatest status." Both Smith and Bird have borrowed their views from Arthur Calhoun, with whose opinions, in matters of American family history, one has always to contend.

> The frontier helped to liberalize the American family. . . . Women stood by their husbands' side and fought for life and little ones against human and other foes. Ladies whose husbands lost everything threw aside ease and luxury and fared boldly into the far West where they endured without complaint toils, danger, sickness and loneliness. Reciprocity in the marriage relation was the logical consequence where woman bore a man's share in the struggle for existence.

This was hardly the assessment of contemporaries. Emigrant women, in their own evaluation, came much closer to the spirit of the frontier aphorism; "This country is all right for men and dogs, but it's hell on women and horses." Perhaps not everyone joined in that consensus, but male and female opinion on the question of the status of women conjoined in a curious but revealing manner. John Ludlum McConnel, in his book of frontier description and proscription, described the frontier wife from the masculine perspective:

> There is no coyness, no blushing, no pretense of fright or nervousness—if you will, no romance—for which the husband has reason to be thankful! The wife knows what her duties are and resolutely goes about performing them. She never dreamed, nor twaddled, about "love in a cottage," or "the sweet communion of congenial souls" (who never eat anything): and she is, therefore, not disappointed on discovering that life is actually a serious thing. She never whines about "making her husband happy"—but sets firmly and sensibly about making him *comfortable*. She cooks his dinner, nurses his children, shares his hardships, and encourages his industry. She never complains of not having too much work to do, she does not desert her home to make endless visits—she borrows no misfortunes, has no imaginary ailings. Milliners and mantua-makers she ignores—"shopping" she never heard of—scandal she never invents or listens to. She never wishes for fine carriages, professes no inability to walk five hundred yards, and does not think it a "vulgar accomplishment" to know how to make butter. She has no groundless anxieties, she is not nervous about her children taking cold: a doctor is a visionary potentate to her—a drug-shop is a depot of abominations. She never forgets whose wife she is,—there is no "sweet confidante" without whom she "can not live"—she never writes endless letters about nothing. She is, in short, a faithful, honest wife: and, in "due time" the husband must make *more* "three-legged stools"—for the "tow-heads" have now covered them all!

Women, when given the chance to speak up for themselves, could describe the same situation from a very different angle. Abigail Scott Duniway, herself an Oregon emigrant of 1853, spoke for farm women when she said a frontier farmer's wife "has to be lady, nurse, laundress, seamstress, cook and dairy-woman by turns, and . . . attends to all these duties unaided, save by the occasional assistance of an indulgent husband who has cares enough of his own." Compare her version of the frontier woman:

> It was a hospitable neighborhood composed chiefly of bachelors, who found comfort in mobilizing at meal time at the homes of the few married men of the township, and seemed especially fond of congregating at the hospitable cabin home of my good husband, who was never quite so much in his glory as when entertaining men at his fireside, while I, if not washing, scrubbing, churning, or nursing the baby, was preparing their meals in our lean-to kitchen. To bear two children in two and a half years from my marriage day, to make thousands of pounds of butter every year for market, not including what was used in our free hotel at home; to sew and cook, and wash and iron; to bake and clean and stew and fry; to be, in short, a general pioneer drudge, with never a penny of my own, was not a pleasant business. . . . My recreation during those monotonous years was wearing out my wedding clothes, or making over for my cherished babies the bridal outfit. . . .
>
> My good husband was not idle; he was making a farm in the timber and keeping a lot of hired men, for whom I cooked and washed and mended, as part of the duties of a pioneer wife and devoted mother.
>
> As I look back over those weary years, the most lingering of my many regrets is the fact that I was often compelled to neglect my little children, while spending my time in the kitchen, or at the churn or wash tub, doing heavy work for the hale and hearty men—work for which I was poorly fitted, chiefly because my faithful mother had worn both me and herself to a frizzle with just such drudgery before I was born.

When Mr. Duniway decided to mortgage their homestead to raise cash for improvements, Abigail remembered:

> It dawned on me suddenly as I was picking a duck that it would ruin us financially if those notes were signed. I tried hard to be silent, being a nonentity in law, but my hands trembled, my heart beat hard, and I laid the pinioned duck on its back and repaired to the living room to investigate. My husband had already signed two notes, and was in the act of signing the third, when I leaned over his shoulder and said, tremulously: "My dear, are you quite certain about what you are doing?" The other fellow looked daggers at me, but said nothing, and my husband answered, as he signed the last note, "Mama, you needn't worry; you'll always be protected and provided for!" I wanted to say: "I guess I'll always earn all the protection I get," but I remembered that I was nothing but a woman; so I bit my lips to keep silent and rushed back to my work, where for several minutes, I fear that duck flesh suffered, for I didn't pluck the feathers tenderly.

There is, in these sexually different perspectives, a reflection of a single reality: the domestic confinement and hard toil of women. Where McConnel and Duniway differed was in their respective estimations of the worth to women in being kept barefoot and pregnant. Some modern observers have noted western women's importance to production and jumped to the conclusion that in consequence their rewards were greater and their equality with men more complete. But in fact the frontier extended the impact that agricultural settings have historically had on relations between the sexes: with men controlling the access to society and controlling the products that were potentially exchangeable on the market, they controlled the acquisition of power and status as well; women, confined to the domestic space, left without social power, were dependent for status upon their relations with their husbands.

The winds of change were blowing in other quarters. In the cities and the industrial countrysides of the East there were growing opportunities for women's employment outside the home—an entry into the public world. Practical equality of the sexes was, and is yet, to be achieved in the social production of the modern world just then being born. The move West called upon people not to change but to transfer old sexual roles to a new but altogether familiar environment.

13

The Know-Nothings

Thomas Horrocks

Thomas Horrocks, holder of a master's degree in history from Villanova University, here raises a topic from the darker side of the American character. Nativism, the fear of and resistance to ideas and peoples different from the American norm, is an emotional movement that ebbs and flows with the passing of years. The antebellum period saw its most powerful direct expression in the American party, but it would crest again in the 1920s and enjoy considerable success through the passage of the National Origins Act in 1924, cutting the flow of nontraditional immigrants to a trickle.

American historians of the past generation have increasingly tended to view politics and the political parties as functions of ethno-cultural factors more than economic or ideological beliefs. While the Democrats had historically been the party most open to non-Anglo immigrants, the Federalists and then the Whigs attracted persons of English extraction and Puritan religious roots —in other words, establishment Americans. When the Whigs split over the slavery issue after

This reading is reprinted by permission of Cowles Magazines Inc., publisher of *American History Illustrated,* January 1983.

the 1852 election, Northern Whigs joined with antislavery Democrats to organize the Republican party. Southern Whigs were adrift. In 1856 they coalesced as the Know-Nothings, then faded. In 1860 they comprised the bulk of the Constitutional Union party. When the Democrats also split over slavery in 1860, they paved the way for Lincoln's victory for the Republicans, and the Civil War ensued.

After Reconstruction, the Southern Whigs continued to be in a quandary. They could not rejoin their ideological soulmates, the Republicans, for that party was anathema in the South because of its role in the war and its aftermath. They lacked sufficient strength to succeed alone. And so, almost by default, they drifted into the Democratic party in the South, and for a century they have contributed to the ideological conservatism and tendency toward nativism of Southern Democrats. Thus, the post-1938 congressional alliance between Republicans and Southern Democrats represents not an aberration but, in essence, a reestablishment of the old Whigs.

In this 1983 article, Horrocks explains how antiforeignism, mixed with longstanding anti-Catholicism, combined to produce the American party, a negative idea wrapping itself in the guise of patriotism — true Americanism. These feelings still lurk in the American character today, generally below the surface, but sometimes erupting in ugly incidents of bigotry.

On the evening of June 22, 1856, former President Millard Fillmore arrived in New York City from a triumphant European tour. A rousing welcome, complete with fireworks and cannon-fire, greeted the former chief executive as his ship, the *Atlantic*, docked.

The several thousand spectators who waited on the pier were there not so much to welcome home their ex-president as to greet their presidential candidate. Fillmore, who had served in the Executive Mansion as a member of the Whig party, was now running for that high office again under the banner of a different party. He was the standard bearer for the American party, popularly known as the "Know-Nothings."

In the bitter presidential campaign of 1856, Fillmore and the Know-Nothings stressed Union over sectional politics. Unionism, however, was not the issue that elevated the Know-Nothings into a position of political prominence. They owed their extraordinary ascent to nativism, an issue equally as explosive as that of slavery in the decades prior to the Civil War.

The Know-Nothing party came into existence in response to the growing influence of both the Catholic church and the immigrant in American life. The political form that nativism embraced in mid-19th-century America was a culmination of more than two centuries of hostility between Protestants and Roman Catholics.

The roots of this hostile relationship reach back to the Protestant Reformation. The first colonists who sailed to America in the 17th century carried with their luggage an intense distrust of Roman Catholicism. This attitude, transported from England and the Continent, pervaded all levels of colonial life. A perfect example of this fact is that, as late as 1700, Catholics were denied full civil and religious rights in all of the colonies except Rhode Island.

This sentiment toward Roman Catholicism rested on a belief held by many Protestants that the Church of Rome was closely linked with monarchism and reaction. During the period of the Early Republic many Americans regarded Catholicism as the antithesis of their democratic ideals. However, during those early years Roman Catholics made up a small part of the population.

But the Catholic church started to exhibit signs of rapid expansion during the 1830s. In the next two decades, five million immigrants, many of them Catholics from Germany and Ireland, sailed to America.

Inspired by an expanding membership, the Catholic hierarchy shed its timid and retiring image, and adopted a more confident and aggressive attitude. Catholic bishops throughout the country, led by Archbishop John Hughes of New York, began to demand legislation favorable to the Church. Catholic church leaders called for the elimination of Bible reading in the public schools, and the division of public school funds to aid a parochial school system. Many Protestants reacted with alarm, believing these demands to be a direct attack on two cherished American institutions, the Bible and the public school system.

In response to the active Catholic position, nativist organizations first started to appear in the 1830s and continued to multiply during the next two decades. Newspapers, pamphlets, and books, all warning of the perils of Catholicism, poured out from the presses into the hands of a receptive public. Whether in a sermon from the pulpit or a speech from the podium, nativist leaders alerted Americans of the imminent Papal plot to subvert the country.

The fervor that accompanied the nativist movement sometimes resulted in violence and destruction. Convent burning and bloody riots occurred in various cities. Mob violence in Philadelphia in 1844 left thirteen dead and over fifty wounded. Although nativist leaders contributed much to this uncontrolled emotion, the Catholic church was not totally blameless. Church leaders committed various blunders in their response to nativist accusations.

One such blunder occurred in November 1850, when Archbishop Hughes delivered a fiery speech to a crowd in Saint Patrick's Cathedral in New York City. The archbishop, known for his oratorical skills and his penchant for controversy, made use of the former and proceeded to become enmeshed in the latter. Responding to the charge that the Church planned to convert America, the archbishop declared that it was true and that "everybody should know it." This error on the part of an eminent Church leader contributed greatly to Protestant hysteria.

Soon all immigrants became a target of nativism, mainly because so many were Catholic. Many American Protestants regarded Catholic immigrants as the soldiers of the Vatican's plot to subvert the country. They also identified foreigners in general as the source of America's many social ills, blaming pauperism, a rising crime rate, and public drunkenness on the foreign element. More importantly, Americans believed the immigrants were taking jobs away from native-born workers and were corrupting the political process by voting in large blocs under the influence of crafty politicians.

By 1840 the nativist movement attracted a large following, especially from the ranks of the working class. Armed with a growing contingent of supporters, nativist leaders called upon politicians to address their concerns. Nativist leaders wanted legislation that would protect the Bible and the public school system. They also demanded a more strict naturalization process and stronger temperance laws.

The Democratic party, for the most part, turned a deaf ear to the nativists. From the beginning the party had vigorously courted the immigrant by representing itself as the voice of the "common man." The Democrats cultivated a strong alliance with foreigners in the large cities of the Northeast, where they tended to settle. The party was not about to alienate vital support by adopting the nativist program.

The Whig party, though more sympathetic toward nativism than were the Democrats, rarely acted on behalf of the nativists. At that time the Whigs were a moribund party. This was no more apparent than in the big cities of the Northeast, where the Whigs were losing the contest for the immigrant voter. Nevertheless, some party members still favored recruiting foreign-born voters. Thus the party failed to take a decisive stand on the controversial issue of nativism.

Nativist leaders found little satisfaction in the meager response from the two major parties. Those Americans who zealously sought restrictions on the Catholic church and the immigrant had to look outside the two-party system for political redress. Their search resulted in the Know-Nothing party.

The Know-Nothings originated in New York City, which had been the scene of intense political involvement by Catholic leaders as well as a city hard hit by immigration. By 1840 New York had become the center of organized nativism. Secret societies such as the Order of United Americans (O.U.A.) and the Order of the Star Spangled Banner were created by citizens who feared the spread of Catholicism and the infiltration of the foreign-born.

The Order of the Star Spangled Banner was founded in 1850 by a thirty-four-year-old New York City businessman, Charles B. Allen. Emphasizing secrecy, members referred to themselves as the "Sires of '76" to conceal their true identity. "I know nothing" was their usual reply when questioned about their activities. Horace Greeley, editor of the *New York Tribune,* referred to them as the Know-Nothings, thus bestowing upon the Order its popular name.

The O.U.A., another secret nativist society established in 1844, played an influential role in the growth of the Know-Nothings. In 1852 members of the O.U.A. took over control of the party. The Know-Nothings then came under the direction of James W. Barker, a dry goods merchant who possessed a talent for organization. Under Barker's leadership the Know-Nothings became a vibrant political machine. By 1853 they had lodges throughout New York, with branches in New Jersey, Connecticut, Maryland, and Ohio.

Naturally the goals of the party reflected the nativist philosophy of its members. The Know-Nothings aimed "to resist the insidious policy of the Church of Rome" and to elect "none but native-born Protestant citizens" to public office. The party also pledged itself to protect the civil and religious rights of all Americans and to defend the Constitution.

The Know-Nothings pursued all of their goals under the rituals of secrecy. Diverse methods of communications, such as passwords, signs, grips, and signals of distress, were employed to conceal party operations. Meetings were called by distributing heart-shaped pieces of white paper. Red pieces sent to the members signaled danger.

By 1853 the Know Nothings were secretly backing their own candidates for political office, or those of other parties, usually conservative Whigs. Because of the secrecy of their actions, Know-Nothing candidates astonished political observers when they were elected. Candidates who believed they were running unopposed and felt assured of victory found themselves on the losing end against an unknown opponent. All that the Democrats and Whigs could do was to watch helplessly as the Know-Nothings achieved success after success.

And successes there were! In the spring elections of 1854 the Know-Nothings recorded dramatic victories in Massachusetts, Delaware, and Pennsylvania. In Massachusetts the Know-Nothings not only elected a governor, but gained control of every state office as well. In the state legislature the Know-Nothings possessed every seat but two. In 1854 the party sent about seventy-five congressmen to Washington.

More surprising victories followed in 1855. By the end of that year the Know-Nothings controlled all the northeastern states except Vermont and Maine. The party also dominated the state governments of California and Tennessee. In many middle-Atlantic and southern states the Know-Nothings had replaced the Whigs as the major Democratic opposition.

The Know-Nothings quickly became the rage of the day. "Know-Nothing Candy," "Know-Nothing Tea," and "Know-Nothing Toothpicks" were popular items on store shelves. The party's name marked the sides of stagecoaches and omnibuses to attract riders. Nativist books appeared bearing the monogram "K.N." on their covers. The *North Carolina Weekly Standard* even printed a Know-Nothing menu for those possessing nativist tastes.

Though the Know-Nothings rose to political power because of the overwhelming popularity of nativism, the slavery issue quickly overshadowed the grievances against foreigners. The controversy over slavery was not new to the American political landscape. Twice before, in 1820 and in 1850, the issue had precipitated national crises, but compromise averted possible confrontation between North and South. With the passage of the Kansas-Nebraska Act in 1854, the avenue of compromise was forever closed.

The Kansas-Nebraska bill, based on the idea of popular sovereignty, allowed the question of slavery in those two territories to be decided by the settlers themselves. Until their decision, slavery would be legal in both territories because the Kansas-Nebraska Act repealed the Missouri Compromise of 1820. (The Missouri Compromise, held sacred by northern opponents of slavery, prohibited southern slaveholders from taking their slaves into any region above 36°30'.)

The passage of the Kansas-Nebraska Act opened the old wounds of sectionalism. Northerners greeted the act with outrage. Opponents of slavery, seeing land once reserved for freedom now open to slaveholding, gathered their forces in an attempt to stop the spread of an institution they considered abominable. The Kansas-Nebraska Act, along with the violence and bloodshed that followed in the wake of its passage, had a profound effect on the Democratic and Whig parties, as well as the Know-Nothings.

Democratic Senator Stephen A. Douglas of Illinois had sponsored the Kansas-Nebraska Act. As a result, many Northern Democrats left the party, feeling that it had fallen under the influence of a Southern slavocracy. These Democrats, together with antislavery Whigs, joined a coalition to fight the expansion of slavery. This coalition became the Republican party.

The disarray of the two-party system left many politicians without a political home. Conservative Whigs, seeing a dim future within their crumbling organization, believed that the Know-Nothing party would best serve their interests. Finding sectional politics distasteful, conservative Whigs turned to the Know-Nothing platform of conservatism, patriotism, and devotion to the Constitution. They also found the Know-Nothings' popularity with the American voter much to their liking.

A group of conservative Whigs, close associates of former President Fillmore, gained control of the Know-Nothing party, which had originally drawn its leaders from the ranks of the young and the working class. These men, attracted to the party by its newness and its concern for the people, were to a large extend politically inexperienced. Consequently, the Whigs had little trouble moving into positions of control within the party.

Once there, the Whigs proceeded to turn the Know-Nothings into an anti-Democratic organization that all men of the conservative Whig persuasion would find appealing. On the issue of slavery, the new Know-Nothing leaders adhered to the standard conservative Whig philosophy: compromise sectional politics. However, the most important change brought about by the new party leaders concerned nativism. The issue that furnished the Know-Nothings with their greatest political victories was now deemphasized to broaden the party's popular appeal, but the shift in emphasis disillusioned ardent Know-Nothing supporters.

With their vision fixed on the 1856 presidential election, the new Know-Nothing strategists now searched for a candidate who would be compatible with their conservative program. To his powerful friends and advisors in the party, Fillmore seemed to be the obvious choice. Fillmore had hopes of reviving the lifeless Whig party, but he soon realized the futility of such an undertaking. Although not a true nativist, he came to see the Know-Nothing party as an excellent vehicle for Whigs like himself to pursue their political goals.

Philadelphia hosted the Know-Nothing nominating convention, which opened on February 22, 1856. Several days before the opening session, party leaders arrived in the city to draft the party platform. The finished document emphasized Unionism and called for restraints on foreigners. In the meantime, the Know-Nothings had changed their name to the American party and lifted their veil of secrecy.

Twenty-seven states sent delegates to the convention. Know-Nothing leaders tried to evade the issue of slavery, but with the South's peculiar institution dominating national politics, the delegates could not escape its divisive effects. Almost immediately, they became involved in a heated debate over the issue. Northern delegates offered a resolution stating that no candidate should be nominated who did not favor the prohibition of slavery north of latitude 36°30′. The Fillmorites in control of the proceedings wanted no part of such a controversial plank; thus the resolution was tabled. As a result, a majority of the Northern delegates walked out of the convention.

Now basically a Southern affair, the Know-Nothing convention nominated Fillmore and Andrew Jackson Donelson of Tennessee as their presidential and vice-presidential candidates. The Republican party nominated the glamorous "Pathfinder of the West," John C. Frémont, with the slogan "Free Speech, Free Soil and Frémont." In denouncing the Kansas-Nebraska Act, the Republicans called for the prohibition of slavery in any new territories. The Democrats, on the other hand, drafted a platform that defended Douglas's doctrine of popular sovereignty. They elected James Buchanan of Pennsylvania, who was minister to England under President Franklin Pierce, as their standard bearer.

Fillmore's advisors, having sent their candidate on a tour of Europe to escape the bitter debate over the Kansas-Nebraska issue, planned a gala reception for the former president's return. The political extravaganza was to mark the beginning of what the Know-Nothings hoped would be a successful campaign. However, when Fillmore walked off the *Atlantic,* his party was politically wounded. The Northern delegates who bolted the party backed the Republican candidate, thus denying the Know-Nothings vital Northern support.

Traveling from New York City to his hometown of Buffalo, Fillmore made twenty-seven public addresses. Throughout all of his speeches, the Know-Nothing candidate condemned the sectional policies of his two rivals and continually stressed the need of preserving the Union. Nativists who listened to Fillmore speak were disappointed because the ex-president seldom referred to their concerns.

Fillmore only mentioned the word "Catholic" once. In a speech to a crowd in Rome, New York, he spoke of his recent visit to another city of the same name and of his meeting with the Pope. The candidate assured his audience that he "had not become a Roman Catholic—far from it." Gone forever were the vitriolic anti-Catholic attacks of previous Know-Nothing campaigns. In fact, the lack of nativism in Fillmore's campaign led the Church hierarchy to believe that the Know-Nothings no longer posed a threat to American Catholics.

The Know-Nothings' attempt to evade the slavery issue and their downplay of nativism left them with an emotionless, ineffective platform. Nor did the party take real advantage of taunting Unionism to the American public. In Fillmore, the Know-Nothings possessed a candidate of restraint and dignity, but these traits were of no value in an emotional campaign marked by bitterness.

Any hopes the Know-Nothings had of electing a president dissipated swiftly as the campaign progressed. When it became clear that Fillmore had no chance of winning, many conservative Whigs deserted the Know-Nothing fold.

Fearing that a Republican victory would dangerously heighten the sectional crisis, many influential Whigs swallowed their anti-Democratic feelings and voted for Buchanan. Among this group were Fletcher Webster and James B. Clay, sons of the former Whig heroes, and Rufus Choate, who believed that it was the Whigs' duty "to defeat and dissolve the new geographical, [Republican] party."

In November 1856, James Buchanan was elected president, defeating Frémont by one-half million votes and Fillmore by a million. The only state that Fillmore carried was Maryland. The Know-Nothing candidate received only twenty-nine percent of the total votes cast nationally, but he received a surprising forty-four percent of the Southern vote.

Upon inspection, the election was much closer than the numbers indicate. Had only about eight thousand voters in Kentucky, Louisiana, and Tennessee cast their lot with Fillmore, those states would have gone to the ex-president and would have sent the election to the House of Representatives, where a Know-Nothing victory would not have been impossible.

The Know-Nothing party suffered a rapid decline after 1856. The party ceased to exist on the national level the next year when its national council held its final meeting. From 1857 through 1860 the Know-Nothings survived only at state and local levels. In the North, Know-Nothing supporters generally migrated into the ranks of the Republican party. In the South, many of the remaining Know-Nothings tended to be vigorously anti-Democratic, supporting the Constitutional Union party in 1860.

The party's legislative record was a dismal failure. Even at the state level, where the party had once won its greatest victories, the Know-Nothings failed to win concrete gains in their nativist campaign. To a great extent their poor record can be attributed to political inexperience. Many Know-Nothing office holders performed ineffectively because they did not understand the process of legislative initiative. Moreover, when the issue of slavery came to dominate debate in Congress, the Know-Nothings lost whatever chance they might have had for a successful program.

By the time Abraham Lincoln became president, the Know-Nothings had passed from the American political scene. Millard Fillmore was in retirement, no longer harboring political aspirations. Newspapers were no longer printing Know Nothing menus, and "Know-Nothing Candy," "Know-Nothing Tea," and "Know-Nothing Toothpicks" gathered dust on the shelves of stores that catered to an eager clientele whose tastes turned to newer fads.

14

The Glorious and the Terrible

Allan Nevins

Allan Nevins (1890–1971), a Columbia University professor for most of his career, stands in the first rank of twentieth-century historians. His writing is well-balanced, judicious, thorough, conscientious, and, as this article demonstrates, very readable. Prior to World War II, Nevins wrote award-winning biographies of Grover Cleveland, Hamilton Fish, and John D. Rockefeller. After the war he turned his attention to the Civil War and worked until his death on the eight-volume Ordeal of the Union, *a detailed study of the nation between 1846 and 1865.*

In this article, written for Saturday Review *on the centennial of the Civil War, Nevins takes issue with historians for overplaying the pageantry and splendor of the war at the expense of the slaughter and destruction we all know to be a part of it. Civil War general William Tecumseh Sherman allegedly originated the cliché "war is hell," but his wisdom has been sadly neglected by historians in favor of "the floating banners, the high-ringing cheers, the humors of the camp, the ardors of the charge," and the romance of it all. Nevins makes the terrible side*

This reading is reprinted by permission of Omni Publications, New York, publisher of the *Saturday Review*, September 2, 1961.

of the war come vividly alive, not least in his depiction of the hatred
engendered by the conflict, a hatred that survived to poison succeeding
generations.

In an age for which total war might very well mean the end of the
human race, Nevins offers a needed corrective to those who see war as
a way to toughen up a nation gone soft. That macho strain within the
national character has ebbed and flowed in popularity, with Theodore
Roosevelt its most famous proponent. In the years following 1961, the
United States fought an undeclared war in Vietnam whose horrors were
brought home vividly to the populace via the television news. Thoroughly
unglamorous, the Vietnam War may have painfully accomplished what
Nevins sought to do.

Every great war has two sides, the glorious and the terrible. The
glorious is perpetuated in multitudinous pictures, poems, novels, statues:
in Meissonier's canvases of Friedland and Austerlitz, Byron's stanzas on
Waterloo and Tennyson's on the Light and Heavy brigades, St. Gaudens's
Sherman riding forward victory-crowned, Freeman's "Lee." The terrible is
given us in a much slighter body of memorabilia: Jacques Callot's grue-
some etchings of the Thirty Years War, Goya's paintings of French atroc-
ities in Spain, Zola's "The Debacle," Walt Whitman's hospital sketches,
and the thousand-page novels that drearily emerged from the Second
World War.

The two aspects do exist side by side. Every student of war comes
upon hundreds of veracious descriptions of its pomp and pageantry, innumerable tales of devotion and heroism. They exalt the spirit. Yet every
such student falls back from this exultation upon a sombre remembrance
of the butchery, the bereavement, and the long bequest of poverty, exhaustion, and despair. In observing the centenary of the Civil War, every
sensible man should keep in mind that the conflict was a terrible reproach
to American civilization and a source of poison and debilities still to
be felt.

If it were not true that its debits far outweighed its credits, we
might conclude that the republic would profit by a civil war in every
generation, and that we should have commemorated Bull Run last July by
again setting Yankee boys and Southern boys to killing each other. The
mind recoils from the thought. But as the Civil War histories, novels, and
motion pictures continue to pour forth, we shall be fortunate if we escape two very erroneous views.

The first view is that the war can somehow be detached from its
context and studied as if it stood alone, without reference to causes or
effects. War in fact, as Clausewitz long ago insisted, does not stand
apart from and opposed to peace. It is simply a transfer of the normal
inescapable conflicts of men from the realm of adjustment to that of

violence. It represents not a complete transformation of national policy, but a continuance of policy by sanguinary means. That is, it cannot be understood without regarding both its causes and its results. Our Civil War, as Walt Whitman insisted, grew peculiarly out of national character. The other erroneous view is that the Civil War was, in the phrase of that graphic military historian Bruce Catton, a "Glory Road."

"Consider it not so deeply," Lady Macbeth says to her husband, stricken by the thought of red-handed murder; and "Consider it not so deeply," people instinctively say to those who remind them of war's inhuman massacre. Who wishes to while away an idle hour by looking at the harrowing pictures in the "Medical and Surgical History" of the war? It is a trick of human memories to forget, little by little, what is painful, and remember what is pleasant, and that tendency appertains to the folk memory as well. One of the finest descriptive pieces of the war was written by the true-hearted Theodore Winthrop, novelist and poet, just after his regiment crossed the Potomac on a spring night in 1861 to encamp on the Virginia side. It is rapturous in its depiction of the golden moon lighting a path over the river, the merry files of soldiers, the white tents being pitched in the dewy dawn. But ere long Winthrop was slain at Big Bethel in an engagement too blundering, shabby and piteous for any pen. We remember the happy march but forget the death.

Or take two contrasting scenes later in the war, of the same day—the day of Malvern Hill, July 1, 1862. That battle of Lee and McClellan reached its climax in the gathering dusk of a lustrous summer evening, no breath of wind stirring the air. The Union army had placed its ranks and its artillery on the slope of a great hill, a natural amphitheatre, which the Southerners assaulted. Participants never forgot the magnificence of the spectacle. From the Confederate and Union guns stately columns of black smoke towered high in the blue sky. The crash of musketry and deeper thud of artillery; the thunder of gunboat mortars from the James River, their shells curving in fiery golden lines; the cavalry on either flank, galloping to attack; the foaming horses flying from point to point with aides carrying dispatches; the steady advance of the Confederate columns and the unyielding resistance of the dense Union lines; then as darkness gathered, the varicolored signal lights flashing back and forth their messages—all this made an unforgettable panorama.

Both novelist and poet almost instinctively turn to the heroic aspects and picturesque incidents of war. Lowell's "Commemoration Ode," one of the half-dozen finest pieces of literature born from the conflict, necessarily eulogizes the heroes; Mary Johnston's "The Long Roll," perhaps the best Southern war novel, celebrates the ardors, not the anguishes, of Stonewall Jackson's foot-cavalry; St. Gaudens's monument on Boston Common to Robert Gould Shaw and his black infantry—the men whose dauntless hearts beat a charge right up the red rampart's slippery swell—shows the fighters, not the fallen. The historian assists in falsifying the picture. Cold, objective, he assumes that both the glorious and horrible sides exist, and need no special emphasis. He thus tends to equate the two, although the pains and penalties of war far outweigh its gleams of grandeur.

Then, too, a problem of expression impedes the realistic writer. It is not difficult to describe the pageantry of Pickett's charge. But when we come to the costs, what can we say except that the casualties were 3,000 killed, 5,000 wounded? It is impossible to describe the agony of even one soldier dying of a gangrened wound, or the heartache of one mother losing her first born; what of 10,000 such soldiers and mothers? Moreover, most historians, like the novelists and poets, have an instinctive preference for the bright side of the coin. Henry Steele Commager's otherwise fine introduction to his valuable compilation "The Blue and The Gray" has much to say about gallantry and bravery, but nothing about the squalor, the stench, and the agony.

If we protest against the prettification of the Civil War, the thoughtless glorification of what was essentially a temporary breakdown of American civilization, we must do so with an acknowledgment that it did call forth many manifestations of an admirable spirit. The pomp and circumstance, the parade and pageantry, we may dismiss as essentially empty. The valor of the host of young men who streamed to the colors we may deeply admire, but as valor we may fortunately take it for granted, for most men are brave. The patriotic ardor displayed in the first months of the war may also be taken for granted. What was highly impressive was the serious, sustained conviction, the long-enduring dedication, of countless thousands on both sides for their chosen cause. This went far beyond the transient enthusiasms of Sumter and Bull Run; far beyond ordinary battlefield courage. Lecky was correct in writing: "That which invests war with a certain grandeur is the heroic self-sacrifice which it elicits." All life is in a real sense a conflict between good and evil, in which every man or woman plays a part. A host of young Americans felt that they were enlisted in this larger struggle, and regarded their service to the North or South as part of a lifetime service to the right.

Those who seek examples of this dedication can find them scattered throughout the war records. Lincoln specially admired his young friend Elmer Ellsworth, who had endured poverty and hardship with monastic devotion to train himself for service; Lee specially admired John Pelham, the daring artillerist. Both gave their lives. Some fine illustrations of the consecrated spirit can be found in the two volumes of the "Harvard Memorial Biographies" edited by Thomas Wentworth Higginson just after the war. The ninety-eight Harvard dead were no better than the farm lads from Iowa or Alabama, the clerks from New Orleans or New York, but some of them had special gifts of self-expression. Hearken, for example, to Colonel Peter A. Porter, who wrote in his last will and testament:

> I can say, with truth, that I have entered on the course of danger with no ambitious aspirations, nor with the idea that I am fitted, by nature, or experience, to be of any important service to the government; but in obedience to the call of duty, demanding every citizen to contribute what he could, in means, labor, or life, to sustain the government of his country—a sacrifice made the more willingly by me when I consider how singularly benefitted I have been, by the institutions of the land. . . .

As we distinguish between the shining glory of the war—this readiness of countless thousands to die for an enduring moral conviction—and the false or unimportant glories, so we must distinguish between the major and the lesser debits of the conflict. Some evils and mischiefs which seemed tremendous at the time have grown less in the perspective of years; some which at first appeared small now loom large.

It was one of the bloodiest of all wars; the total deaths in the Union and Confederate armies have been computed at about 620,000; and one of the facts which appalls any careful student is the enormous amount of suffering on the field and in the hospitals. The evidence of this, while not within the view of general readers, is incontrovertible. Armies the world over in 1860 were *worse* provided with medical and surgical facilities than in Napoleon's day. The United States, after its long peace, began the war with practically no medical service whatever. Surgical application of the ideas of Pasteur and Lister lay in the future. Almost every abdominal wound meant death. Any severe laceration of a limb entailed amputation, with a good chance of mortal gangrene or erysipelas. The North systematically prevented shipments of drugs and surgical instruments to the South, a measure which did not shorten the conflict by a day, but cost the Southern troops untold agony. Had it not been for the Sanitary Commission, a body privately organized and supported, Northern armies would have duplicated the experience of British forces in the Crimea; yet Secretary of War Stanton at first deliberately impeded the Commission's work.

The story of battle after battle was the same. Night descended on a field ringing with cries of agony: Water! Water! Help!—if in winter, Blankets! Cover! All too frequently no help whatever was forthcoming. After some great conflicts the wounded lay for days, and sometimes a week, without rescue. Shiloh was fought on a Sunday and Monday. Rain set in on Sunday night, and the cold April drizzle continued through Tuesday night. On Tuesday morning nine-tenths of the wounded still lay where they fell; many had been there forty-eight hours without attention; numbers had died of shock or exhaustion; some had even drowned as the rain filled depressions from which they could not crawl. Every house in the area was converted into a hospital, where the floors were covered with wretches heavily wounded, sometimes with arms or legs torn off, who after the first bandages, got no nursing, medical care, or even nourishment. "The first day or two," wrote a newspaper reporter, "the air was filled with groans, sobs, and frenzied curses, but now the sufferers are quiet; not from cessation of pain, but mere exhaustion." Yet at this time the war was a year old.

Still more poignant versions of the same story might be given. Lee and Pope fought Second Manassas on the last Friday and Saturday in August, 1862, so near Washington that groups standing on housetops in the capital heard the rumble of artillery. The battleground, five miles long and three wide, was thickly strewn with dead and wounded. Pope retreated in confusion; many in Washington feared the city might be taken. In these circumstances, as late as the following Wednesday one member of the inadequate body of surgeons estimated that 2,000 wounded had received no attention. Many had not tasted food for four days; some were dying of hunger and thirst. A reporter for the Washington *Republican* wrote on Thursday that some dying men could yet be saved by prompt help. And on Friday, a week after the battle began, a correspondent of the New York *Tribune* told of heart-rending scenes as the doctors searched among heaps of putrefying dead men for men yet clinging to life—men who, when anyone approached, would cry "Doctor, come to *me*; you look like a kind man; for God's sake come to *me*."

Anyone who is tempted to think of Gettysburg only in terms of its heroic episodes, its color and drama, should turn to the pages in "Battles and Leaders" in which General John D. Imboden describes the transport of the Confederate wounded, after their defeat, back into Maryland. He was ordered to ride to the head of the long wagon column as, in darkness and storm, it moved south:

> For four hours I hurried forward on my way to the front, and in all that time I was never out of hearing of the groans and cries of the wounded and dying. Scarcely one in a hundred had received adequate surgical aid, owing to the demands on the hard-working surgeons from still worse cases that had to be left behind. Many of the wounded in their wagons had been without food for thirty-six hours. Their torn and bloody clothing, matted and hardened, was rasping the tender, inflamed, and still oozing wounds. Very few of the wagons had even a layer of straw in them, and all were without springs. The road was rough and rocky from the heavy washings of the preceding day. The jolting was enough to have killed strong men, if long exposed to it. From nearly every wagon as the teams trotted on, urged by whip and shout, came such cries and shrieks as these:
>
> "My God! Why can't I die?"
>
> "My God! Will no one have mercy and kill me?"
>
> "Stop! Oh, for God's sake stop just for one minute; take me out and leave me to die on the roadside."
>
> Occasionally a wagon would be passed from which only low, deep moans could be heard. No help could be rendered to any of the sufferers.

No heed could be given to any of their appeals. Mercy and duty to the many forbade the loss of a moment in the vain efforts then and there to comply with the prayers of the few. On! On! We must move on. The storm continued and the darkness was appalling. There was no time even to fill a canteen with water for a dying man; for, except the drivers and the guards, all were wounded and utterly helpless in that vast procession of misery. During this one night I realized more of the horrors of war than I had in all the preceding two years.

After such a description, we can understand why a radical Northern Senator, looking across the battlefield of the Wilderness as fighting ended, told Hugh McCulloch that if in 1861 he had been given one glimpse of the agonies he there beheld, he would have said to the South: "Erring sisters, go in peace." John Esten Cooke was right in his elegy for Pelham; the living were brave and noble, but the dead were the bravest of all.

Yet *this* was far from being the ugliest side of war. Nor was the suffering in the huge prison camps, South and North, part of the worst side of war; the suffering which MacKinlay Kantor describes in his novel and to which Benet briefly adverts in "John Brown's Body":

> The triple stockade of Andersonville the damned,
> Where men corrupted like flies in their own dung
> And the gangrened sick were black with smoke and their filth.

What maims the bodies of men is less significant than what maims their spirit.

One ugly aspect of the Civil War too generally ignored is the devastation, more and more systematic, that accompanied it. For three reasons too little has been said of this devastation; the facts were kept out of official reports, the tale is too painful, and the recital easily becomes monotonous. Yet by 1862 the war in the South had become one of general depredation; by 1863, of wanton destruction; and by 1864, of an organized devastation which in terms of property anticipated the worst chapters of the two world wars. Georgia and the Shenandoah suffered in 1864 almost precisely as Belgium and Serbia suffered in 1914—the executions omitted. It was barbaric, and the only excuse to be made is that war is barbarism.

The turning point in the attitude of Northern military men was reached when General John Pope on July 18, 1862, issued from Washington headquarters a set of Draconian general orders. Order No. 5 directed that the army should subsist as far as practicable upon the country, giving vouchers for supplies seized. Order No. 7 decreed the summary execution of persons caught firing upon Union troops from houses. Order No. 11 (five days later) required officers to arrest immediately all disloyal males within reach, to make them take the oath of allegiance or go South, and to shoot all who violated their oath or who returned from the Confederacy.

The order for living on the country, widely publicized East and West, changed the attitude of troops, and inspired private looting as well as public seizures of property. Pope was soon ousted, but the moral effect of his orders persisted.

Though most of the facts were excluded from official reports, their sum total, insofar as one shrewd observer could arrive at it, may be found in John T. Trowbridge's graphic volume written in 1866, "A Picture of the Desolated States." In his preface Trowbridge speaks of the Union forces not as our heroic armies but our destroying armies. Even this practiced reporter is less graphic, however, than the people who suffered under the onslaught and wrote while their emotions, like their property, still burned. Hear a lady of Louisiana tell what occurred when N. P. Banks's army passed:

> I was watching from my window the apparently orderly march of the first Yankees that appeared in view and passed up the road, when, suddenly, as if by magic, the whole plantation was covered with men, like bees from an overthrown hive; and, as far as my vision extended, an inextricable medley of men and animals met my eye. In one place, excited troopers were firing into the flock of sheep; in another, officers and men were in pursuit of the boys' ponies, and in another, a crowd were in excited chase of the work animals. The kitchen was soon filled with some, carrying off the cooking utensils and the provisions of the day; the yard with others, pursuing the poultry. . . . They penetrated under the house, into the outbuildings, and into the garden, stripping it in a moment of all its vegetables. . . . This continued during the day . . . and amid a bewildering sound of oaths and imprecations. . . . When the army had passed, we were left destitute.

Sherman believed in total war; that is, in waging war not only against the Southern armies, but the Southern people. His theory was that every man, woman, and child was "armed and at war." He wrote his wife in the summer of 1862 that the North might fall into bankruptcy, "but if they can hold on the war will soon assume a turn to extermination, not of soldiers alone, but the people." He denied, in effect, that Southerners had a right to resist invasion. When Union steamers were fired on near Randolph, Mississippi, in the fall of 1862, he destroyed Randolph, and a little later had all houses, farms, and cornfields devastated for fifteen miles along the banks.

When he drove his red plowshare across Georgia and the Carolinas, his object was to leave only scorched earth behind. He had already written of his Western operation: "Not a man is to be seen; nothing but women with houses plundered, fields open to the cattle and horses, pickets lounging on every porch, and desolation sown broadcast; servants all gone, and women and children bred in luxury . . . begging . . . for soldiers' rations." His aim was that which Phil Sheridan avowed: to leave them nothing but their eyes to weep with.

The final devastation of half the South was horrible to behold, and it was distressing to think that these savage losses had been inflicted by Americans upon fellow Americans. Yet this was far from being the worst aspect of the conflict, or the least easily reparable. Damages on which we can fix the dollar sign are important not in themselves, but as they become translated into cultural and spiritual losses; into the intellectual retardation caused by poverty, for example. The physical recovery of the South was rapid. As it was primarily an agricultural section, a few good crops at fair prices did much to restore it; and the swiftness with which housing, railroads, bridges, and public facilities were rebuilt astonished observers of the 1870s just as the swift postwar recovery of Germany and Poland has astonished observers of our day.

Infinitely worse were the biological losses—the radical hurts—inflicted by the Civil War. The killing of between 600,000 and 700,000 young men in a nation of 33,000,000 and the maiming or permanent debilitation of as many more had evil consequences projected into the far-distant future. We lost not only these men, but their children, and their children's children. Here, indeed, was a loss that proved highly cumulative. During the First World War, Lord Dunsany wrote a slender volume called "Tales of War." One of his apologues showed the Kaiser, as the embodiment of German militarism, commanded by a spirit to come on a tour. They crossed the German plain to a neat garden. Look, said the spirit:

> The Kaiser looked; and saw a window shining and a neat room in a cottage; there was nothing dreadful there, thank the good German God for that; it was all right, after all. The Kaiser had had a fright, but it was all right, there was only a woman with a baby sitting before a fire, and two small children and a man. And it was quite a jolly room. And the man was a young soldier; and, why, he was a Prussian Guardsman—there was a helmet hanging on the wall—so everything was all right. They were jolly German children; that was well. How nice and homely the room was. . . . The firelight flickered, and the lamp shone on, and the children played on the floor, and the man was smoking out of a china pipe; he was strong and able and young, one of the wealth-winners of Germany.
>
> "Have you seen?" asked the phantom.
>
> "Yes," said the Kaiser. . . .
>
> At once the fire went out and the lamp faded away, the room fell sombrely into neglect and squalor, and the soldier and the children faded away with the room; all disappeared phantasmally, and nothing remained but the helmet in a kind of glow on the wall, and the woman sitting all by herself in the darkness.
>
> "It has all gone," said the Kaiser.
>
> "It has never been," said the phantom.
>
> The Kaiser looked again. Yes, there was nothing there, it was just a vision. . . .
>
> "It might have been," said the phantom.

Just so, we can say that the multitude of Civil War dead represent hundreds of thousands of homes, and hundreds of thousands of families, that might have been, and never were. They represent millions of people who might have been part of our population today and are not. We have lost the books they might have written, the scientific discoveries they might have made, the inventions they might have perfected. Such a loss defies measurement.

The only noteworthy attempt to measure the biological losses was made by David Starr Jordan and his son Harvey in a volume called "War's Aftermath" (1914). The authors circulated carefully drawn questionnaires in Spottsylvania and Rockbridge Counties in Virginia, and in Cobb County in Georgia, inquiring particularly into the eugenic effects of the conflict. One of their queries brought out evidence that by no means all casualties were among the men; numerous girls and women succumbed to the hardships and anxieties of the conflict in the South. Another question elicited unanimous agreement that "the flower of the people" went into the war at the beginning, and of these a large part died before the end. President Jordan, weighing all the responses, reached two conclusions: first, that the evidence "leaves a decided evidence in favor of grave racial hurt," and second, that "the war has seriously impoverished this country of its best human values."

Even the terrible loss of young, productive lives, the grave biological injury to the nation, however, did not constitute the worst side of the war. One aspect of the conflict was still more serious. It was the aspect to which Lowell referred in lines written a few years after Appomattox:

> I looked to see an ampler atmosphere
> By that electric passion-gust blown clear
> I looked for this; consider what I hear. . . .
> Murmur of many voices in the air
> Denounces us degenerate,
> Unfaithful guardians of a noble fate. . . .

The war, as Walt Whitman truly said, had grown out of defects in the American character; of American faults it cured few, accentuated a number, and gave some a violently dangerous trend. Far behind the lines, it added to the already discreditable total of violence in American life. Applying to industry a great forcing-draft, the bellows of huge wartime appropriations, it strengthened the materialistic forces in our civilization. Its state and federal contracts, its bounty system, its innumerable opportunities for battening on the nation's woes, made speculation fashionable, and corruption almost too common for comment. Its inflation bred extravagance and dissipation.

Every month heightened the intolerance of war; it began with mobs in New York threatening newspaper offices, a mob in Philadelphia trying to lynch Senator James A. Bayard, and mobs in the South flogging and exiling Union men; as it went on, freedom of speech almost disappeared over broad areas. The atmosphere of war fostered immorality; Richmond and Washington alike became filled with saloons, brothels, and gambling dens, and such occupied cities as Memphis and Nashville were sinks of iniquity. For every knightly martyr like James Wadsworth or Albert Sidney Johnston there arose two such coarse, aggressive, selfish careerists as Ben Butler and Dan Sickles. Wadsworth and Johnston died in battle, but Butler and Sickles remained to follow postwar political careers. Seen in perspective, the war was a gigantic engine for coarsening and lowering the American character even while it quickened certain of our energies.

Parson Brownlow, a Tennessee Unionist, went from city to city in the North in 1862 demanding "grape for the Rebel masses, and hemp for their leaders"; saying that he himself would tie the rope about the necks of some rebel generals; calling for the confiscation of all Southern property; proclaiming that he would be glad to arm every wolf, bear, catamount, and crocodile, every devil in hell, to defeat the South; and declaring he would put down the rebellion "if it exterminates from God's green earth every man, woman, and child south of Mason and Dixon's Line."

In the South two famous leaders, Robert Toombs and Howell Cobb, united that year in an address to their people just as vitriolic. "The foot of the oppressor is on the soil of Georgia," it began. "He comes with lust in his eye, poverty in his purse, and hell in his heart. How shall you meet him? . . . With death for him or for yourself!" Better the charnel house for every Southerner, they continued, than "loathsome vassalage to a nation already sunk below the contempt of the civilized world." Thaddeus Stevens nursed his hatred until he spoke of "exterminating" or driving into exile *all* Southerners, just as Sherman declared he would "slay millions" to assure the safety of the Mississippi. Women of the South meanwhile expressed the most vindictive detestation of all Yankees. "I hate them," wrote one Mississippi woman after a raid on her community, "more now than I did the evening I saw them sneaking off with all we cared for, and so it will be every day I live."

Hatred was seen in its most naked form in those communities divided against themselves and racked by guerrilla war; in Missouri, Arkansas, parts of Kentucky, and east Tennessee. Writes Charles D. Drake, a distinguished Missouri leader, of his state: "Falsehood, treachery, and perjury pervaded the whole social fabric." He went on: "Could there be written a full account of all the crimes of the rebels of Missouri, and the outrages and wrongs inflicted by them upon her loyal inhabitants, during the four years of the rebellion, the world would shrink aghast from a picture which has no parallel in the previous history of any portion of the Anglo-Saxon race." Confederate sympathizers in Missouri would have said the same of Union irregulars. One atrocity provoked another. These hatreds long survived the conflict, and indeed in some spots the embers still smoulder. Typifying the whole range of spiritual injuries wrought by the war, they justify the poet Blake's cry:

> The soldier, armed with sword and gun,
> Palsied strikes the summer sun.

The historian Mendelssohn Bartholdy, in his volume entitled "War and German Society," written as part of the Carnegie Endowment's huge economic history of World War I, concluded that the moral effects of war are much worse than the material effects. He also concluded that they are radically bad, for they strike at the very heart of a country's character; "modern war, with its robot-like disregard of individual values, is bound to make the peculiar virtue of a nation an object of attack." As respects the Civil War, we can agree. If it was necessary for preserving the Union and extinguishing slavery, it was of course worth more than it cost; but should it have been necessary? Could not better leadership from 1830 to 1860 have averted it? This is a bootless question. But it is certain that the conflict, so much the greatest convulsion in our history, so tremendous in its impact on our national life, so fascinating in its drama, was in spite of all compensating elements, all the heroism, all the high example we find in Lee's character and Lincoln's wisdom, materially a disaster and morally a tragedy.

It is unfortunate that of the flood of books on the war ninety-nine in a hundred are on military topics and leaders, and that a great majority fasten attention on the floating banners, the high-ringing cheers, the humors of the camp, the ardors of the charge; the whole undeniable fascination and romance of the first true *volkskrieg* in history. It is right, within measure, to let them lift our hearts. But the long commemoration will pass essentially unimproved if it does not give us a deeper, sterner, more scientific study of the collision of two creeds and two ways of life as related to an examination of war in general.

We should probe more deeply into its roots, a process that will expose some of the weaknesses of our social fabric and governmental system. We should pay fuller attention to its darker aspects, and examine more honestly such misrepresentations as the statement it was distinguished by its generosity of spirit, the magnanimity with which the combatants treated each other; a statement absurd on its face, for no war which lasts four years and costs 600,000 lives leaves much magnanimity in its later phases. We should above all examine more closely the effects of the great and terrible war not on the nation's politics—we know that; not on its economy—we also know that; but on its character, the vital element of national life.

This examination will lead into unpleasant paths, and bring us to unhappy conclusions; but it will profit us far more than stirring battle canvases. All nations must be schooled in such studies if the world is ever to find an answer to a question uttered just after World War I by William E. Borah, a question that still rings in men's ears: "When shall we escape from war? When shall we loosen the grip of the monster?"

15

The New View
of Reconstruction

Eric Foner

Eric Foner (1943   ), both educated and educator at Columbia Univer-
sity, is one of the fine young scholars engaged in exploring the gaps be-
tween perception and reality in the Civil War and Reconstruction era.
Like Eugene Genovese, he takes particular interest in blacks and radical-
ism. Two of his books indicate his area of expertise: Politics and Ideology
in the Age of the Civil War *(1981) and* Nothing but Freedom: Emancipation and Its Legacy *(1983). In 1988 he published a full-length and*
well-received treatment of the subject of this article: Reconstruction:
America's Unfinished Revolution, 1863–1877.

In this 1983 selection from American Heritage, *Foner offers a clear*
picture of the view of Reconstruction that prevailed from the 1870s
through the 1950s and explains why it is no longer convincing. Recon-
struction provides a good case study of historiography, the history of
history. As long as white racism was the social and historical norm, radi-
cal northern attempts to force black equality in the South during Recon-
struction appeared misguided, if not downright malevolent. The civil

rights movement in the 1960s forced historians to reevaluate both their attitudes toward current racial issues and their interpretations of the past. This new look led to a shift in the roles of heroes and villains in Reconstruction: Now the Radical Republicans became the good guys and President Andrew Johnson and southern obstructionists the obstacles to racial progress.

Foner suggests that a new, more radical, view has emerged: Reconstruction was simply not radical enough. The failure of the Radical Republicans to provide "forty acres and a mule" or any economic stake in the new postwar society left the freedmen at the mercy of their former masters—with the resultant economic gap lasting down to the present. Nevertheless, the door of hope was opened and blacks have been struggling through it ever since what W. E. B. DuBois termed the "splendid failure" of Reconstruction.

The American character is not static. Frederick Jackson Turner argued that the frontier was the most important factor forging it. Foner's article depicts human, political attempts to reshape it. The debate over Reconstruction is in part a debate over whether the Radical Republicans, promoting greater racial equality, or the Southern Redeemers, seeking continued racial supremacy, were truer to what the American character has been—or could be.

In the past twenty years, no period of American history has been the subject of a more thoroughgoing reevaluation than Reconstruction— the violent, dramatic, and still controversial era following the Civil War. Race relations, politics, social life, and economic change during Reconstruction have all been reinterpreted in the light of changed attitudes toward the place of blacks within American society. If historians have not yet forged a fully satisfying portrait of Reconstruction as a whole, the traditional interpretation that dominated historical writing for much of this century has irrevocably been laid to rest.

Anyone who attended high school before 1960 learned that Reconstruction was an era of unrelieved sordidness in American political and social life. The martyred Lincoln, according to this view, had planned a quick and painless readmission of the Southern states as equal members of the national family. President Andrew Johnson, his successor, attempted to carry out Lincoln's policies but was foiled by the Radical Republicans (also known as Vindictives or Jacobins). Motivated by an irrational hatred of Rebels or by ties with Northern capitalists out to plunder the South, the Radicals swept aside Johnson's lenient program and fastened black supremacy upon the defeated Confederacy. An orgy of corruption followed, presided over by unscrupulous carpetbaggers (Northerners who ventured south to reap the spoils of office), traitorous scalawags (Southern whites who cooperated with the new governments for personal gain), and the ignorant and childlike freedmen, who were incapable of properly exercising the political power that had been thrust upon them. After much needless suffering, the white community of the South banded together to overthrow these "black" governments and restore home rule (their euphemism for white supremacy). All told, Reconstruction was just about the darkest page in the American saga.

Originating in anti-Reconstruction propaganda of Southern Democrats during the 1870s, this traditional interpretation achieved scholarly legitimacy around the turn of the century through the work of William Dunning and his students at Columbia University. It reached the larger public through films like *Birth of a Nation* and *Gone With the Wind* and that best-selling work of myth-making masquerading as history, *The Tragic Era*, by Claude G. Bowers. In language as exaggerated as it was colorful, Bowers told how Andrew Johnson "fought the bravest battle for constitutional liberty and for the preservation of our institutions ever waged by an Executive" but was overwhelmed by the "poisonous propaganda" of the Radicals. Southern whites, as a result, "literally were put to the torture" by "emissaries of hate" who manipulated the "simple-minded" freedmen, "inflaming the negroes' egotism" and even inspiring "lustful assaults" by blacks upon white womanhood.

In a discipline that sometimes seems to pride itself on the rapid rise and fall of historical interpretations, this traditional portrait of Reconstruction enjoyed remarkable staying power. The long reign of the old interpretation is not difficult to explain. It presented a set of easily identifiable heroes and villains. It enjoyed the imprimatur of the nation's leading scholars. And it accorded with the political and social realities of the first half of this century. This image of Reconstruction helped freeze the mind of the white South in unalterable opposition to any movement for breaching the ascendancy of the Democratic party, eliminating segregation, or readmitting disfranchised blacks to the vote.

Nevertheless, the demise of the traditional interpretation was inevitable, for it ignored the testimony of the central participant in the drama of Reconstruction—the black freedman. Furthermore, it was grounded in the conviction that blacks were unfit to share in political power. As Dunning's Columbia colleague John W. Burgess put it, "A black skin means membership in a race of men which has never of itself succeeded in subjecting passion to reason, has never, therefore, created any civilization of any kind." Once objective scholarship and modern experience rendered that assumption untenable, the entire edifice was bound to fall.

The work of "revising" the history of Reconstruction began with the writings of a handful of survivors of the era, such as John R. Lynch, who had served as a black congressman from Mississippi after the Civil War. In the 1930s white scholars like Francis Simkins and Robert Woody carried the task forward. Then, in 1935, the black historian and activist W. E. B. DuBois produced *Black Reconstruction in America,* a monumental reevaluation that closed with an irrefutable indictment of a historical profession that had sacrificed scholarly objectivity on the altar of racial bias. "One fact and one alone," he wrote, "explains the attitude of most recent writers toward Reconstruction; they cannot conceive of Negroes as men." DuBois's work, however, was ignored by most historians.

It was not until the 1960s that the full force of the revisionist wave broke over the field. Then, in rapid succession, virtually every assumption of the traditional viewpoint was systematically dismantled. A drastically different portrait emerged to take its place. President Lincoln did not have a coherent "plan" for Reconstruction, but at the time of his assassination he had been cautiously contemplating black suffrage. Andrew Johnson was a stubborn, racist politician who lacked the ability to compromise. By isolating himself from the broad currents of public opinion that had nourished Lincoln's career, Johnson created an impasse with Congress that Lincoln would certainly have avoided, thus throwing away his political power and destroying his own plans for reconstructing the South.

The Radicals in Congress were acquitted of both vindictive motives and the charge of serving as the stalking-horses of Northern capitalism. They emerged instead as idealists in the best nineteenth-century reform tradition. Radical leaders like Charles Sumner and Thaddeus Stevens had worked for the rights of blacks long before any conceivable political advantage flowed from such a commitment. Stevens refused to sign the Pennsylvania Constitution of 1838 because it disfranchised the state's black citizens; Sumner led a fight in the 1850s to integrate Boston's public schools. Their Reconstruction policies were based on principle, not petty political advantage, for the central issue dividing Johnson and these Radical Republicans was the civil rights of freedmen. Studies of congressional policy-making, such as Eric L. McKitrick's *Andrew Johnson and Reconstruction,* also revealed that Reconstruction legislation, ranging from the Civil Rights Act of 1866 to the Fourteenth and Fifteenth Amendments, enjoyed broad support from moderate and conservative Republicans. It was not simply the work of a narrow radical faction.

Even more startling was the revised portrait of Reconstruction in the South itself. Imbued with the spirit of the civil rights movement and rejecting entirely the racial assumptions that had underpinned the traditional interpretation, these historians evaluated Reconstruction from the black point of view. Works like Joel Williamson's *After Slavery* portrayed the period as a time of extraordinary political, social, and economic progress for blacks. The establishment of public school systems, the granting of equal citizenship to blacks, the effort to restore the devastated Southern economy, the attempt to construct an interracial political democracy from the ashes of slavery, all these were commendable achievements, not the elements of Bowers's "tragic era."

Unlike earlier writers, the revisionists stressed the active role of the freedmen in shaping Reconstruction. Black initiative established as many schools as did Northern religious societies and the Freedmen's Bureau. The right to vote was not simply thrust upon them by meddling outsiders, since blacks began agitating for the suffrage as soon as they were freed. In 1865 black conventions throughout the South issued eloquent, though unheeded, appeals for equal civil and political rights.

With the advent of Radical Reconstruction in 1867, the freedmen did enjoy a real measure of political power. But black supremacy never existed. In most states blacks held only a small fraction of political offices, and even in South Carolina, where they comprised a majority of the state legislature's lower house, effective power remained in white hands. As for corruption, moral standards in both government and private enterprise were at low ebb throughout the nation in the postwar years—the era of Boss Tweed, the Credit Mobilier scandal, and the Whiskey Ring. Southern corruption could hardly be blamed on former slaves.

Other actors in the Reconstruction drama also came in for reevaluation. Most carpetbaggers were former Union soldiers seeking economic opportunity in the postwar South, not unscrupulous adventurers. Their motives, a typically American amalgam of humanitarianism and the pursuit of profit, were no more insidious than those of Western pioneers. Scalawags, previously seen as traitors to the white race, now emerged as "Old Line" Whig Unionists who had opposed secession in the first place or as poor whites who had long resented planters' domination of Southern life and who saw in Reconstruction a chance to recast Southern society along more democratic lines. Strongholds of Southern white Republicanism like east Tennessee and western North Carolina had been the scene of resistance to Confederate rule throughout the Civil War; now, as one scalawag newspaper put it, the choice was "between salvation at the hand of the Negro or destruction at the hand of the rebels."

At the same time, the Ku Klux Klan and kindred groups, whose campaign of violence against black and white Republicans had been minimized or excused in older writings, were portrayed as they really were. Earlier scholars had conveyed the impression that the Klan intimidated blacks mainly by dressing as ghosts and playing on the freedmen's superstitions. In fact, black fears were all too real: the Klan was a terrorist organization that beat and killed its political opponents to deprive blacks of their newly won rights. The complicity of the Democratic party and the silence of prominent whites in the face of such outrages stood as an indictment of the moral code the South had inherited from the days of slavery.

By the end of the 1960s, then, the old interpretation had been completely reversed. Southern freedmen were the heroes, the "Redeemers" who overthrew Reconstruction were the villains, and if the era was "tragic," it was because change did not go far enough. Reconstruction had been a time of real progress and its failure a lost opportunity for the South and the nation. But the legacy of Reconstruction—the Fourteenth and Fifteenth Amendments—endured to inspire future efforts for civil rights. As Kenneth Stampp wrote in *The Era of Reconstruction*, a superb summary of revisionist findings published in 1965, "If it was worth four years of civil war to save the Union, it was worth a few years of radical reconstruction to give the American Negro the ultimate promise of equal civil and political rights."

As Stampp's statement suggests, the reevaluation of the first Reconstruction was inspired in large measure by the impact of the second—the modern civil rights movement. And with the waning of that movement in recent years, writing on Reconstruction has undergone still another transformation. Instead of seeing the Civil War and its aftermath as a second American Revolution (as Charles Beard had), a regression into barbarism (as Bowers argued), or a golden opportunity squandered (as the revisionists saw it), recent writers argue that Radical Reconstruction was not really very radical. Since land was not distributed to the former slaves, they remained economically dependent upon their former owners. The planter class survived both the war and Reconstruction with its property (apart from slaves) and prestige more or less intact.

Not only changing times but also the changing concerns of historians have contributed to this latest reassessment of Reconstruction. The hallmark of the past decade's historical writing has been an emphasis upon "social history"—the evocation of the past lives of ordinary Americans—and the downplaying of strictly political events. When applied to Reconstruction, this concern with the "social" suggested that black suffrage and officeholding, once seen as the most radical departures of the Reconstruction era, were relatively insignificant.

Recent historians have focused their investigations not upon the politics of Reconstruction but upon the social and economic aspects of the transition from slavery to freedom. Herbert Gutman's influential study of the black family during and after slavery found little change in family structure or relations between men and women resulting from emancipation. Under slavery most blacks had lived in nuclear family units, although they faced the constant threat of separation from loved ones by sale. Reconstruction provided the opportunity for blacks to solidify their preexisting family ties. Conflicts over whether black women should work in the cotton fields (planters said yes, many black families said no) and over white attempts to "apprentice" black children revealed that the autonomy of family life was a major preoccupation of the freedmen.

Indeed, whether manifested in their withdrawal from churches controlled by whites, in the blossoming of black fraternal, benevolent, and self-improvement organizations, or in the demise of the slave quarters and their replacement by small tenant farms occupied by individual families, the quest for independence from white authority and control over their own day-to-day lives shaped the black response to emancipation.

In the post–Civil War South the surest guarantee of economic autonomy, blacks believed, was land. To the freedmen the justice of a claim to land based on their years of unrequited labor appeared self-evident. As an Alabama black convention put it, "The property which they [the planters] hold was nearly all earned by the sweat of *our* brows." As Leon Litwack showed in *Been in the Storm So Long,* a Pulitzer Prize–winning account of the black response to emancipation, many freedmen in 1865 and 1866 refused to sign labor contracts, expecting the federal government to give them land. In some localities, as one Alabama overseer reported, they "set up claims to the plantation and all on it."

In the end, of course, the vast majority of Southern blacks remained propertyless and poor. But exactly why the South, and especially its black population, suffered from dire poverty and economic retardation in the decades following the Civil War is a matter of much dispute. In *One Kind of Freedom,* economists Roger Ransom and Richard Sutch indicted country merchants for monopolizing credit and charging usurious interest rates, forcing black tenants into debt and locking the South into a dependence on cotton production that impoverished the entire region. But Jonathan Wiener, in his study of postwar Alabama, argued that planters used their political power to compel blacks to remain on the plantations. Planters succeeded in stabilizing the plantation system, but only by blocking the growth of alternative enterprises, like factories, that might draw off black laborers, thus locking the region into a pattern of economic backwardness.

If the thrust of recent writing has emphasized the social and economic aspects of Reconstruction, politics has not been entirely neglected. But political studies have also reflected the postrevisionist mood summarized by C. Vann Woodward when he observed "how essentially nonrevolutionary and conservative Reconstruction really was." Recent writers, unlike their revisionist predecessors, have found little to praise in federal policy toward the emancipated blacks.

A new sensitivity to the strength of prejudice and laissez-faire ideas in the nineteenth-century North has led many historians to doubt whether the Republican party ever made a genuine commitment to racial justice in the South. The granting of black suffrage was an alternative to a long-term federal responsibility for protecting the rights of the former slaves. Once enfranchised, blacks could be left to fend for themselves. With the exception of a few Radicals like Thaddeus Stevens, nearly all

Northern policy-makers and educators are criticized today for assuming that, so long as the unfettered operations of the marketplace afforded blacks the opportunity to advance through diligent labor, federal efforts to assist them in acquiring land were unnecessary.

Probably the most innovative recent writing on Reconstruction politics has centered on a broad reassessment of black Republicanism, largely undertaken by a new generation of black historians. Scholars like Thomas Holt and Nell Painter insist that Reconstruction was not simply a matter of black and white. Conflicts within the black community, no less than divisions among whites, shaped Reconstruction politics. Where revisionist scholars, both black and white, had celebrated the accomplishments of black political leaders, Holt, Painter, and others charge that they failed to address the economic plight of the black masses. Painter criticized "representative colored men," as national black leaders were called, for failing to provide ordinary freedmen with effective political leadership. Holt found that black officeholders in South Carolina mostly emerged from the old free mulatto class of Charleston, which shared many assumptions with prominent whites. "Basically bourgeois in their origins and orientation," he wrote, they "failed to act in the interest of black peasants."

In emphasizing the persistence from slavery of divisions between free blacks and slaves, these writers reflect the increasing concern with continuity and conservatism in Reconstruction. Their work reflects a startling extension of revisionist premises. If, as has been argued for the past twenty years, blacks were active agents rather than mere victims of manipulation, then they could not be absolved of blame for the ultimate failure of Reconstruction.

Despite the excellence of recent writing and the continual expansion of our knowledge of the period, historians of Reconstruction today face a unique dilemma. An old interpretation has been overthrown, but a coherent new synthesis has yet to take its place. The revisionists of the 1960s effectively established a series of negative points: the Reconstruction governments were not as bad as had been portrayed, black supremacy was a myth, the Radicals were not cynical manipulators of the freedmen. Yet no convincing overall portrait of the quality of political and social life emerged from their writings. More recent historians have rightly pointed to elements of continuity that spanned the nineteenth-century Southern experience, especially the survival, in modified form, of the plantation system. Nevertheless, by denying the real changes that did occur, they have failed to provide a convincing portrait of an era characterized above all by drama, turmoil, and social change.

Building upon the findings of the past twenty years of scholarship, a new portrait of Reconstruction ought to begin by viewing it not as a specific time period, bounded by the years 1865 and 1877, but as an episode in a prolonged historical process—American society's adjustment to the consequences of the Civil War and emancipation. The Civil War, of course, raised the decisive questions of America's national existence: the relations between local and national authority, the definition of citizenship, the balance between force and consent in generating obedience to authority. The war and Reconstruction, as Allan Nevins observed over fifty years ago, marked the "emergence of modern America." This was the era of the completion of the national railroad network, the creation of the modern steel industry, the conquest of the West and final subduing of the Indians, and the expansion of the mining frontier. Lincoln's America—the world of the small farm and artisan shop—gave way to a rapidly industrializing economy. The issues that galvanized postwar Northern politics—from the question of the greenback currency to the mode of paying holders of the national debt—arose from the economic changes unleashed by the Civil War.

Above all, the war irrevocably abolished slavery. Since 1619, when "twenty negars" disembarked from a Dutch ship in Virginia, racial injustice had haunted American life, mocking its professed ideals even as tobacco and cotton, the products of slave labor, helped finance the nation's economic development. Now the implications of the black presence could no longer be ignored. The Civil War resolved the problem of slavery but, as the Philadelphia diarist Sydney George Fisher observed in June 1865, it opened an even more intractable problem: "What shall we do with the Negro?" Indeed, he went on, this was a problem *"incapable* of any solution that will satisfy both North and South."

As Fisher realized, the focal point of Reconstruction was the social revolution known as emancipation. Plantation slavery was simultaneously a system of labor, a form of racial domination, and the foundation upon which arose a distinctive ruling class within the South. Its demise threw open the most fundamental questions of economy, society, and politics. A new system of labor, social, racial, and political relations had to be created to replace slavery.

The United States was not the only nation to experience emancipation in the nineteenth century. Neither plantation slavery nor abolition were unique to the United States. But Reconstruction was. In a comparative perspective Radical Reconstruction stands as a remarkable experiment, the only effort of a society experiencing abolition to bring the former slaves within the umbrella of equal citizenship. Because the Radicals did not achieve everything they wanted, historians have lately tended to play down the stunning departure represented by black suffrage and officeholding. Former slaves, most fewer than two years removed from bondage, debated the fundamental questions of the polity: What is a republican form of government? Should the state provide equal education for all? How could political equality be reconciled with a society in which property was so unequally distributed? There was something inspiring in the way such men met the challenge of Reconstruction. "I knew nothing more than to obey my master," James K. Greene, an Alabama black politician later recalled. "But the tocsin of freedom sounded and knocked at the door and we walked out like free men and we met the exigencies as they grew up, and shouldered the responsibilities."

"You never saw a people more excited on the subject of politics than are the negroes of the south," one planter observed in 1867. And there were more than a few Southern whites as well who in these years shook off the prejudices of the past to embrace the vision of a new South dedicated to the principles of equal citizenship and social justice. One ordinary South Carolinian expressed the new sense of possibility in 1868 to the Republican governor of the state: "I am sorry that I cannot write an elegant stiled letter to your excellency. But I rejoice to think that God almighty has given to the poor of S. C. a Gov. to hear to feel to protect the humble poor without distinction to race or color. . . . I am a native borned S. C. a poor man never owned a Negro in my life nor my father before me. . . . Remember the true and loyal are the poor of the whites and blacks, outside of these you can find none loyal."

Few modern scholars believe the Reconstruction governments established in the South in 1867 and 1868 fulfilled the aspirations of their humble constituents. While their achievements in such realms as education, civil rights, and the economic rebuilding of the South are now widely appreciated, historians today believe they failed to affect either the economic plight of the emancipated slave or the ongoing transformation of independent white farmers into cotton tenants. Yet their opponents did perceive the Reconstruction governments in precisely this way—as representatives of a revolution that had put the bottom rail, both racial and economic, on top. This perception helps explain the ferocity of the attacks leveled against them and the pervasiveness of violence in the postemancipation South.

The spectacle of black men voting and holding office was anathema to large numbers of Southern whites. Even more disturbing, at least in the view of those who still controlled the plantation regions of the South, was the emergence of local officials, black and white, who sympathized with the plight of the black laborer. Alabama's vagrancy law was a "dead letter" in 1870, "because those who are charged with its enforcement are indebted to the vagrant vote for their offices and emoluments." Political debates over the level and incidence of taxation, the control of crops, and the resolution of contract disputes revealed that a primary issue of Reconstruction was the role of government in a plantation society. During presidential Reconstruction, and after "Redemption," with planters and their allies in control of politics, the law emerged as a means of stabilizing and promoting the plantation system. If Radical Reconstruction failed to redistribute the land of the South, the ouster of the planter class from control of politics at least ensured that the sanctions of the criminal law would not be employed to discipline the black labor force.

An understanding of this fundamental conflict over the relation between government and society helps explain the pervasive complaints concerning corruption and "extravagance" during Radical Reconstruction. Corruption there was aplenty; tax rates did rise sharply. More significant than the rate of taxation, however, was the change in its incidence. For the first time, planters and white farmers had to pay a significant portion of their income to the government, while propertyless blacks often escaped scot-free. Several states, moreover, enacted heavy taxes on uncultivated land to discourage land speculation and force land onto the market, benefiting, it was hoped, the freedmen.

As time passed, complaints about the "extravagance" and corruption of Southern governments found a sympathetic audience among influential Northerners. The Democratic charge that universal suffrage in the South was responsible for high taxes and governmental extravagance coincided with a rising conviction among the urban middle classes of the North that city government had to be taken out of the hands of the immigrant poor and returned to the "best men"—the educated, professional, financially independent citizens unable to exert much political influence at a time of mass parties and machine politics. Increasingly the "respectable" middle classes began to retreat from the very notion of universal suffrage. The poor were no longer perceived as honest producers, the backbone of the social order; now they became the "dangerous classes," the "mob." As the historian Francis Parkman put it, too much power rested with "masses of imported ignorance and hereditary ineptitude." To Parkman the Irish of the Northern cities and the blacks of the South were equally incapable of utilizing the ballot: "Witness the municipal corruptions of New York, and the monstrosities of negro rule in South Carolina." Such attitudes helped to justify Northern inaction as, one by one, the Reconstruction regimes of the South were overthrown by political violence.

In the end, then, neither the abolition of slavery nor Reconstruction succeeded in resolving the debate over the meaning of freedom in American life. Twenty years before the American Civil War, writing about the prospect of abolition in France's colonies, Alexis de Tocqueville had written, "If the Negroes have the right to become free, the [planters] have the incontestable right not to be ruined by the Negroes' freedom." And in the United States, as in nearly every plantation society that experienced the end of slavery, a rigid social and political dichotomy between former master and former slave, an ideology of racism, and a dependent labor force with limited economic opportunities all survived abolition. Unless one means by freedom the simple fact of not being a slave, emancipation thrust blacks into a kind of no-man's land, a partial freedom that made a mockery of the American ideal of equal citizenship.

Yet by the same token the ultimate outcome underscores the uniqueness of Reconstruction itself. Alone among the societies that abolished slavery in the nineteenth century, the United States, for a moment, offered the freedmen a measure of political control over their own destinies. However brief its sway, Reconstruction allowed scope for a remarkable political and social mobilization of the black community. It opened doors of opportunity that could never be completely closed. Reconstruction transformed the lives of Southern blacks in ways unmeasurable by statistics and unreachable by law. It raised their expectations and aspirations, redefined their status in relation to the larger society, and allowed space for the creation of institutions that enabled them to survive the repression that followed. And it established constitutional principles of civil and political equality that, while flagrantly violated after Redemption, planted the seeds of future struggle.

Certainly, in terms of the sense of possibility with which it opened, Reconstruction failed. But as DuBois observed, it was a "splendid failure." For its animating vision—a society in which social advancement would be open to all on the basis of individual merit, not inherited caste distinctions—is as old as America itself and remains relevant to a nation still grappling with the unresolved legacy of emancipation.